C++ Programming
and Fundamental Concepts

Arthur E. Anderson, Jr.
William J. Heinze, Ph.D.

PRENTICE HALL P T R, Englewood Cliffs, NJ 07632

Editorial production supervision: *Barbara Marttine*
Cover designer: *Lundgren Graphics*
Photo Illustration: *Image Bank*
Illustration by: *Akio Matsuyoski*
Manufacturing buyer: *Susan Brunke*
Prepress buyer: *Mary McCartney*
Acquisitions editor: Gregory Doench

© 1992 by Prentice Hall P T R
Prentice-Hall, Inc.
A Simon & Schsuter Company
Englewood Cliffs, New Jersey 07632

The publisher offers discounts on this book when ordered
in bulk quantities. For more information write:

Special Sales/College Marketing
Prentice-Hall, Inc.
College Technical and Reference Division
Englewood Cliffs, New Jersey 07632

Printed in the United States of America

10 9 8 7 6 5 4 3

ISBN   0-13-118266-8

Prentice-Hall International (UK) Limited, *London*
Prentice-Hall of Australia Pty. Limited, *Sydney*
Prentice-Hall Canada Inc., *Toronto*
Prentice-Hall Hispanoamericana, S.A., *Mexico*
Prentice-Hall of India Private Limited, *New Deli*
Prentice-Hall of Japan, Inc., *Tokyo*
Simon & Schuster Asia Pte. Ltd., *Singapore*
Editora Prentice-Hall do Brasil, Ltda., *Rio de Janero*

Together, we dedicate this book to

Everett Ross Dempster
who inspired us to do our best,

the world's programmers who are enchanted by their craft,

and
Bjarne Stroustrup for providing all of us a powerful media
to pursue our quests.

Art:
To Cheryl, Heath, and Twyla
who provided the unity of happiness.

Bill:
To Beverly
for 25 years of joy.

Contents

Preface

This book is a comprehensive text on the C++ programming language version 2.1 and its iostream library. It also discusses the pre–2.1 versions of the language and how pre–ANSI C and ANSI C differ from C++. Templates (a C++ version 3.0 feature) and nested classes are also discussed.

This book services two audiences. The first audience is professional C programmers who need to expand their knowledge of C++, which is rapidly becoming a major force in software development. This audience includes software engineers such as graphics, database, systems, network, and applications programmers, as well as technical managers who need to determine what language is best suited for the projects they manage. The second audience is universities and colleges which are beginning to offer courses in C++ to their computer science students.

Our goal in writing this book is to provide C programmers with a description of the new features provided in the C++ programming language so they can incorporate these features into their C programming style. Experienced C programmers will likely first incorporate non–object–oriented features such as code–inlining, function prototyping, and function overloading into their programs. Soon they will begin to use the class construct of C++ to provide data abstraction, operator overloading, and separation of interfaces and implementations in their code. Finally, they will use the feature of inheritance to create object–oriented programs. At this time, they will be C programmers no longer but will have become C++ programmers. We assume the reader has obtained at least the level of proficiency that comes from reading and understanding a C textbook such as *The C Programming Language* by Kernighan and Ritchie.

Bjarne Stroustrup developed the C++ language in the 1980s at AT&T's Bell Laboratories. The language is a superset of the C language which, up to this time, was the language of choice of many programmers because of its efficiency, its use as the implementation language of the UNIX operating system, and its use for providing system calls to the UNIX kernel. However C lacks many features that are considered by many to be essential for use in large software engineering applications: strong type checking, data abstraction, and the distinction between interfaces and implementations. While these features are provided in Xerox's Mesa language, Nicholas Wirth's Modula2 language, and the U.S. Department of Defense's Ada language, these three languages lack the simplicity and efficiency of the C language. C++ provides these features and retains C's efficiency and simplicity.

Recently, the concept of object–oriented programming has appeared and promises to revolutionize programming in the 1990s much in the same way as structured programming revolutionized programming in the 1970s. Many traditional languages are being modified to provide object–oriented features (Pascal, Lisp, Prolog, etc.) and object–oriented languages have also been developed (Smalltalk, Objective–C, and C++). However, of the object–oriented languages, only C++ retains the simplicity and efficiency of the C language. We strongly believe that C++ will become the major programming language of the 1990s.

Acknowledgements

The authors gratefully acknowledge the assistance of the following people: Robert P. Medlin, Dr. Robert L. Jenks, William Bulley, Dr. Clovis L. Tondo, Jon Shapiro, Richard M. Kelly, Stephen J. Friedl, and Allen R. Lorenz who gave us careful and thoughtful comments on the manuscript; and the staff of Prentice Hall for their patience during the writing of this book and their support during the final phase of production.

We also give a very special thanks to our students for their questions, comments, discussions, and suggestions which provided special inspiration for this book.

1

Introduction to C++

Many of you are interested in the technology of object–oriented programming and want to use the object–oriented language C++ to do your programming. For you, we have good news and bad news.

The bad news is that C++ is not an object–oriented programming language. Smalltalk™ is an object–oriented language. For example, to add two integers in Smalltalk and place the result in a third integer, each integer is an object, as well as the + operator. When the executable is produced, it is very large because the entire Smalltalk programming environment would be part of the executable. C++ is a dialect of C and retains all the benefits and efficiency of using the C programming language. In C++, to add two integers and place the result in a third, you might write the following program:

```
main()
{
     int       a, b, c;
     a = 7;
     b = 5;
     c = a + b;
}
```

As you can see, the program looks just like a C program.

The good news is that C++ supports object–oriented programming. You may use the mechanisms of data abstraction, inheritance, and polymorphism using C++. A brief example is shown below. Do not worry if you do not understand it; after reading this book, you will find this example trivial.

```
#include <iostream.h>
#include <string.h>

// Use data abstraction to create a user–defined data type
```

```cpp
class Oop_program {
private:
    int x;
protected:
    char* y;
public:
    Oop_program()        { x = 57; y = new char[strlen("B") + 1];
                            strcpy(y, "B"); }
    virtual ~Oop_program() {delete y;}
    virtual void display() {cout << y << x << '\n';}  // Polymorphism
    int get() {return x;}
};


// Use inheritance to inherit data and functionality from parent


class Child_of_oop : public Oop_program {
private:
    char* a;
public:
    Child_of_oop() { a = new char[strlen("Bill") + 1];
                     strcpy(a, "Bill");}
    ~Child_of_oop() { delete a;}
    void display() { cout << a << '\t' << y << get() << '\n';}
};


main()
{
    Oop_program        parent;
    Oop_program        *op = &parent;
    parent.display();            // Call a function through an object
    op -> display();             // Call a function virtually

    cout << '\n';
    Child_of_oop       child;
    op = &child;
    child.display();             // Call a function through an object
    op -> display();             // Call a function virtually
}
```

——————— **Program's Output** ———————
B57
B57

Bill B57
Bill B57

Obviously, there are many additional features in the C++ language that are not found in previous dialects of C. These features will be described in section 1.2.

1.1   Dialects of C

The first dialect of C was developed in the 1970s and became very popular in the 1980s. We refer to this dialect as pre–ANSI C. This dialect is still found on many workstations today. Perhaps its most serious defect is that it does not support type checking of arguments passed to function calls or type checking on return values from function invocations. However, this language provided the programmer with great flexibility in writing extremely efficient programs. The prevalent attitude at the time seemed to be that the programmer knew what he wanted to do and the language was not going to prevent him from doing it. We use the "tree paradigm" to express this attitude. *Here is a rope and a box. Over there is a tree. You know what to do.* If the programmer put the rope around his neck, climbed on the box, and threw the rope over a branch of the tree, he knew what he was doing and the language would not prevent this. We refer to this as *the spirit of C.*

In the 1980s an ANSI committee formed to produce a standard for the C language. One very important feature that the committee added to the language (there were many) was type checking. However, type checking was not required and could be avoided (*the spirit of C* still prevails), but if type checking were used, many potential problems could be eliminated. Although ANSI C was a major advance over pre–ANSI C, you were still restricted to using the standard set of data types (we refer to these as the *built–in* types; they are the ones provided to you by the compiler writer). The mechanism of data abstraction (the ability to produce your own data types) was not included. And, although you could do object–oriented programming using the two existing C dialects, the language did not support this programming style (you can do object–oriented programming in any language; however some languages such as Smalltalk, Eiffel, and C++ support it).

In the 1980s Bjarne Stroustrup was developing his dialect of C (originally called C with classes), which provided many of the software engineering enhancements which are required when working on large software projects:

- Data abstraction

- Inheritance

- Polymorphism.

The name of the dialect was changed to C++ (see Stroustrup's original book for a discussion on how the name was chosen) and this dialect is the one covered in this book. Much effort has gone into the language to make it *type–safe*. In other words, you are prevented from accidentally doing bad things with built–in and user–defined data types but, *in the spirit of C*, you are not prevented from deliberately doing bad things.; for sometimes your program requires deviations from the *normal* way.

Because C++ is just another dialect of C (being biased, we think that it is the best dialect), you are an 80% C++ programmer by virtue of being a C programmer. Almost everything that you can do in C you can do in C++. After reading this book, you will find many new things are also possible.

1.2 Modern Language Features

Every author has his bias and we have ours. Below is a list of features that we believe should be in modern computer languages:

- Strong data typing

- Strong type checking

- Memory addressing

- Data abstraction

- Data encapsulation

- Access restriction

- Information hiding

- Automatic initialization and cleanup

- Inheritance

- Dynamic binding

- Parametric types

- Exception handling.

Data Typing

Most computer languages deal with data types; the C language is extremely rich in the number of built–in data types that you can use. All of these built–in data types are available in C++. However, a unique feature of C++ is that it allows you, the programmer, to create your own user–defined data types. Therefore, C++ is a much more typed language than its predecessor.

Strong Type Checking

Although C was a very typed language, the pre–ANSI version did no type checking on arguments passed to functions or on values returned from functions. In ANSI C, although type checking was provided, it was possible to avoid its use by declaring functions without providing an argument list. In languages which do not support strong type checking, it is possible to pass the wrong type of argument of a function call, e.g.,passing a double when an int should have been passed. These programs will often compile and produce an executable file but generate runtime errors. To prevent runtime errors (i.e., catch the errors during compilation) strong type checking must used. Strong type checking is a feature of Pascal, Modula2, Ada, and C++. In C++, all functions must be declared with the types of their return values and function arguments. This declaration is called the function prototype. When a function is called, the type of arguments that are passed are checked with the type of arguments in the function prototype and any non–coercible differences will invoke a compiler error.

Memory Addressing

A very useful feature of C is the ability to work with the memory address of a variable instead of the value of the variable. In functional languages such as C , pointers provide the means by which a function can modify its calling arguments. Pointers are also used to dynamically allocate memory. Finally, pointers can improve the efficiency of certain routines. C++ supports the use of pointers as a memory addressing mechanism. Pointers also provide another mechanism, references.

Data Abstraction

When you use the new features in the C++ language, you may create your own user–defined data types. These data types should reflect a data abstraction. An example of such an abstraction is a stack. When creating an abstraction, you are responsible for providing all the necessary states required by the abstraction and all of the abstraction's required behavior. A well–designed abstraction allows users to use the abstraction in the same way they would use a built–in abstraction, such as double. In C++, an abstraction is implemented as a class definition.

Data Encapsulation

When creating data abstraction, it would be nice to have the abstraction's state and behavior packaged into a capsule. The data abstraction would be that capsule (class). The abstraction is your new user–defined data type and instances of that type (objects) would contain all the necessary state (data members) and behavior (member functions) to operate on the state. We would like to require the user to use the particular functions that reflect the abstraction's behavior to read or alter the abstraction's state. The mechanism for this is provided in the C++ class definition and it is very easy to use.

Access Restriction

C++ provides a mechanism which restricts access to the state found in objects of an abstraction. These are the access regions *private*, *protected*, and *public*. Without going into too much detail at this time, only functions that are declared in structs or classes of C++ can see the private and protected data of an abstraction. In other languages, this feature is referred to as *data hiding*; however, we prefer the term *access restriction* because a user can see what data a class contains by viewing the class's definition with any text editor (the class definition is in an ASCII file), but the user cannot necessarily access the data. The requirement of having to use functions declared inside an abstraction to access private and protected data provides an enforceable interface to the abstraction's state.

Information Hiding

Often you want the user of your routines to know what an interface looks like: what functions are available, what they return, what arguments they require, and comments on what the routines do. However, you do not want the user to know how the functions are implemented. The standard approach is to place function declarations in header files and function code in libraries. Users of your functions should write their code against your interface and not the function implementation. Then, you change how you implement your functions, users' programs will not break. The classic example is implementing a stack abstraction as an array. The push() function adds another element to the array and the pop() function removes an element. A user of your push() and pop() routines may decide to access the array directly and make whatever changes he wants directly. If you later implement your stack abstraction as a linked list of structs, the user's code will be broken. If the user does not know how the stack abstraction is implemented, the user will write code against your abstraction, which is desirable. In C and particularly in C++, you provide the abstraction in an ASCII header file and all the function implementations are in object code or library files.

Automatic Initialization and Cleanup

When an object of a given class is created, its member variables have no values. You must assign values to these variables before they are used. For some variables, it may become necessary to allocate some memory dynamically. When an object goes out of scope, the memory for the local variables is automatically reclaimed, but any dynamically allocated memory remains. A mechanism should exist that allows the member variables to be automatically initialized and dynamic memory allocated. When a local object goes out of scope, the dynamic memory should be automatically reclaimed. C++ provides a mechanism for the user to create a special function called the constructor, which is used to automatically initialize objects. It also provides a mechanism for the user to create a second special function called the destructor that is used to do automatic cleanup for an object.

Inheritance

Inheritance is the mechanism through which a new user–defined type is created from an existing user–defined type. The new or derived class will contain all the state and behavior of its parent, which it may or may not use, and can create a new state and behaviors not seen in its parent(s). The derived class can also redefine the state and behaviors inherited from a parent. The ability to derive new classes from existing classes provides the capability to better organize applications and the mechanism to reuse.

Dynamic Binding

A philosophy in C++ is to do all type checking and function binding at compile time. Any errors that occur can be detected and corrected before a program is executed. This is very useful; however, there are times when you want to delay until runtime the choice of just what function in an inheritance hierarchy will be executed. Dynamic binding is the ability to defer until runtime the decision of what code to execute when a function is invoked. In C++, virtual functions use dynamic binding.

Parametric Types

In C, when you create a routine for manipulating a linked list, you specify the type of data that is in the list. If you create the code for a linked list of integers and you want to use a linked list of employee records, you must write a routine for that linked list, even though the underlying code may be the same for both routines. Using parameterized types (synonym: templates), you would write a generic routine that manipulates a linked list and contains all the required public list functions. However, you would not specify what type of data is to be found in the list until the list was actually used. At that time, the list would be instantiated to the data type it will contain. This feature is similar to the generics of the Ada language. Although this feature is not present in C++, the ANSI C++ committee has said that it will be a feature of the next major release of the language. Currently, C++ provides this feature with a set of macros that are defined in generic.h.

Exception Handling

Whenever a major error occurs in C and C++, either the program crashes on its own, or if you detect the error, you may write error routines to handle it (usually followed by an exit(1) in your code). What you require to correct program errors is a mechanism for the language to have the ability to detect errors and quickly dispose of them while allowing the program to continue to execute. This is referred to as exception handling and it is a major feature of languages such as Ada. Although this feature is not present in C++, it is needed in the next major release of the language.

Keywords in C++

The following are keywords in C++ that were not keywords in pre–ANSI C:

asm	class	const	delete
friend	handle	inline	new
operator	overload	private	protected
public	signed	template	this
virtual	volatile		

2

Non–object–oriented Extensions to C++

C++ was designed by its creator Bjarne Stroustrup to be a superset of the C programming language. It retains the syntax and to a large extent the semantics of its predecessor, making it appealing to C programmers. One of the major extensions to C was the extension of C's struct to C++'s class. Using the class, a programmer can create an abstract data type which can be used anywhere a built–in data type can be used. Further major extensions included the mechanism of inheritance and delayed function binding. C++ also provides many small enhancements to C which are useful. With these non–object–oriented enhancements, a C programmer can write better C code. The authors believe that when experienced C programmers begin to program in C++, they will first use many of the enhancements covered in this chapter. Later they will use the data abstraction features and finally the object–oriented features provided by C++. The ability to increase productivity while learning and using a new language makes using C++ unique.

2.1 Topics Covered in this Chapter

At the end of this chapter, the reader should recognize the following small enhancements that were made to the C language and should be able to use these C++ enhancements in programming. These enhancements include

- To the end–of–line comments

- Void data type

- Declaration position within blocks

- Constant specifier

- Scope resolution operator

- Aggregate names (struct, enum, union, class)

- Functional style of type conversion

- Function prototypes

- Default function arguments

- Functions with a variable number of arguments

- Function overloading and type–safe linkage

- Inlining of function code

- Memory addresses in C++

- Memory management operators new and delete

- Stream I/O.

2.2   Comments in C++

Comments that are used in programming are intended for the readers of the source code and are not compiled into object code. Although each programmer and programming shop have their own coding styles, a few general comments are in order. Comments should document features of the programming that can be unclear to others who must read the code. C++ provides two forms of comment delimiters:

- The comment pair (/* ... */)

- The double slash (//)

The /* ... */ form of comment (the C style of comment) is treated as whitespace (a space character, tab character, or new line character) and can occur wherever whitespace is allowed. The reader should note that no whitespace can occur between the / (virgule) and the * (asterisk) in a correctly formatted comment.

A comment can be found within a single line:

const float pi = 3.14159; /*pi is used in math functions*/

Comments can also span multiple lines:

/* This comment is used to inform some future user what the intention and logic is for the following function. */

One possible danger with this form of comment is the inadvertent creation of a nested comment. For example,

```
#include <stdio.h>

main()
{
    float x, r = 5.5;
    const float pi = 3.14159; /*pi is used in math functions*/
    x = pi * r * r;
    printf("%f\n", r);
}
```

To comment out part of the code, the following scheme may be implemented:

```
#include <stdio.h>

main()
{
    float x, r = 5.5;
    /*
    const float pi = 3.14159; /*pi is used in math functions*/
    x = pi * r * r;
    */
    printf("%f\n", r);
}
```

The above scheme will generate a compile error because the first comment ends with the */ combination following the word *functions*. When the compiler reaches the line

x = pi * r * r;

it does not recognize pi. Another error will be generated when the final */ is reached because this token is not recognized as valid C++ syntax.

C++ provides a form of comment that starts with // and goes to the end–of–line. This comment is totally enclosed within one line. Below are some examples of this comment form:

const float pi = 3.14159; // pi is used in math functions

Comments can also span multiple lines if each line proceeded by //:

// This comment is used to inform
// some future user what the intention
// and logic is for the following
// function.

To comment out part of the code, the following could be done:

```
#include <stdio.h>

main()
{
    float x, r = 5.5;
//    const float pi = 3.14159; /*pi is used in math functions*/
//    x = pi * r * r;
    printf("%f\n", r);
}
```

There is no problem with the C style comment that exists within the const line. However, there is a potential problem on non–C++ preprocessors with the end–of–line commenting style. Consider the following program:

```
#include <stdio.h>
#define PI 3.14159  // PI is used in math functions

main()
{
    float x, r = 5.5;
    x = PI * r * r;
    printf("%f\n", r);
}
```

C++ preprocessors strip out the comment before doing the macro substitution; however, if a non–C++ preprocessor is used, everything following PI in the program line is commented out including the semicolon. A compile error will be generated because the following statement does not make sense:

x = 3.14159 printf("%f\n", r);

Therefore, end–of–line comments should not be used with preprocessor directives if the corresponding code used is in a header file that is used by both C and C++ functions.

2.3   The Void Data Type

In C, a function always returns a value. In cases where a returned value is neither needed nor wanted, typically an int is returned and ignored. ANSI C and some later versions of C supported the concept of the void data type, which was used to indicate that no data were being returned from a function call. C++ supports the void data type, which specifies an empty set of values.

In C++, if you specify that a return value is void, and then try to use the function in an expression, a compile error is generated.

The void data type is used

1) To specify the return type from a function call.

2) To specify that a function takes no arguments.

3) As a generic pointer.

Functions that Return a Void

In C++, specifying that a function returns a void means that the function returns nothing. Because a void expression indicates a nonexistent value, it can only be used as an expression statement or as the left operand of a binary comma operator. The comma operator is a binary operator that evaluates its left operand, throws away the value (but retains any side effect), and then evaluates its right operand and returns this value. The following example shows the use of void in a function declaration as the value returned from a function call:

void f(int a);   **// nothing is returned by this function**

We have seen some C programmers resort to a trick of creating their own pseudo–void data type:

#define void int

void print();

In this example, the function still returned an int value but the documentation clearly states that the return value is not to be used in an expression.

In C++, you can explicitly declare a function as returning a void value. If a return value is specified within a function, the compiler generates an error message.

```
void internalAdd()
{
    int x = 25, y = 32;
    x += y;
    return x;        // Error: function returns a void
    return;          // Valid: no value is being returned
}
```

If you try to use a void function in an expression where a value is required, the compiler will detect this and will return an error message.

```
void internalAdd()
{
    int x = 25, y = 32;
    x += y;
}

main()
{
    int z;
    z = internalAdd();  // Compile error
}
```

Because type checking is very important in C++, the compiler makes sure that the value returned from a function is the type expected or can be coerced to the type expected. If not, the compiler generates an error message.

Functions that Take Void as an Argument

In reality, there is no void value that is a function argument. When you specify that a function takes void as an argument, you are just providing added documentation, explicitly stating that this function takes no arguments. This was not a problem in C, because function prototypes were not used. In ANSI C, a function with an empty parameter list means that argument type checking is turned off; in C++, it means that no arguments are passed:

```
void internalAdd()
{
    int x = 25, y = 32;
    x += y;
}
```

This format is also permissible in C++ and its meaning is identical to specifying void:

```
void internalAdd(void)
{
    int x = 25, y = 32;
    x += y;
}
```

In C++, the choice of using void or an empty argument list to specify that a function takes no arguments is a coding style issue and is up to you. Interestingly, the authors each have a different preference.

Pointers to Void

ANSI C and C++ provide the ability to create generic pointers to void. In C, a pointer variable always points to a specific data type as the type of data is important for pointer arithmetic. If you try to initialize a pointer variable with the wrong data type, the compiler generates an error message. In C, you can cast the data to the correct data type.

```
main()
{
    int a = 57, *p;
    double x = 47.48;
    p = &a;          // Legal: pointer and variable are ints
    p = &x;          // Error: pointer type mismatch
    p = (int *)&x;   // Legal: double cast to int * type
}
```

In C++, you can create a *generic pointer* which can receive the address of any data type.

```
main()
{
    void *p;
    int a = 57;
    double x = 47.48;
    p = &a;
    p = &x;
}
```

However, unlike ANSI C, in C++ there is no predefined conversion of void * to a pointer of any other type because this conversion is potentially unsafe. In C++, to assign the void pointer to another pointer type, you must explicitly cast the pointer types.

```
main()
{
    void  *vp1,  *vp2;
    int a = 57, *ip;
    float x = 47.48, *fp;
    ip = &a;
    fp = &x;
    vp1 = &a;
    vp2 = &x;
    ip = (int *)vp1;
    fp = (float *)vp2;    // This is allowed but dangerous
    vp1 = vp2;            // This is valid
}
```

You cannot de–reference a void pointer. The following example would not compile:

```
main()
{
    void* vp;
    double x = 33.33;
    vp = &x;
    *vp = 57.57;          // Error: de–referencing a void pointer
    x = *vp;              // Error
}
```

The most important use of void pointers in C++ is to pass the addresses of different data types in a function call when you do not know in advance what type of data is being passed.

```
#include <iostream.h>

enum dataType{character, real, integer, string};

void print(void *, dataType);

main()
{
    char a = 'B';
    int x = 57;
    float d = 47.48;
    char* name = "Bill";
    print(&a, character);
    print(&x, integer);
    print(&d, real);
```

```
            print(name, string);
    }
    void print(void *input, dataType data)
    {
        switch(data) {
            case character:
                printf("%c\n",  *(char *) input);
                break;
            case  integer:
                printf("%d\n",  *(int *) input);
                break;
            case real:
                printf("%f\n",  *(float *) input);
                break;
            case string:
                printf("%s\n",  (char *) input);
                break;
        }
    }
```

In the example, you do not know in advance what type of value will be passed as an argument to print. The address of a variable is passed along with a description of its data type. Because the function requires a void pointer as an argument, the system implicitly converts your pointer to a void pointer when it is passed. Inside the print function a switch statement is used to determine which code to execute based on the type of input data. The reader should note that because the input was a void pointer, it first had to be cast it to the appropriate data type and then the pointer had to be de–referenced to get the correct value, which was then passed as an argument to printf().

2.4   Declarations

In C++ there is an important distinction made between declarations and definitions. A declaration introduces a name into a program but does not reserve any memory storage for that name. A definition allocates memory for a variable or object and also acts as a declaration that introduces a name to a program. For example,

   int x = 57;

is a definition which reserves memory for an int and also introduces the variable x to the program. However, the following struct, day, is introduced into the program but no memory is allocated for the struct until an object of that type is declared. It acts only as a template.

```
struct day {
      char* today;
};
```

Declarations and Definitions

The terms declaration and definition have very specific meanings, but in the C and C++ communities they are used very loosely. Often the word declaration is used when definition is meant.

Declarations are used to introduce a name to the compiler but they they do not allocate any memory for what is being declared.

~~Declarations are used to introduce a name to the compiler but they they do not allocate any memory for what is being declared.~~

When dealing with built–in data types (int, float, char, etc.), a definition allocates memory for a variable.

With functions, a definition is the signature of the function (function prototype) and also the code which is executed when the function is called.

```
void  f(int);              // Function declaration

void f(int alpha)          // Function definition
{
      int beta = alpha;
      return;
}
```

With user–defined data types, a definition is the description of the state and behavior of the type; however, no memory is allocated until there is an instance of the user–defined data type. In C++, where you declare a struct, a user–defined data type, you introduce its name to the compiler.

```
struct alpha;
```

When you define the struct, no memory is allocated (this is really only specifying the properties and behavior of the data type).

```
struct alpha {
      int x;
      double y;
};
```

When you create an instance of a struct, memory is allocated for the object.

alpha bet;

The following table shows the difference between declarations and definitions:

DECLARATIONS	DEFINITIONS
extern float y;	**float y;**
extern const int x;	**extern const int x = 57;**
int get(void);	**int get(void) {return x;}**

class obj;	**class obj {**
	    int x;
	public:
	    obj() {x = 57;}
	};

typedef int up, down;	**enum {up, down};**

Declaration Position within a Block

In the C programming language, all declarations that are made within a block (the region of code between an opening { and a closing }) must come before the first line of executable code or the program will not compile. The following examples show how to declare variables in C:

```
main()
{
    int a = 54;
    int b = 9;
    int c, i;
    c = a/b;                        // First executable  statement
                                    // in main block
if (c < 10) {
        float a = 33.33;
        float b = 11.1;
        float c;
        c = a/b;                    // First executable statement
                                    // in if sub–block

        printf("%f\n", c);
```

```
        }
        else
            for(i=0; i < c; ++i){
                int d = 57;
                printf("%d\t%d\n", c,d);      // first  executable  statement
                                              // in for
            }                                 // sub=block
    }
```

The variables a, b, and c were originally declared as ints in the main() function block. Once the first line of executable code was encountered (c=a/b;), no more declarations were allowed in that block. The variables a, b, and c were declared again within the nested block that was associated with the **if** statement. Once again, within this block, the declarations occurred before the first executable statement. The variable d was declared again within the nested block associated with the **for** statement. Once again, within this block, the declarations occurred before the first executable statement.

In C++, declarations can occur anywhere within a block, as long as they are made before the identifier is used. A declaration can be placed anywhere a statement can be placed. In the following example, the declaration of the variable i occurs within the for statement after executable statements have occurred in the block:

```
#include <stdio.h>
main()
{
    int a = 54;
    int b = 9;
    int c = 57;
    c = a/b;                // First executable statement
    if (c < 10) {
        float a = 33.33;
        float b = 11.1;
        float c;
        c = a/b;            // First executable statement  in block
        printf("%f\n", c);


    } else
        char d = 'B';       // Declaration made after   executable statements
        for(int i=0; i < c; ++i)
            printf("%c%d\n",d,  c);
}
```

The choice of where to put the declarations within blocks is largely a matter of style. Some programmers prefer them at the top of the block where they can be easily found and changed. Other programmers believe that declarations should be made very close to where they are used. In either case, the declaration of the control variable within the for loop in C and C++ and will discussed in the next chapter in the section on function prototyping.

for(int i = 0; i < c; ++i)

seems useful and should be adopted as a C++ convention.

The astute reader should have noticed the preprocessor directive #include <stdio.h> was used with the C++ program but not the C program. This results from the different style of function declarations in C and C++ and will discussed in Chapter 3.

2.5   The Constant Specifier

A constant is something whose value cannot be changed, and in C++, the keyword const is used to declare a constant. The C++ language prevents consts from being accidentally changed directly or indirectly. The pre–ANSI C compilers did not support a constant type. This lack was perceived as a flaw in the language; therefore, constants have been implemented in both ANSI C and C++.

Why are constants useful? The following C program fragment shows three arrays declared with 81 elements:

```
main()
{
    char    buffer[81];
    int     array[81];
    double  incore[81];
    // ...
}
```

In this program, the literal integer constant 81 is used three times. The significance of this number is not apparent. To make changes to this program which involve changes in the array sizes, you would have to find every place that 81 was used and then change the value, which is both cumbersome and prone to error. If you missed an occurrence of 81 you would have a run–time error that would be very hard to debug.

As a work–around, you might declare an integer variable and assign it the appropriate value; then, you might use that variable within the program.

```
main()
{
    int    c = 81;
    char   buffer[c];
    int    array[c];
    double incore[c];
    // ...
}
```

However, neither C nor C++ allows you use a variable as an array subscriptor. Therefore this program will not compile.

Experienced C programmers avoided this problem by using the preprocessor. Instead of creating an integer variable, they use #define to create a named constant. This is seen in the following segment:

```
#define BUFFERLENGTH  81

main()
{
    int    c = 81;
    char   buffer[BUFFERLENGTH];
    int    array[BUFFERLENGTH];
    double incore[BUFFERLENGTH];
    // ...
}
```

This approach is not without its own problems.

- The named constants are outside the scope of the compiler because the preprocessor replaces them with their values before the compiler sees the code.

- No type checking can be performed on the named constant identifier.

- Symbolic debuggers cannot work on the named constant identifier because the preprocessor removes all information about the name.

C++ introduces the concept of symbolic constants. To declare a symbolic constant, you use the keyword **const,** followed by the data type, followed by the identifier, followed by an initialization. For example,

```
const int bufferLength = 81;
const int stringLength; // Error: uninitialized constant
```

Once a constant is declared it cannot be changed within the program because it can only be used as an rvalue (rvalues are values that can be read but not changed). Because the left operand of an assignment operator is an lvalue (lvalues are memory locations whose values can be changed) and the right operand is an rvalue, the following is illegal:

bufferLength = 35; //Error: bufferLength is not an lvalue

Once the program containing the constant has been compiled, the constant value cannot be changed. When you want to change the value, you must do it in the source program and then recompile. Our program is now rewritten using the following symbolic constant:

```
main()
{

    const  int  c = 81;
    char   buffer[c];
    int    array[c];
    double incore[c];
    // ...
}
```

In C++, unlike ANSI C, you can use constants as array subscripts when defining arrays.

Constants in C++ and ANSI C

Although both C++ and ANSI C have implemented constants, they have not implemented them in the same way. In ANSI C, the const is treated as a special case of a variable whose value cannot be changed; therefore it has program scope (default storage class is static and not extern). The compiler creates space for the const and, therefore, you cannot have two different consts with the same name in different files, or include the const definition in a header file.

In C++, the definition of a const is meant to replace #define and should go in a header file; therefore it has file scope. Because you can use a named constant inside an array declaration, you can also use a symbolic constant (see the last example). However in ANSI C, you cannot use a const in any expression where the compiler expects to see a constant expression, such as the size of a declaration. For example,

```
const int bufferLength = 81;
char arrayValue[bufferLength];
```

would be valid in C++, but not in ANSI C.

In C++, a constant must be initialized when it is declared, whereas in ANSI C, an uninitialized constant defaults to 0. For example,

```
main()
{
    const int x = 57;          // Valid in C++ and ANSI C
    const int y;               // 0 in ANSI C and not valid in C++
}
```

In C++, memory space is not always reserved for a constant, whereas in ANSI C space is always reserved. In C++ however, if you declare a constant as an extern or take the address of a constant, the space will be reserved. For example,

```
main()
{
    extern const int x = 57;
    const int y = 48;
    const int *ip = &y;
}
```

Perhaps the most important difference in the treatment of constants between C++ and ANSI C is how constants which are declared outside of functions are handled. In ANSI C, they are treated as global constants (they have external linkage) and can be seen by any file which is part of the program. The following program will compile in ANSI C but not in C++:

```
/* file1.c */
#include <stdio.h>

const int x = 57;

void print(int a)
{
    printf("%d\n", a);
}

/* file2.c */

extern const int x;

void print();
```

```
main()
{
    print(x);
}
```

In C++, constants which are declared outside of a function have file scope (they have internal linkage) by default and cannot be seen outside of any file in which they are declared. Therefore, the above program will not compile in C++. If you want a constant to be seen in more than one file, you must explicitly give it program scope when you declare it by using the keyword extern. The following modified program will compile in C++:

```
// file1.cc

#include <stdio.h>

extern const int x = 57;

void print(int a)
{
    printf("%d\n", a);
}

   // file2.cc

extern   const int x;
void     print(int);

main()
{
    print(x);
}
```

Because constants are usually placed in header files, their C++ static (file scope) defaulting is typically what you want and the header file can be included in several other files without any extra problems or work.

Pointers and Constants

You can create pointer constants in C++ just as you can make integer constants. However, there are some subtleties in using pointers and constants.

Pointers and Addresses of Symbolic Constants

You cannot assign the address of a symbolic constant to a non–constant pointer. If you did however, you could de–reference the pointer and change the value of the constant. For example,

```
const int x = 57;
int *ip;
ip = &x;              // Error: you cannot assign the address of
                      // a constant to a non–const pointer

*ip = 50;
```

If the above code fragment would have compiled, you would have changed the value of x from 57 to 50, which is not possible for a constant.

Pointers to a Constant Data Type

You can declare a pointer to a constant data type but you cannot de–reference this type or pointer as an lvalue. For example,

```
#include <stdio.h>

main()
{
      const int x = 57, y = 48;
      const int *ip;
      int z;
      ip = &x;
      ip = &y;
      ip = &z;
      *ip = 50;              // Error: you cannot de–reference this
                            // type of pointer and alter z
      z = 46;               // Valid: z is not a constant and can be
                            // changed directly
      printf("%d\t%d\t%d\n", x, y, z);
}
```

One way to understand a pointer declaration is to read it from right to left (ip is a pointer to an integer constant). This type of pointer can be assigned the address of any integer variable or constant integer. The data it points to cannot be changed through the pointer, although the data may be changed directly. This prevents you from accidentally changing constant data through this type of pointer declaration. The pointer to a constant type is very useful when you want to pass a pointer variable as an argument to a function but do not want the function to change the value of the variable that is pointed to. For example,

```
struct foo {
    int x;
    int y;
};

void  function(const foo*);

main()
{
    foo  bar = {47, 57};
    function(&bar);                      // A standard conversion will
                                         // convert a non–const pointer
                                         // to a const pointer

}

function(const foo* ref)
{
    foo ump;
    ump.x = ref –> x;
    ump.y = ref –> y;
    ref–>x = 57;                         // Error: you cannot de–reference
                                         // ref as an lvalue

}
```

Because a constant pointer to a foo variable was passed as an argument to function(), you could copy the struct by using its constant pointer but not change any of its values inside the called function. You can read but you cannot write to what a constant pointer points to. Passing a pointer to a constant type as an argument to a function is the normal use of a pointer to a constant type in C++.

The astute reader should have noticed that when we declared the variables of struct foo, the keyword struct was omitted. The reason for the omission is covered in Section 2.7.

Constant Pointers

You can also define a pointer constant in C++. Pointer constants must be initialized at the time that they are declared. They can also be read from right to left. For example,

```
#include <stdio.h>
```

```
main()
{
    int x = 57, y;

    int *const xp = &x;      // xp is a constant pointer to an int
    xp = &y;                 // Error: the pointer is a constant and
                             // cannot be assigned to
    *xp = 33;                // Constant pointers can be de-referenced
    printf("%d\n", x);
}
```

In the above example, the address contained at xp's memory location cannot be changed. However, xp can be de–referenced and the value at the memory location pointed at can be changed.

Constant Pointers to Constant Variables

It is also possible in C++ to create a constant pointer to a constant variable. For example,

```
#include <stdio.h>

main()
{
    int *yp;
    const int x = 57;
    const int const *ip = &x;
    yp = &x;                 // Error: address of a constant
                             // cannot be assigned to a
                             // non-constant pointer

    *ip = 48;                // Error: you cannot de-reference a
                             // pointer to constant  data
}
```

In the above example, neither the address contained in the pointer variable nor the value of the variable pointed at can be changed. The following figure summarizes the four types of associations between pointers and data:

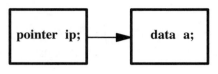

variable   variable

int a, *ip;
p = &a;

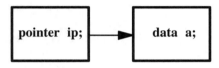

variable   constant

const int *ip;
ip = &a;

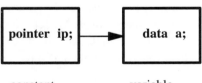

constant   variable

int *const ip = &a;

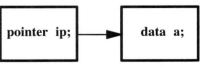

constant   constant

const int *const ip = &a;

2.6   Scope Resolution Operator

C++ provides two new operators that are used to resolve scope. One is the unary :: operator and the other is the binary :: operator. This only section covers the unary operator; discussion of the binary operator is deferred until Chapter 5.

In C, if you compiled the following program:

```
int scoper = 57;                        /* First program scope */

main()
{
    float scoper = 33.33;               /* Local to current block */
    printf("%f\n", scoper);
    {                                   /* Creating a nest block within
                                           main */

        char scoper = 'B';              /* Local to current block */
        printf("%c\n", scoper);

    }                                   /* Closing nest block */
}
```

——————— **Program's Output** ———————

```
33.33
B
```

Even though the same identifier, scoper, was used in three places in the program, there were no compile errors because inner scope masks outer scope. In each block within the main() function, the value of the most local scoper identifier is printed. It would be impossible to print the integer value associated with the global identifier within the scope of main() or the block nested within main().

In C++, it is possible to reference a global variable within the scope of another variable with the same identifier name. For example,

```
#include <stdio.h>

int scoper = 57;

main()
{
    float scoper = 33.33;
    printf("%f\t%d\n", scoper, ::scoper);
```

```
        {
            char scoper = 'B';
            printf("%c\t%d\n", scoper, ::scoper);
        }
    }
```

The output is

33.33   57
B   57

This C++ program behaves much like the C program, except the value of the global int variable, scoper, can be accessed using the :: operator within the scope of the main() function and again within the nested block within main(). Note that it is still impossible to access the float variable, scoper, from within the scope of the nested block. Therefore, the unary version of the scope resolution operator can only be used to access global or file static variables.

2.7   Aggregate Names

In C, an aggregate is a collection of things, not necessarily of the same type. It is possible to have aggregates of specific data types. An aggregate of a single type is called an array. For example,

int integerArray[200];

Aggregates of mixed types are called structs. For example,

```
struct record {
    char*     name;
    int       idNumber;
    char*     address;
};
```

An aggregate called a union has only one element but the element, can be of different types. For example,

```
union employee {
    char   name[25];
    int    idNumber;
    float  salary;
};
```

You can also have enumerated types. For example,

enum workdays{mon, tues, weds, thurs, fri};

These aggregate types are also present in C++ but are treated differently than they are in C.

struct, enum, and union Names in C

In C, you would define a struct as follows:

```
struct record {
    char*       name;
    int         idNumber;
    char        address[45];
};
```

You would use the following syntax when you declare a variable for the struct:

struct record sun;

The use of the keyword struct is necessary because the tag name record is not a C data type and therefore cannot be used as a type identifier.

The same logic applies to enumerated types and unions. In enumerations, you would define the enum as follows:

enum workdays {mon, tues, weds, thurs, fri};

You would declare a variable of that type as

enum workdays sun;

The definition of a union is

```
union employee {
    char        name[25];
    int         idNumber;
    float       salary;
};
```

And the declaration of a union variable is

union employee bill;

Because the tag names and variable identifiers for the above aggregates are in different namespaces, the following is legal (although not a very good coding practice):

struct record record;

```
enum    workdays   workdays;
union   employee   employee;
```

The following is also valid in C:

struct	**record**	**salaryHistory;**
enum	**workdays**	**sun;**
union	**employee**	**personnel;**
float		**salaryHistory;**
char		**sun[25];**
char*		**personnel;**

The preceding example is syntactically legal because the aggregate tag names and variable identifiers are in different namespaces in C, and therefore the identifiers do not clash. In C++, there is only one namespace.

You may prefer to use typedef to produce synonyms for your structs, enums, and unions. For example,

```
typedef  struct {
     char*      name;
     int        idNumber;
     char       address[45];
} record;


record      sun;
```

In this example, record appears to be a new data type of the language and a variable sun is declared for that type. This is not true. The data type is still a struct and record is a synonym for that data type. The same is true for enumerated types.

```
typedef  enum{mon, tues, weds, thurs, fri} workdays;


workdays    sun;
```

Finally, for unions:

```
typedef union {
     char    name[25];
     int        idNumber;
     float      salary;
} employee;


employee        sun;
```

The typedef allows you to use aggregate tag names as if they represented a user–defined type; however, they are still the built–in types of structs, enums, and unions.

Aggregate Names in C++

In C++, you can create user–defined data types that are extensions to the language and typically can be used anywhere compiler–provided built–in data types can be used. You create these user–defined data types whenever you define a struct, enum, union, or class (classes will be discussed later). Technically, enums are a distinct integral type. The tag names of these aggregates become new data types in the language.

struct Aggregates

In C++, the following creates a new data type in the language called a record:

```
struct record {
     char*      name;
     int        idNumber;
};
```

By declaring **struct record**, you declare a new data type in the language. This new data type can be used anywhere a built–in data type, such as **int**, can be used. The new data type is defined and can have instances when the closing brace of the struct is encountered. You can declare objects of this type as follows:

```
record sun;
```

Once again, the astute reader should have noticed that we ~~object~~ *declare* *object* of type record and not *variable* of type record. We use the following distinction:

- If you are using the built–in data types of the language such as int, char, float, etc., you declare *variables* of these data types

- If you create user–defined data types with struct, enum, class, or union, you declare *objects* of the user–defined data types.

enumeration Aggregates

For the enumeration data type, the following definition and declaration are valid:

```
enum workdays{mon, tues, weds, thurs, fri};

workdays sun;
```

union Aggregates

For unions, you would use the following:

```
union  employee  {
      char          name[25];
      int           idNumber;
      float         salary;
};
```

```
employee  sun;
```

The tag name of a union is optional. In the following example, the union is part of a struct:

```
struct  record  {
      union  {
            char          name[25];
            int           idNumber;
            float         salary;
      } field;
      char*         address;
};
```

```
record sun;
```

To access the name field within this struct, you would use the following notation:

```
sun.field.name;
```

C++ also provides a method of declaring unions that use neither tag names nor object declarations. These unions are called anonymous unions and are found within struct and class objects. For example,

```
struct record  {
      union  {
            char          name[25];
            int           idNumber;
            float         salary;
            char*         address;
      };
      char*         phone;
};
```

```
record sun;
```

To access the name field within this struct, you would use the following notation:

```
sun.name;
```

class Aggregates

C++ provides another type specifier called the class, which is the subject of most of this book. For now, you should only know that classes are very similar to structs. A class's tag name becomes a user–defined type as does a struct's tag name. For example,

```
class record {
public:
        char*       name;
        char*       street;
        char*       city;
        char*       state;
        int         zip;
        char*       phoneNumber;
};
```

```
record      art;
```

To access the name field in this class, you would use the following notation:

```
art.name;
```

Once again, the astute reader should have noticed the inclusion of the keyword *public*. This keyword specifies the access region of the class. For structs, the default access is public, but for classes, the default access is private. Levels of access control is a subject described in Chapter 3.

Namespace in C++

In C++, the tag name of a struct, class, enum, or union is in the same namespace as object and variable identifiers; C++ has only one namespace. This is logical because it prevents you from using the same name for a user–defined data type and a variable identifier without creating extra work. You would not want to have the same name for built–in type identifiers, such as

```
int      alpha;
float    int;
char     float;
```

It stands to reason that you would not want the same name used for a user–defined type and an object of that type. For example,

```
record      sun;
int         record;
```

The compiler would not know, except by context, whether a record represented a user–defined type or a variable of an int type. Placing aggregate tag names and object and variable identifiers in the same namespace thus simplifies the language.

C++ allows

record   record;

Object record is of type record. But when this is done (not recommended), in some contexts it is necessary to use

struct record   another_record;

when you refer to the type because there is an instance record from the statement

record record;

2.8   Type Conversions

Although C++ provides all the implicit type conversions that are available in the C language, there will be times when you will want to use explicit type conversions. In addition, C++ provides many implicit conversions that work with user–defined data types. These will be discussed in Chapter 10. Additionally, appendix B contains a program that instructs the compiler to tell us how it converts various types.

Explicit Type Conversions

In both C and C++, you can explicitly convert data from one type to another. To cast a variable to another type, you must put the desired type, including all modifiers, inside parentheses and place it to the left of the variable which is being converted. Both languages use this casting operation. For example, if you have a char variable, but want to use it in your program as an integer variable, you can explicitly cast the char to an int as follows:

```
#include <stdio.h>

main()
{
    char c = 'B';
    int i = 57;
    printf("%c%d\n", c, i);
    printf("%d%d\n", (int)c, i);
}
```

The first printf() statement prints B57 while the second printf() statement prints 4157 because c was converted to an integer value for the ASCII character B.

C++ provides another style of casting that resembles a function call. For example, the previous program could be rewritten as

```
#include <stdio.h>

main()
{
    char c = 'B';
    int i = 57;
    printf("%c\t%d\n", c, i);
    printf("%d\t%d\n", int(c), i);
}
```

Although the cast looks like a function call, there can be no function called int in C++ (int is a reserved word). This functional style of casting puts the desired type (no modifiers) on the left and outside of parentheses and the data being converted on the right, inside parentheses. For example, the code that casts a char to an int could be rewritten as follows:

```
char c = 'B';
int i;
i = int(c);              // functional cast
```

The functional style would not work if you tried to use modifiers. For example,

```
char x = 'b';
char * cp = &x;
int *ip = int *(cp);    // error
```

This notational style usually causes no difficulty when using built–in data types and also causes no confusion to the compiler when using user–defined data types. However, you may be confused when reading code that uses this casting style. For example, is

```
print(x);
```

a function call or a conversion of type x to a print type?

There are times when the old style of conversion is necessary. For example, if you wish to convert a pointer to a function that takes no arguments and returns a double to a pointer to a function that returns an int, the following code does the conversion:

```
double (*a) ();
int (*fp) ();
fp = (int (*))()a;
```

Trying to use the functional style of casting here would cause a compile error.

Unsafe Conversions

There are potential dangers of making type conversions. It is possible to lose information when narrowing type conversion. For example,

```
double x, y = 33.33;
int z;
z = (int)y;                    // Explicit conversion from double to int
x = z;                         // Implicit conversion from int to double
```

The first conversion loses the fractional part of y. The second (implicit) conversion promotes a copy of z to x but the lost data are not recovered. You may not believe that this could be a problem because you would detect this situation and not allow it; however, the first conversion may occur in one part of the program and the second conversion much later and you might therefore miss it.

In the following example, the interpretation of the bit pattern can change because of the conversion:

```
unsigned     char     to_upper;
signed       char     c;

c = (signed char)to_upper;
```

Half of the values, from 128 to 255, will have the left–most bit interpreted as the sign bit.

In the next example, any values that require bits to be used beyond what is stored in a variable of type short will have undefined results:

```
long x;
short y, z;
y = short(x);                  // Explicit conversion
z = x;                         // Implicit conversion
```

The safety of conversions is often machine dependent. On a machine that uses four bytes for short, int, and long, the last example would have been safe.

2.9   Function Code Inlining

To avoid the cost of a function call in C, you would use the preprocessor to create a macro that would be expanded when it was encountered in a program. For example,

```
#define min(x,y)  (((x) < (y)) ? (x) : (y))
#define max(x,y)  (((x) > (y)) ? (x) : (y))

main()
{
    int x = 57, y = 48, z;
    z = min(x,y);
    printf("%d\n", z);
    z = max(x,y);
    printf("%d\n", z);
}
```

However, there are problems with using macros within your programs:

- Macros are tricky to write correctly.

- There cannot be any type checking of their arguments.

- You cannot debug macros because they are outside the scope of the program.

- You cannot assign pointers to macros so you cannot pass them as arguments to functions.

Inlining in C++

C++ provides the keyword *inline* to allow you to create a function whose code is placed inline in your program at each point of call. The use of inline allows you to avoid the cost of a function call. The reasons for inlining a function instead of just writing the code inline yourself are:

- If you need to change the function, you only change it in one place in your code and not everywhere that the code is used.

- Each occurrence of the function is guaranteed to be the same (you will not forget to change the code in some parts of your program).

- The function is more easily understood than the raw code:

  (x) < (y) ? (x) : (y)

- It is easy to change a function from inlined to not inlined to performance–tune a program.

Using C++ inline functions rather than preprocessor macros to define inline functions has the following advantages:

- The arguments are typed checked at compile time.

- The address of the function can be obtained when it is needed (passing the address of one function as an argument to another function).

- Debuggers can work on inlined functions but not on macros.

- They are not tricky to code.

Many of the advantages of declaring a function are, therefore, attained using inline functions.

Because inline functions avoid the cost of function call overhead, their use can speed up the execution of a program. Below is an example of a program with inline functions:

```
#include <stdio.h>

inline int min(int x, int y)
{
    return x < y ? x : y;
}

inline int max(int x, int y)
{
    return x > y ? x : y;
}

main()
{
    int x = 57, y = 48, z;
```

```
        z = min(x,y);
        printf("%d\n", z);
        z = max(x,y);
        printf("%d\n", z);
}
```

When the compiler encounters the keyword inline it does not generate code at this time, but remembers the code and inserts it whenever a call to the inline function is made. At this time, type checking and then inline insertion occurs. Therefore, the keyword inline must be associated with the function definition which contains the code and not the function declaration. The function definition should be in a header file.

Inline insertion of code will not take place under the following conditions:

- The function is too large.

- The function is used recursively.

- Function arguments cannot be resolved at compile time.

- A pointer to the function is used (the code will not be inlined here but will still be inlined elsewhere in the code where a pointer is not used).

Under the above circumstances, the compiler ignores the request to inline the code and treats the function as a non–inline function for the given call.

Inline functions must be defined, not declared, before the first call to the function so that the source code to be inserted is known. To assure that the above is true, inline function definitions should be placed in header files and included in files in which they are needed.

Advantages and Abuses of Inline Functions

Inline functions can improve execution speed by avoiding the cost of a function call. However, they do this by increasing the code size of a program, which can eventually offset the advantage gained by avoiding a function call. If an inline function is never called in a program, no code is ever generated for it; code is generated for non–inlined functions whether they are called or not. Because inline functions are easier to read than code inserted directly into a program or defined in a macro, you may be tempted to use them whether or not they are required. In general, inline functions should be used only with very small functions (three or less lines of executable code) that are called repeatedly.

2.10   Function Name Overloading

In C, each function identifier must be unique. If you had two functions with the same identifier, the linker would not be able to resolve the identifiers at link time and an error would occur. If you had functions that printed integers, floats, characters, and strings, each would have to have its own identifier. For example,

> **void print_int(int);**
> **void print_float(float);**
> **void print_char(char);**
> **void print_string(char *);**

Overloading Function Names

In C++ you can use the same function identifier to represent different functions. Such function identifiers are said to be overloaded.

Function Identifier Mangling

In C++, the function name that is in the C++ source code is different from the function name generated by the C++ system. C++ function names are said to be mangled, that is, they contain additional information. For example, in the following program:

```
int          f(int x)      { return x;}
double       g(double x)  {return x;}
void         h()           {}

main()
{
    int x = f(57);
    double y = g(57.57);
    h();
}
```

the function call **f(57)** would be mangled to **f__Fi (57)**, the function call **g(57.57)** would be mangled to **g__Fd (57.57)**, and the function **h()** would be mangled to **h__Fv()**. This mangling appends to the function identifier information about the type of data passed. Note: different compilers may have different mangling schemes.

Version 1.2

In version 1.2 of C++, the function identifier had to be preceded by the keyword overload before the overloaded function was declared. For example,

```
overload print;
void print(int);
void print (float, int)
void print(char *);
void print(char, char);
```

The first occurrence of the identifier (print(int) in this example) uses the identifier print. However, all subsequent declarations mangle the functional external name to include some additional information about the type and number of arguments passed (this change in the identifier is referred to as name mangling). For example, the subsequent print() functions' external names would be modified as follows:

```
void      print__float__Ffi(float, int);
void      print__FPc(char *);
void      print__FcT1(char, char);
```

The fact that the first name was not mangled caused difficulty when combining C and C++ functions in the same program. It became important to declare the C version of the function before the C++ versions of the function. Subsequent versions of the compiler fixed this problem.

Version 2.0 and Later Versions

In version 2.0 and later versions of C++, all function identifiers are mangled whether the keyword overload is used or not, making the use of the keyword overload redundant (its use is now archaic). Also, the requirement that C function declarations occur before C++ functions is no longer critical or necessary in these later versions.

Argument Matching

When an overloaded function is called, the compiler checks the arguments to the functions and sees if there is a direct match between the arguments passed in the call and the arguments in the function declaration. If an exact match is found, the definition for that function is used. For example,

```
#include <stdio.h>

int swap(int, int);
int swap(int*, int*);
```

```
main()
{
    int a = 5, b = 7;
    swap(a, b);                       // Calls swap(int, int)
    printf("%d\t%d\n", a, b);
    swap(&a, &b);                     // Calls swap(int*, int*)
    printf("%d\t%d\n", a, b);
}
```

If an exact match is not found, the compiler sees if implicit conversions can produce a match between the arguments passed and any of the function declarations. If so, the arguments are converted and the appropriate code called. For example,

```
#include <stdio.h>
int swap(int, int);
int swap(int*, int*);

main()
{
    short a = 5, b = 7;
    swap(a, b);                       // Calls swap(int, int)
    printf("%d\t%d\n", a, b);
    swap(&a, &b);                     // Calls swap(int*, int*)
    printf("%d\t%d\n", a, b);
}
```

In the following example, a compile error would be generated because the compiler would not know whether to convert the two shorts to ints or to convert them to doubles:

```
#include <stdio.h>
int swap(int, int);
int swap(double, double);

main()
{
    short a = 5, b = 7;
    swap(a, b);                       // Error, ambiguous
    printf("%d\t%d\n", a, b);
}
```

Because of implicit conversions, the compiler could not tell which of the following functions to use when integer, short, long, or float data are passed:

```
void swap(int, int);
void swap(double, double);
```

Because there is more than one choice, the choice is ambiguous and the compiler does not know what you want; therefore, the compiler generates an error. *The compiler will never guess what you want.*

It is important to note that the compiler does not check the return value from a function when trying to determine which version of a function to use. For example, the following two functions look exactly the same to the compiler:

```
int swap(int, int);
double swap(int, int);                    // Error
```

Issues in Function Name Overloading

While overloading allows a set of functions that perform similar tasks to share the same function name identifier, its use is not without certain problems. If the functions do not perform similar operations, their names should not be overloaded. Likewise, if they perform similar functions, they should be overloaded.

```
void     initialize(char*, char*, int);
void     initialize(char*, char*);
void initialize(char*, int);
void initialize();
```

The four initialize( ) functions are overloaded. In the following example, the additional three functions could also be used:

```
void       initialize(char*, char*, int);
void       initialize(char*, char*);
void       initialize(char*, int);
void       initialize();
record*    set(record *, char *, char *, int);
record*    change(record*, int);
void       print(record*);
```

These three functions do not perform similar operations and should not be overloaded.

Functions taking default arguments (default argument values will be discussed shortly) should be overloaded carefully because the compiler may not be able to tell which function to use. For example,

```
void    initialize(char* a = "", char* = "", int = 0);
void    initialize(char* = "", char* = "");           // Error
```

```
void      initialize(char* = "", int = 0);                 // Error
void      initialize();                                    // Error
```

If you called this function with no arguments, the compiler would not know which function code to execute. Default arguments will be discussed in Section 2.11.

Implicit conversions can also create unexpected problems with function name overloading. For example, ints may be correctly converted to doubles.

Resolving Overloaded Functions

When a call is made to an overloaded function, the compiler attempts to resolve which code to execute through argument matching. For example,

```
void      change(char);
void      change(char *);
void      change(char, char*);
void      change(char *, int);
```

For the following program:

```
main()
{
      char*       a = "Bill";
      char        b = 'B';
      long        c = 48;
      int         d = 57, *ip;
      ip = &d;
      change(a);
      change(b);
      change(a, c);
      change(ip);                              // Error
}
```

the call change(a) results in a direct match with change(char*). The call change(b) results in a direct match with change(char). However the call change(a, c) does not result in any direct match. However, the long can be converted implicitly to an int and therefore be matched with change(char*, int). The call change(ip) cannot be converted and this function call therefore causes a compile error.

2.11   Passing Default Function Arguments

In C, if a function requires two arguments, both arguments must be passed when the function is called. For example, the following function is used to position the cursor within a window. The cursor will have an X and a Y location on the screen.

```
move(int a, int b)
{
      static int x, y;
      x = a;
      y = b;
}
```

Whenever you want to position the cursor at the home position (0,0), you would call the move() function and pass it the zero values:

```
 move(0,0);
```

Because it is common to reposition the cursor to the home position, which is always (0,0), it would be convenient to provide default values for a and b. In C++, you can provide default values as follows:

```
move(int a = 0, int b = 0)
{
      static int x, y;
      x = a;
      y = b;
}
```

This function can be called in three ways:

1)   **move(35, 70);//Positions the cursor at 35,70**

2)   **move(10);   //Positions the cursor at 10,0**

3)   **move();   //Positions the cursor at 0,0**

The astute reader should notice that a was never defaulted when a function call was made, unless b was first defaulted. It is impossible to provide a value for the last parameter and take any default values for previous parameters. For example, in the previous program, the following calls would be illegal:

```
move(, 34);
move(b = 34);
```

Rules for Using Default Values

If default values are to be used, the right–most value must be given a default value before arguments to its left are defaulted; the two right–most arguments must be defaulted before any arguments to their left are defaulted, etc.

You cannot use positional notation (letting a comma take the place of a defaulted argument) when calling a function with defaults. For example

> **move(, 34);**

does not assign the value 34 to b and take the default value for a.

You cannot use named notation (giving the name of the value not to be defaulted along with a value). The following function call is incorrect:

> **move(b = 34);**

b is not given the value of 34 and a default value is not taken for a.

Because of the restrictions on how default functions are called, you should carefully design your functions so that parameters that are likely to have user–supplied values are listed first and parameters that are likely to be defaulted are listed last.

Defaults are typically made in the function declaration and are often included in a header file. This header file is included in all files that use the defaulted function.

2.12 Function Prototypes

The C programming languages use the function as a mechanism of modularity, and have the requirement that all functions must be either declared or defined before they are used. Because C uses functions instead of procedures, all arguments to a function are input and a function can return at most, one value. If a function returns an int value, it need not be declared; by default, the compiler will assume that a function that returns an int is defined with that identifier.

A major difference exists between how function declarations are handled in pre–ANSI C, ANSI C, and C++ dialects. Both ANSI C and C++ use a *function prototype* in which the type of the return value, as well as the types of the arguments, are declared when declaring functions. For example,

```
void move(int, int);            // Two ints passed
int get_x(void);                // No arguments passed
double min(double, double);     // Two doubles passed
```

The function move() takes two arguments and returns no values. The function get_x() takes no arguments and returns an int. The function min() takes two doubles and returns a double. In pre–ANSI C, the types of the arguments passed to the function are not declared. For example,

```
void move();
int get_x();
double min();
```

These functions in pre–ANSI C are equivalent to those in ANSI C and C++ above. In pre–ANSI C and ANSI C, the get_x() function does not have to be declared because it returns an int; however, in C++ it must be declared.

The function prototype is referred to as the *function's signature*.

Type Checking

After a function has been declared, it must be defined with a code body so that the local variables and executable can be made known to the system. Function definition in C++ is similar to that of ANSI C but not pre–ANSI C. The signature in the function definition must be exactly the same as the signature in the function declaration. For example,

```
int min(int, int);                          // Declaration signature

// Lots of inserted code would be found here

int min(int first, int second)              // Definition signature
{
    return  first < second ? first : second;
}
```

The compiler checks that the types of arguments to the function and the return value type from the function match in number and type in the declaration with each call to the function. If the types do not match, the compiler checks to see if parameters have been defaulted and if, by taking defaults, a match can occur. Next, the compiler checks to see if any implicit conversion can be used to achieve a match. If no match can be achieved, the compiler generates an error message and will not compile the program. This behavior assures that most errors occurring because of type clashes are detected at compile time when it is easy to detect and correct them, rather than at runtime, when they are difficult to detect and correct.

Function Prototypes and Header Files

Every function in C++ must be declared or defined before the function can be used. Also, a function can be declared only once; it is a compile error to have multiple declarations. The standard practice is to place declarations in a header file and then include the header file wherever the declarations are required. For example, you might place the following function declarations in a header file called myHeader.h:

```
void display(int, int);
int min(int, int);
int max (int, int);
```

You would then create another file called myFunctionsImpl.cc, which would contain the function definitions. For example,

```
#include <stdio.h>
#include "myHeader.h"

void display(int x, int y)
{
     printf("%d\t%d\n", x, y);
}

int min(int x, int y)
{
     return x < y ? x : y;
}

int max(int x, int y)
{
     return x > y ? x : y;
}
```

This file would then be compiled but not sent to the linker. Under UNIX, it is compiled to an object file (module), myFunctionsImpl.o.

As a user of the header file, you would write a driver routine (the driver routine is the file that contains the main() function) called myDriver.cc much like the following:

```
#include "myHeader.h"

main()
{
    int a = 5, b = 7;
    display(a, b);
    b = min(a,b);
    a = max(a, b);
    display(a, b);
}
```

The following command on our system would then compile and link the elements of the program:

CC myDriver.cc myFunctionsImpl.o –o execute

You could then execute the program by issuing the following command:

execute

If you had not included the header file, myHeader.h, in myDriver.cc, you would get error messages and the program would not compile because you had not included your function declarations. You should also take care to avoid the potential problem of including a header file twice in a file (this mistake is easier to do then you might think). You should place the following code in your header file to avoid this problem:

```
#ifndef MYHEADER_H
#define MYHEADER_H
    // Place function declarations here
#endif   // MYHEADER_H
```

The first time the header file is included, MYHEADER_H is not defined and the rest of the header file is included the file. More importantly, MYHEADER_H becomes defined. The next time you try to include this file within the scope of a previous inclusion, it will not be included because #ifndef MYHEADER_H will evaluate to false.

You should be careful when creating header files. Their contents get compiled into your program and if they are too large, the time required to compile may be very long. Therefore, you should create small, homogeneous header files that contain a logical grouping of declarations. It is also a good idea not to include a global definition in a header file because it is possible for two different source files in a program to include a header file which has the same definition. The linker would detect multiple definitions of the symbols and, because this is not allowed in C++, the program would not link.

2.13   Functions with Variable a Number of Arguments

In C, you can create functions in which the type and number of arguments are not known at compile time. Classical examples are printf() and scanf(). printf() takes one required argument, a pointer to char, and then it has zero or more additional arguments. The information contained in the required string provides runtime instructions about the number and type of additional arguments, which it then uses to process the arguments.

You can also create functions with a variable number of arguments in C++. These functions must also have some mechanism to inform the routine at runtime about additional arguments. The function prototype contains the required arguments, if any, followed by an ellipsis. For example, the function prototype for printf() in C++ is

int printf(char * ...);

An optional comma may precede the ellipsis. To process a function with a variable number and type of arguments, you must include the header file

stdarg.h

if you are using the standard library routines to process them. In pre–ANSI C, you would use the following header file:

vararg.h

These header files contain the necessary declarations and definitions required by your function to process a variable number of arguments. The important ones are

va_list
va_start()
va_arg()
va_end()

Inside your function definition of a function with a variable number of arguments, you must declare a variable of the type va_list. For example,

va_list mac_pointer;

This variable is a pointer to a list which contains the variable number of arguments. This pointer will be used to process the list. However, before any processing can be done, this pointer must be initialized with the address of the list which contains the variable number of arguments.

To create a list and to initialize the va_list pointer, use the following macro:

va_start(pointer, type)

This macro takes two arguments:

1) The va_list pointer

2) The last specified argument in your function definition. For example, with printf(char* string ...), the argument would be string.

The va_start syntax for your implementation of **print()**

va_start(mac_pointer, string);

To extract arguments from your variable list, use the following macro:

va_arg(pointer, data type)

This macro also takes two arguments:

1) A pointer variable of type va_list

2) The type of data to be extracted.

For example, if the next argument you wanted to extract from the list was an integer, you would use the following syntax:

va_arg(mac_pointer, int);

Note that you do not pass a variable of the data type to be extracted, but instead, the data type itself. If you wanted to extract a double instead of an int, you would have to specify double. va_arg not only returns the data extracted but also advances the mac_pointer so the subsequent item will be extracted next.

After the variable argument list has been processed, you must use the following macro:

va_end(pointer)

This macro completes the access to the list of data and will do any necessary cleanup processing required by the implementation on your system. The following shows the syntax of this macro:

va_end(mac_pointer);

The following is an example of processing a function with a variable number of arguments:

```
#include <iostream.h>
#include <stdarg.h>
void print(int ...); // Declare with at least one argument
```

```
main()
{
    print(3, 5, 7, 57);
}


void print(int input ...)
{
    va_list  mac_pointer;
    va_start(mac_pointer, input);
    int temp;
    for(int i = 0; i < input; ++i)  {
        temp = va_arg(mac_pointer, int);
        printf("%d\n",  temp);
    }
    va_end(mac_pointer);
}
```

The first argument to print() tells how many following integers there will be. Its major use in this function is in the for loop. When print() is called, the pointer, mac_pointer is created and is used in the other macros because it points to the list to be processed. Next, va_start() initializes the pointer and includes in the list all data following input.

Within the for loop, va_arg() extracts an integer argument from the list pointed to by mac_pointer and assigns that value to temp. The pointer is then advanced one integer. The temp value is written to the screen and the loop starts again. This processing occurs until the list is empty.

Finally, the macro, va_end() is called and processing ceases.

2.14   Using Memory Addresses in C++

In C and C++, you can use the memory address of a variable in your program when it is required. It is often more efficient to pass the address of an aggregate to a function or return the address of an aggregate when a function returns. Because C and C++ are functional languages, only one value can be returned from a function call back to the calling program. If more than one variable in a called function must be changed and the change is to occur in the calling function, the memory addresses of the variables to be changed must be passed to the called function, not the variables themselves.

Pointers

C++ supports pointers to data types. A pointer variable contains the memory address of another variable. To assure correct pointer arithmetic when processing aggregates, it is necessary to know what type of variable is being pointed at.

In the following example, the main() function calls two different functions named increment() which increment two variables that are passed as arguments. The two variables are then written to the screen by a printf() call in the main() function.

```
#include <stdio.h>
void increment(int, int);
void increment(int*, int*);

 main()
{
    int x = 33, y = 44;
    increment(x, y);              // Does not affect x and y
    printf("%d\t%d\n", x,y);      // Prints 33  44
    increment(&x, &y);            // Affects x and y
    printf("%d\t%d\n", x,y);      // Prints 34  45
}

inline void increment(int a, int b)
{
    ++a;
    ++b;
}

inline void increment(int* a, int* b)
{
    ++(*a);
    ++(*b);
}
```

The first call to increment() passes the two variables by value. Although the values are changed in the *called* program, they are not changed in the *calling* program. The second call to increment() passes the addresses of the two variables and the values at their memory locations are changed, which is reflected in the calling program.

Of course you can use pointers in many other ways than simply passing them as arguments to a function call. There are two difficulties with pointers: you must remember to pass the memory addresses when making a function call and you must remember to de–reference the pointers when required in the called program. You can get around the first difficulty by creating pointer variables and then using the variables, such as

```
main()
{
    int x = 33, y = 44;
    int *a = &x, *b = &y;
    increment(x, y);
    printf("%d\t%d\n", x,y);
    increment(a,  b);
    printf("%d\t%d\n", x,y);
}
```

However, you must still de–reference these values in the called program or you may create more identifiers that may conflict with other identifiers.

References

C++ provides another mechanism for representing a variable, called a reference. You can declare a reference to a variable. Like a pointer, a reference contains the memory address of some other variable and is used to create an alias for that variable. However, the system handles any de–referencing that needs to be done to the reference (it is important to realize that you cannot de–reference a reference yourself, nor can you do any reference arithmetic). You would use it just as you would use any other variable once it is declared. Chapter 8 covers references in more detail.

Passing Arguments by Reference

The following program illustrates passing arguments by reference (C does not have this capability):

```
#include <stdio.h>
void increment(int&, int&);          // Pass by reference arguments

main()
{
    int x = 33, y = 44;
    increment(x, y);
```

```
        printf("%d\t%d\n", x,y);        // Prints 34  45
        increment(x, y);
        printf("%d\t%d\n", x,y);        // Prints 35  46
}

inline void increment(int &a, int &b)
{
        ++a;
        ++b;
}
```

The function prototype specifies that the two arguments are to be passed as references. Each of the local parameters inside the function is a reference to the corresponding argument in the calling program. Using the operator **&** in a function declaration and/or a function definition specifies that the variable is used as a reference. Using the & operator in a function call takes the address of the variable and treats the variable in the called function as a pointer. Note that & was not used in the function call. The context of how the & operator is used should make clear whether the variable is a reference or a pointer. When a call is made to increment(), a temporary reference variable is created and passed to the called function. It does not have to be de–referenced within the called program.

A Reference to a Variable

It is also possible to create references directly within a program as follows:

```
main()
{
        int x, y;
        int &a = x;
        int &b = y;
        a = 33;                 // Means the same as x = 33
        b = 44;                 // Means the same as y = 44
        increment(x, y);
        printf("%d\t%d\n", x,y);
        increment(a, b);
        printf("%d\t%d\n", x,y);
}
```

a is now another name (an alias) for x and b is another name for y; a contains the address of x and b contains the address of y. The syntax for declaring a reference is as follows:

type &reference = initializer_variable;

A reference must be initialized to the variable to which it refers when it is declared. The following would be an error:

```
int x;
int &a;                  // error, must initialize a reference
a = x;                   // error, assignment to a reference
```

Once a reference is initialized and contains a memory address, it cannot be changed to contain another memory address (it behaves like a pointer constant). Once a reference is made, its use as an lvalue refers to the variable that it references. For example,

```
int x = 33, y = 44;
int &a = x;
a = y;                   // Now x = 44
```

x and y are declared integer variables and are assigned the values of 33 and 44, respectively. The variable a is declared as an int reference and is initialized with the memory address of x.

The assignment

```
a = y;
```

assigns x (what a refers to) the value of y. Now both x and y have the value 44.

References cannot be explicitly de–referenced because they are implicitly de–referenced by the system and an explicit de–reference would try to use the value contained in what the reference referred to as a memory address. This situation would most likely result in a core dump. You also cannot use reference arithmetic because this would have the effect of changing the memory address of the reference, which is not allowed.

A Comparison of Pass–by–value, Pass–by–pointer and Pass–by–reference

The following example shows the uses of three different swap routines:

```
#include <stdio.h>
void Swap(int, int);                  // Notice the capital S
void swap(int*, int*);
void swap(int&, int&);

main()
{
    int x = 33, y = 44;
```

```
        printf("x = %d\ty = %d\n", x, y);
        Swap(x, y);                        // Call by value
        printf("x = %d\ty = %d\n", x, y);
        swap(x, y);                        // Call by reference
        printf("x = %d\ty = %d\n", x, y);
        swap(&x, &y);                      // Call by pointer
        printf("x = %d\ty = %d\n", x, y);
}

void Swap(int a, int b)                    // A do nothing function
{
        int temp;
        temp = a;
        a = b;
        b = temp;
}

void swap(int *a, int *b)
{
        int temp;
        temp = *a;
        *a = *b;
        *b = temp;
}

void swap(int &a, int &b)
{
        int temp;
        temp = a;
        a = b;
        b = temp;
}
```

In Swap(int, int), the two arguments are passed by value and, although they are swapped in the called function, they are not swapped in the calling function.

In swap(int*, int*), the function passes the arguments by pointer and the arguments are swapped in both the called and calling functions. However, must insure that the addresses of the variables are passed and also that all the requisite de–referencing in the called function is done.

In swap(int&, int&), the function passes the arguments by reference and the arguments are swapped in the called and calling functions. Note that the addresses of the variables are not passed in the function call and that you do not have to de–reference the variables in the called program. Once again, the system knows to de–reference the variables when they are used.

The astute reader should have noticed that the versions of swap() that used pass–by–pointer and pass–by–reference were overloaded, but the function that used pass–by–value was not because its name was different (capitalized). The compiler cannot distinguish between a pass–by–value argument and a call with an argument passed–by–reference by looking at the arguments to the function when called, and therefore, generates an error message if these two are overloaded.

Given the following call:

swap(x, y);

the system does not know whether to call

void swap(int x, int y);

or

void swap(int& x, int& y);

therefore, the program will not compile.

A Comparison of Return–by–value, Return–by–pointer, and Return–by–reference

Values may be returned from a function call by value, pointer, or reference. If a value is returned–by–value, a copy of the value is made and returned, not the variable itself. Return–by–pointer and return–by–reference both return the address of the variable.

The following program has three functions that return variables:

```
#include <stdio.h>
int     f(int x)     {return x;}
int*    g(int *x)    {return x;}
int&    h(int &x)    {return x;}

main()
{
     int a = 57;
```

```
        int b = f(a);
        printf("b = %d\n", b);        // Print the value of b

        int *c = g(&a);
        printf("c = %d\n", *c);       // Print the value of *c

        int &d = h(a);
        printf("d = %d\n", d);        // Print the value of d
}
```

When you look at the printf() functions, you see that the function that was returned by point-er had to be de–referenced when we wanted to print an int. The function that returned–by–reference also returned a memory address but, there was no need to de–reference the refer-ence (it looks like a return–by–value). More will be said about references in Chapter 8.

2.15 Memory Management

In C, you have functions in the C Standard Library that can be used to dynamically allocate and then deallocate memory. These functions are

- **calloc()**

- **malloc()**

- **realloc()**

- **free()**

These functions can also be used in C++. calloc(), malloc(), and realloc() must be told how much memory to allocate and all return a void* pointer to the dynamically allocated mem-ory, which may have to be explicitly cast to a different type of pointer. C++ also provides two additional *operators* (not functions) that can be used to manage memory:

- **new**

- **delete**

These operators are used to manage memory on the free store (also referred to as the heap). In C++, new and delete are typically used instead of the C memory management functions because they are type–safe.

The Free Store

The program process model is discussed in detail in Chapter 4. However, every executing program has a pool of memory that can be used for dynamic allocation of memory. This pool is referred to as the free store. Because this pool is finite, you will want to carefully manage its contents. When you need to dynamically allocate memory in your program, you will use new to allocate a block of memory in the free space and it will then return the address of a block. The address is assigned to a pointer variable declared in the program; the pointer is used to access the new memory. When the dynamically allocated memory is no longer needed by the program, it is deallocated through the pointer with delete and it becomes available for further allocation. If the pointer variable is assigned a new memory address before the original memory is deallocated, the memory can no longer be referenced or reused (some programmers refer to this memory as garbage and C++ does not support garbage collection, which is the return to the free store of memory which has no pointer referencing it). Therefore, you must be careful to deallocate any memory that you dynamically allocate.

The new Operator

C++ provides an *operator* called new which you use to dynamically allocate memory in the free store. The new operator is applied to a data type, memory is allocated to hold the data type, and the memory address of that type is returned. The type of the pointer returned by new is the same as the type that new allocated. For example,

```
char* cp;
double* dp;
int* ip;

dp = new double;
ip = new int[15];
cp = new char[81];
```

For the double, eight bytes (on our workstation) is allocated in the free store and the address of that memory is assigned to dp. For the int, 60 bytes are allocated in the free space (enough memory to hold an array of 15 ints) and the address of that memory is assigned to ip. For the string, 81 bytes are allocated in the free space (enough memory to hold an array of 81 characters) and the address of that memory is assigned to cp. The data contents of these allocated blocks in the free store are not specified. It is your responsibility to provide them with values. For example,

```
main()
{
    int *ip = new int[100];
    for(int i = 0; i < 100; ++i)
        ip[i] = i;
}
```

As memory is allocated in the free space, it exists for the lifetime of the process or until you explicitly deallocate it. If new cannot allocate enough memory in the free store, it returns a 0. It is your responsibility to check for a zero return or to provide a handler that executes when a zero is returned.

The delete Operator

C++ provides the delete *operator* to deallocate dynamically allocated memory. For example,

```
main()
{
    int *ipp = new int;
    *ip = 57;
    delete ipp;                      // Deletes a single int

    double *dp ≠ 0;     ← ? does not hurt
    dp = new double;
    *dp = 57.33;
    delete dp;                       // Deletes a single double

    int *ip = new int[100];
    for(int i = 0; i < 100; ++i)
        ip[i] = i;
    delete ip;                       // Deletes an array of ints
}
```

The delete operator should only be used on a pointer variable which contains the memory address of memory that is allocated on the free store. If an attempt to allocate memory using new fails, its pointer variable would contain the value 0. A delete on a pointer variable which contains the value zero (0) is safe because the delete operator will do nothing. A delete on a pointer variable which is set to dynamically allocated memory succeeds and the memory is returned to the free store for reuse. The result of a delete on a pointer variable that is not pointing to dynamically allocated memory or zero is undefined and can lead to unexpected program behavior during execution. For example,

```
main()
{
    int *ip1, *ip2, *ip3 = 0, x = 57;
    ip1 = &x;
    ip2 = new int[1000];
    delete ip1; //Unsafe: No dynamic memory
    delete ip2; //Safe: Dynamic memory
    delete ip3; //Safe: Pointer to zero
}
```

The _new_handler Exception Handler

In C++, when new cannot allocate enough memory on the free store, an exception handler called _new_handler is invoked. This exception handler is defined as a pointer to a function that takes no arguments and returns no values. For example, the declaration is

```
void (* _new_handler)();
```

By default, this pointer is set to zero.

```
_new_handler = 0;
```

Nothing happens when this exception handler is invoked. However, you can provide your own exception handler function that you want executed when new fails. For example,

```
void myHandler()
{
    fprintf(stderr, "Not enough memory on the heap.\n");
    exit(1);
}
```

Next, you would change the memory address in _new_handler.

```
_new_handler = myHandler;
```

Whenever new could not allocate enough memory, the _new_handler pointer would point to the myHandler function which, when executed, would print out an error message and then terminate the program. You may also use a function that is declared in new.h called set_new_handler() which takes as an argument the address of your exception handler. This function will set _new_handler to your function and will return the previous value of _new_handler.

> **set_new_handler(myHandler);**

2.16   Stream I/O

C++ provides an alternative to the I/O that is used with C. The details of this form of I/O require the understanding of the concept of a class (explained in detail in chapter 8). However, a brief description of stream I/O and standard input and output is given here. C++ allows you to read from the standard input using an object, cin, and the operator >>. You can also write to standard output with the object, cout, and the operator <<. To use stream I/O, you must include the header file, iostream.h. It is also permissible to intermix standard I/O with stream I/O. There are many advantages of stream I/O over standard I/O. These include complete type checking of both built–in and user–defined data types.

Writing to the Standard Output

The standard output is connected by default to your terminal but it can be redirected to other output devices. The following program shows how to write a string to your terminal:

```
#include <iostream.h>

    main()
{
        cout << "Hello world.\n";
}
```

Stream I/O requires an output stream object (in this example, cout) to be used. The insert operator (output operator), <<, is used followed by a data value, in this case, a char* value. The << operator has been overloaded (overloaded operators will be discussed in Chapter 7) to output any of the C++ language built–in data types. The following program shows the output of various built–in data types:

```
#include <iostream.h>

main()
{
        int x = 57;
        float y = 33.33;
```

```
    char a = 'B';
    char* b = "Hello world.\n";
    cout << x;
    cout << y;
    cout << a;
    cout << b;
}
```

Unlike printf() (which you can also use), in which you must specify with a format character in the control string the type of data being sent to output, the C++ system knows the type of data which is being output because all identifiers must be declared before they are used.

If you want, you can cascade or chain together your output stream operations for standard output. For example, the above program can be rewritten as follows:

```
#include <iostream.h>

main()
{
    int x = 57;
    float y = 33.33;
    char a = 'B';
    char* b = "Hello world.\n";
    cout << x << y  << a << b;
}
```

Cascading makes the meaning of the output statement clearer but it does not avoid function call overhead. The above statement represents six function calls for output. How this works is explained in Chapter 11.

Reading from the Standard Input

By default, the standard input is your keyboard but it can be redirected to other input devices. The following program shows how to read an integer into your program:

```
#include <iostream.h>

main()
{
    int x;
    cin >> x;
    cout << x << '\n';
}
```

Stream input requires an input stream object, in this case, **cin**. The extractor operator (input operator), **>>**, is used followed by a variable identifier. The input from the keyboard is placed at the memory address where **x** resides. The >> operator has been overloaded to handle all the C++ built–in data types. The system knows, through the declaration of the identifier, which type of data to expect for input, which is unlike **scanf()** in which you had to specify with a format character in the control string the type of data expected. Another important difference between **scanf()** and **cin** is that you do not have to specify the memory address operator.

Consider the following program which shows the difference between **scanf()** and **cin**:

```
#include <stdio.h>
#include <iostream.h>

main()
{
    int x;
    float y;
    scanf("%d%f", &x, &y);
    printf("X = %d\tY = %f\n", x, y);
    cin >> x >> y;
    cout << "X = " << x << '\t' << "Y = " << y << "\n";
}
```

The s**canf()** function required both format characters and address operators; **cin** requires neither. Like **scanf()**, **cin** reads the input stream until white space is encountered (a blank, a newline character, a tab character, or a comment) at which time, input for the present variable stops. If white space occurs before the actual data are reached, this white space is ignored and the input starts with the first non–white space character. As with cout of standard output, cin can also be cascaded. You might have noticed that you can handle a newline as either a character, '\n', or as a string, "\n".

3

Overview of Data Abstraction and Object–oriented Features

Although the C++ features discussed in the last two chapters allow programmers to write better C code and increase their productivity, you will find the real power of the C++ language comes from the use of its data abstraction and object–oriented features.

3.1   Introduction

What we intend in this chapter is to provide the reader with a high–level overview of the language; details are provided in the remaining chapters. Therefore, do not worry if you still have many questions after reading this chapter; we promise that we will answer them.

The topics included in this chapter are

- Object–oriented programming in C

- Using structs and classes in C++

- Access regions in structs and classes

- Friend functions

- Constructors and destructors

- Operator overloading

- Inheritance and virtual functions

- Stream I/O and user–defined types

- A comprehensive example.

3.2 Object–oriented Programming in C

In object–oriented programming, the user creates objects that contain both state and behavior (in English, data and the functions that operate on these). An object should be an abstraction that exists in the application domain and that can be represented in some C data structure. For example, a window abstraction can be represented as an object. This abstraction consists of an initial x, y position and a diagonal x, y position. With these two sets of coordinates, a window frame can be drawn. By changing these x, y values, the window can be moved and/or resized.

To manipulate an object, the end–user should use only those functions declared inside the object to initialize and/or alter the x, y coordinates. The C aggregate, the struct, can be used to create this abstraction. However, because functions cannot be declared inside a struct in C, pointers to functions are used and their corresponding functions are declared and defined outside the struct.

If you were not using the data abstraction and object–oriented features of C++, your program might look as follows:

```
typedef struct {
    float   x0, x1, y0, y1;
    void (*initialize)(void *, float, float, float, float);
    void (*display)(void *);
}window;

void initialize_window(window *this, float a, float b, float c, float d)
{
    this->x0 = a;
    this->y0 = b;
    this->x1 = c;
    this->y1 = d;
}

void display_window(window *this)
{
    printf("%f : %f \n", this -> x0, this -> x1);
    printf("%f : %f \n", this -> y0, this -> y1);
}
```

```
main()
{
     window top;
     window sub;
     top.initialize = initialize_window;
     top.display = display_window;
     top.initialize(&top,  0.0, 0.0, 0.0, 0.0);
     top.display(&top);
     sub.initialize = initialize_window;
     sub.display = display_window;
     sub.initialize(&sub, 1.0, 1.0, 2.0, 2.0);
     sub.display(&sub);
     top.x0 = 1.1;
     sub.y1 = 2.2;
}
```

In this example, we created a window structure that contains four floats that are used to determine the minimum and maximum x, y coordinates of the window. We also declared two pointers to functions in the struct. Two functions were defined and, inside the main function, their addresses were assigned to the struct's pointers to functions. We therefore made a social contract; the user of this struct can only use these pointers to functions when assigning to or changing the x, y coordinates of the window object.

Inside the main function we created window objects called top and sub and used the appropriate pointers to functions to initialize and draw our window frame. According to the rules of object–oriented programming, only these functions should be used to read from or write to the object's data. However, in the last two lines of the main function, we directly altered the x, y coordinates. There is nothing in a C object that forces us to use the pointers to functions; in other words, there is no enforceable interface. This C example demonstrates one of the potential flaws of trying to do object–oriented programming in a language that does not support it. The following sections will show that C++ can support our window abstraction by providing an enforceable interface and will solve the problem of directly accessing data.

3.3   structs and classes in C++

A major difference between C and C++ is that in C++, you can declare functions inside a struct (you are not required to declare pointers to functions). These are true function declarations and not pointers to functions. Structs can also have access regions specified (by access region, we mean that we can control how data are accessed). In C, you can access any member of a struct by using a dot operator with the struct variable. By default, everything inside a C++ struct is public and can be accessed in the same way as struct members are accessed in C, through the struct tag name with the dot membership operator.

```
struct example {
      int a;              float b;
};

example get_element;             // Create get_element
get_element.a = 33;
```

By using the keyword *private* followed by a colon, we can change the access. No longer can we use the struct tag name and the dot membership operator to access the struct element. Now, only those functions that are declared inside the struct can access (read from or write to) the struct's data. Let us rewrite our previous example.

```
struct window {
private:                           // Private access region starts here
      float    x0, x1, y0, y1;
public:                            // Public access region starts here
      void initialize(float, float, float, float);
      void display();
};

void window::initialize(float a, float b, float c, float d)
{                                  // Note the use of the :: operator
      x0 = a;
      y0 = b;
      x1 = c;
      y1 = d;
}

void window::display()
{
      printf("%f : %f \n",  x0, x1);
      printf("%f : %f \n", y0,  y1);
}

main()
{
```

```
            window  top;
            window  sub;
            top.initialize(0.0, 0.0, 0.0,0.0);
            top.display();
            sub.initialize(1.0,1.0, 1.0 1.0);
            sub.display();
       }
```

There are a few things that should be noted about the previous example:

1. The struct is divided into two access regions: the *private* region contains the data
    and the *public* region contains the function declarations (not pointers to functions).

2. Only the two functions which have been declared inside the struct can access the
    private data in the struct – these functions represent the public interface to the data
    type. What is important to note here is that this interface is enforceable – there is no
    other way to access the data. These functions are called member functions.

3. The function definitions are written differently from those in C. When a function
    that is declared inside a struct is defined outside the struct, the function definition
    must contain information about the struct to which it belongs. The C++ binary op-
    erator, ::, is used; the left operand is the struct to which the function belongs, and
    the right operand is the function identifier. For example,

    void window:: display() { /* Do some work */}

    All member functions use this notation.

4. The address of the struct object is not passed as an argument to the member func-
    tions as it was in the C example (the member functions can see directly into the
    struct data).

    ```
    void display_window(window *this)
    {
        printf("%f : %f \n", this –> x0, this –> x1);
        printf("%f : %f \n", this –> y0, this –> y1);
    }
    ```

```
void window::display()
    {
    printf("%f : %f \n",  x0, x1);
    printf("%f : %f \n",  y0,  y1);
}
```

5. It is not necessary to assign the address of the member functions to pointers to functions as it was in C.

6. Functions are called by using an object tag name with the dot membership operator. This is similar to accessing variables from a C struct. We can think of this as having the object come first, followed by the data or function that is inside the object, which demonstrates the object–oriented style used with this language.

```
window        graphics;          // Create the object graphics
graphics.initialize(0, 0, 1, 1);      // Style is object.function()
graphics.display();
graphics.initialize(0.5, 0.5, 0.5, 0.5);
graphics.display();
```

7. It is not necessary to use the keyword struct when declaring objects of a structure

C++ structs

Structs can be used in C++ to hold both data variables and function declarations. This makes them different from C structs which can contain pointers to functions within a struct, but not function declarations. The data declarations made within a struct are referred to as *data members*. Data members can be standard data types, such as ints, floats, char*, etc. and they can also be user–defined data types. In our window struct, x0, y0, x1, and y1 are data members. The functions declared within a struct are called *member functions*. Member functions can only be used when there is an object of the struct. Member functions are called by using the object and the dot membership operator, as is seen in the following code segment:

```
graphics.initialize(0, 0, 1, 1);
graphics.draw();
graphics.move(0.5, 0.5);
graphics.resize(0.1, 0.2);
graphics.draw();
```

Public member functions provide the interface to a struct's data and to enforce this interface, the data should be placed in a private access region. By default, everything declared inside a struct in both C and C++ is public and can be accessed directly. You must explicitly place data in a restricted access region by using the keyword *private*.

```
struct access {    // By default, everything is public
    int x;
    double y;
    void set(int, double);
    void display();
};

main()
{
    access region;
    region.x = 57;
    region.y = 33.33;
    printf("%d/t%lf", region.x, region.y);
}
```

If all data members were public, as they are in the above example, the users of the struct would not have to use any interface provided in the struct (set() and display()). By using the keyword private (followed by a colon), the following data members of the struct would be private and only member functions that were declared inside the struct could access these members:

```
#include <stdio.h>

struct access {                     // Public member functions
    void set(int, double);
    void display();
private:                            // Private data members
    int x;
    double y;
};
```

```
main()
{
    access  region;          // Create object of type access
//  region.x = 57;           // Error: cannot access private  member
//  region.y = 33.33;        // Error: cannot access private  member
    region.set(57, 33.33);
//  printf("%d/t%lf", region.x, region.y);  // Error
    region.display();
}
```

Only the member functions set() and display() can write to the data members or read from them. Because the member functions are in the public part of the struct, they can be accessed through the object (this is how we call member functions).

Structs share many properties with classes. In fact, the only difference between a struct and a class in C++ is that *everything inside a struct is public by default and everything inside a class is private by default*. Structs remain in the language for two reasons: 1) because C++ is a dialect of C and 2) to handle porting C applications to C++.

C++ classes

C++ provides another aggregate, the *class*. As was previously mentioned, classes are exactly like structs except for their default access. Classes can have the following associated attributes:

- Tag name

- Data members

- Member functions

- Access regions

- Self–referencing pointer (*this*).

As we saw in Chapter 2, every class has a tag name that serves as the type specifier of the class; a class tag name represents a *user–defined type* that can be used anywhere in a C++ program that a *built–in type,* such as an int, can be used. For example,

```
class alpha {          // Creates the user–defined type, alpha
                       // some internal data
};
```

```
main()
{
    alpha      bet;      // bet is an object of type alpha
    int        x;        // x is a variable of type int
}
```

An *object* is an instance of a user–defined type. Similarly, a *variable* is an instance of a built–in data type.

A class can have zero or more data members (variable and/or object declarations) and zero or more member functions.

```
class alpha {                    // All members are private by default
    int x;                       // Data member x
    float y;                     // Data member y
    char z;                      // Data member z
public:
    void set(int, float, char);  // Member function
    void display();              // Member function
};

main()
{
    alpha   bet;
    bet.set(3, 4.4, 'c');
    bet.display();
}
```

The function definitions of the member functions in the above example are not shown; this program will not run until you provide the member functions with some appropriate definitions.

A class can have up to three levels of access (access regions):

1. Private

2. Protected

3. Public

These regions control access to members of the class. By default, everything declared inside a class is private and can only be accessed by member functions declared inside the class or by friend functions (friend functions will be discussed in Section 3.5). Members that are declared in the protected region of a class can only be accessed by member functions declared within the class, by friend functions, or by member functions in classes derived from this class (derived classes will be discussed in Section 3.9). Members that are declared in the public region of a class can be accessed through any object of the class in the same way that members of a C struct are accessed.

Generally, data members are declared within the private region and member functions are declared within the public region of a class.

```
class alpha {
        int         x;              // Private data members
        float   y;
        char    z;
public:
        double  y;                  // Public data member
        void set(int, float, char);
        void display();             // Public member function
};

main()
{
        alpha         bet;          // Declaring a local object
        bet.set(3, 4.4, 'c');       // Invoking a member function
        bet.display();              // Invoking a member function
        bet.x = 57;                 //Error: cannot access private  data
        bet.y = 33.33;              //Valid: y is in the public region
}
```

When defining a class member function, you must specify to which class the member function belongs. This is done by specifying the class name, followed by the scope resolution operator :: (double colon), followed by the function definition. For example,

```
class alpha {
        int x;
public:
        void set(int);                    // Declaration
};

class aero {
        double x;
```

```
public:
      void set(double);                    // Declaration
};

void alpha::set(int a) {x = a;}
void aero::set(double a) {x = a;}
```

The preceding are function definitions that are written using the C++ style of putting short functions on one line. We realize that now this looks strange, but shortly it will look normal.

Whenever a member function is called, the address of the object through which the function is called is implicitly passed by the compiler as the first argument. Therefore, the above set() function actually has two arguments, the implicit address of the object calling the function and the explicit value that is passed in. The address of the object is referred to as the *this* pointer and it is used to determine the memory location of the object.

```
main()
{
      alpha       bet;
      bet.set(3);                 // Call function set on object bet
      aero        plane;
      plane.set(33.44);           // Call function set on object plane
}
```

In the first function call, the first argument would be the address of bet and 3, and in the second argument would be the address of plane and 33.44.

Classes support the following computer language concepts:

- Data encapsulation

- Abstract data types.

We have seen that *data encapsulation* occurs when the internal representation of an object, along with its operations, are enclosed in the same structure. This is precisely what happens within a class. When data hiding (access regions) is also used with a class, we are actually specifying an enforcable interface for our object.

For example, when coding the class astronomy, we would first create a header file that contains the class definition, which includes the data members and declarations for the member functions. This header file is called *astronomy.h* and it is provided to the user as an ASCII text file. From the header file, the user can determine the programmatic interface (what functions are available to work on what data). The definitions for the member functions are included in a second file called *astronomy.cc*, which is compiled with the –c option to the CC command on our compiler. The output is an object file, *astronomy.o*, which is provided to the user along with the header file (the user does not get a copy of the source file, *astronomy.cc*).

The user can now use the member functions from *astronomy.o* to manipulate the data members but does not know how the member functions are implemented. If we were to change the implementation, we would have to recompile *astronomy.cc* after modifying it and the users would have to relink their code using the new object module if they wanted to take advantage of the new module. However, they would not have to alter their source code because they do not depend on a particular implementation of the code.

The class defines a type which is represented by the class's tag name. A set of operations have been developed that work with objects of that type. This is a *user–defined type* which can be used in the same way as any predefined data type. This is an example of an *abstract data type*. The essence of C++ programming is the design and implementation of these user–defined types.

3.4   Access Regions in a Class

As previously stated, there are three access regions in C++ classes:

- Private

- Protected

- Public.

Below is an example of inheritance (a base class and its derived class) that shows the use of all three access regions (inheritance will be discussed in Chapter 9):

```
class parent {                        // Base class
    int  car;
protected:
    float money;
public:
    char    food;
    init(int a, float b, char c);
```

```
        int get_car();
        float get_money();
} ;

class son : public parent {              // Derived class
    int keys;
public:
    void init(int x, int y, float z, char a)
        {    keys = x; parent::init(y, z, a);}
    int get_keys() {return keys;}
    int get_car()
        {    return  parent::get_car();}
    float get_money()
        {    return money;}
};


parent        dad;         son            junior;
```

A *private* member can be accessed only by member functions and friend functions of the class. A class that enforces data hiding declares its data members as private.

A *protected* member in a base class behaves like a private member. However, a derived class and any class derived from the derived class can access the protected data through their member functions. Protected members will be discussed in more detail in Chapter 9.

A *public* member of an object can be accessed anywhere within a program where the object is visible; the member can be accessed using the dot membership operator. Classes that enforce data hiding declare their data members as private and their member functions as public.

In the above example, class parent has the car in the private part and only a member function of this class can access this variable. The money variable is in the protected part and a member function in the parent class or a member function in the son class can access the money. The food variable is in the public part of the parent class and can be accessed directly by anyone through the dot membership operator. In class son, the code

: public parent

declares the class to be a publicly derived class from the parent. The keys variable that was declared in the derived class can only be accessed through a member function of the derived class.

3.5 Friend Functions

Data hiding is an important feature of C++. However, occasionally it is necessary that private data members be accessed by ordinary functions that are not members of a class. Reasons for this will be provided in Chapter 7.

C++ provides the mechanism of friend functions that allows non–member functions access into the private and protected regions of a class. The following program shows the use of a friend function:

```
#include <stdio.h>

class friendly  {
     int x;
public:
     void  init();
     friend void display(friendly);     // Declare function display() a friend
};

void  friendly::init()
{
     this –> x = 57;
}

void display(friendly programmer)     //Define function display()
{
     printf(”%d\n”, programmer.x);
}

main()
{
     friendly  trainer;               // Create the object
     trainer.init();                  // Member function call
     display(trainer);                // Regular function call
}
```

To be a *friend function* of a class, a function must be declared inside the class definition, but the declaration must be preceded by the keyword *friend* (*friend* can only be used inside the class definition). Because friend functions are not member functions of a class, the *this* pointer is not implicitly passed as the first argument of a function call. Because friend functions are not called through a class object, the only way that they know what object to read from or write to is by having the object passed as an argument. Therefore friend functions must take at least one argument, which is an object, pointer, or reference of the class to which they are a friend.

In the following example, init() is a member function of class friendly, and display() is a friend function. Notice how the two functions are defined.

```
void friendly::init()
{
    this -> x = 57;
}

void display(friendly  programmer)
{
    printf("%d\n", programmer.x);
}
```

init() uses the class tag name with the :: operator and can directly access the data member x using this –> x. However, display() is defined as a non–member function, and must pass an object of class friendly as an argument; through that object then, the function is able to access the data member x using (programmer.x).

Member functions are called through an object (trainer.init();), whereas friend functions are called like any other C++ function (display(trainer);). The astute reader should notice that a friend function is not really required here; a member function would do the same. However, this is only an example to show you how friend functions are declared, defined, and called.

3.6   Constructor Functions

After a class object is created, you need to initialize its data members. Until now, we have used a function called init() to initialize our data. C++ provides a special function called a constructor that is automatically called when an object is created; class data members are typically initialized with a constructor.

Below is an example of a class that contains a constructor:

```
#include <stdio.h>

class saywhat  {
    int x, y, z;
```

```
public:
     saywhat();              // Constructor declaration
     void print(void);
};


saywhat::saywhat()          // Constructor definition
{
     printf("Constructor called\n");
     x = 57; y = 58; z = 59;
}


inline void saywhat::print(void)
{
     printf("%d   %d   %d\n\n", x, y, z);
}


main()
{
     saywhat a, b, c;
     a.print();
     b.print();
     c.print();
}
```

A constructor is a member function that has the same name as the class and has no return value specified (a compile error would result if a constructor returned void). Whenever an object of a class is declared, the system first allocates memory for the object and then, if the class has a constructor, the constructor is automatically and implicitly called by the system (constructors are never explicitly called by a programmer). *If a class has a constructor, a constructor will be called when creating an object of that class.* Constructors are generally used to initialize data members of a class but they can be used for other purposes (these will be discussed in Chapter 6). In the example, a class called saywhat ~~with~~ which has three data members is declared . The class also contains two member functions, one of which is the constructor, saywhat(). In the main() function, three objects of class saywhat are declared. For each object declaration, a constructor is called that notifies us that it was called and initializes the data members. The member function print() is called for each object.

It is often useful to put an output statement in constructors when code is being developed so that you can see when a constructor is called. Once a program is completely debugged and operating properly, the output statement can be removed.

A class may have several overloaded constructors. We will discuss this topic in Chapter 6.

3.7   Destructor Functions

Frequently, a class data member is a pointer to dynamically allocated memory on the heap. If you dynamically allocate memory for a class object, you should de–allocate the memory when the object is destroyed (C++ does not provide garbage collection). You can write a member function to do the de–allocation, but you must remember to explicitly call it before the object goes out of scope, or the dynamically allocated memory will remain on the heap as garbage. C++ provides a special member function called a destructor that is automatically called when an object goes out of scope. It is often used to automatically de–allocate dynamically allocated memory.

A destructor has the same name as its class but is preceded by a tilde, ~, and does not specify a return value or take any arguments. Whenever an object of a class goes out of scope, if the class has a destructor, the destructor is automatically called.

Destructors are generally used to de–allocate dynamic memory that was allocated for the class but they can be used for other purposes (these will be discussed in Chapter 6). It is often useful to put an output statement in destructors when code is being developed so that you can see when a destructor is called. Once a program is completely debugged and operating properly, the output statement can be removed.

The following program shows the use of a destructor:

```
#include <stdio.h>
#include <string.h>

class whale  {
    char* species;              // Pointer
public:
    whale(char* string);        // Constructor that takes a string
    ~whale();                   // Destructor
    void print(void);
};
```

```
whale::whale(char* string)          // Define the constructor
{
     species = new char[strlen(string) + 1];
     strcpy(species, string);
     printf("Constructor %s called\n", species);
}
```

✗

repeated!

```
whale::whale(char* string)          // Define the constructor
{
     species = new char[strlen(string) + 1];
     strcpy(species, string);
     printf("Constructor %s called\n", species);
}
```

```
whale::~whale()                     // Define the destructor
{
     printf("Destructor %s called\n", species);
     delete species;                // de–allocate heap memory
}
```

```
void whale::print(void)
{
     printf("%s \n", species);
}
```

```
main()
{
     whale alpha("red"), beta("white"), gamma("blue");
     alpha.print();
     beta.print();
     gamma.print();
}
```

The notation

```
whale    alpha("red")
```

creates a whale object named alpha and passes its constructor the string "red". We will discuss the methods of passing arguments to constructors in Chapter 6.

──────── **Program's Output** ────────

Constructor red called
Constructor white called
Constructor blue called
red
white
blue
Destructor blue called
Destructor white called
Destructor red called

In the example, a class called whale, which has one data member is declared. The class also contains three member functions, one of which is a destructor, ~whale().

In the main() function, three objects of class whale are declared. For each object declaration, a constructor is automatically called by the system, notifies us that it was called, and initializes the data members. The member print() function is called for each object. Finally, when the objects go out of scope, their destructors are called by the system. Thus, the objects of class whale are automatically initialized when they are created and automatically de–initialized when they go out of scope. Also note that the objects are destroyed in the reverse order in which they were created.

3.8 Operator Overloading

The C++ language provides a set of operators that can be used on built–in data types of the language. For example, the + operator can be used with shorts, ints, longs, floats, and doubles. For these data types, it has the meaning of adding together two data types and returning the result so that it can be assigned to a third data type.

```
#include <stdio.h>

main()
{
    int a = 5, b = 6, c;
    c = a + b;
    printf("c is %d", c);
}
```

The operators of C++ have no idea what to do with user–defined data types. When designing a class, you may want to provide a set of operators that work on the objects of the class. C++ provides the capability to redefine operators that work on predefined data types of C++ to work on your user–defined data types. This capability is referred to as *operator overloading*.

Below is a program that allows the + operator to be used with the user–defined data type, complex:

```
#include <iostream.h>

class complex {
    double  real, imag;
public:
    complex() {}                                        // Constructor
    complex(double r, double i ) {real=r; imag=i;} // Another
    void display() {cout << real << " + " << imag << " i\n";}
    complex  operator+(complex);
};

complex  complex::operator+(complex a)
{
    complex     temp;
    temp.real = this–>real +  a.real;
    temp.imag = this–>imag + a.imag;
    return temp;
}

main()
{
    complex  x(1.1, 3.3), y(2.6, 1.4),  z;
    z = x + y;                          // Add two complex numbers
    z.display();
    double  a = 1.1, b = 2.2, c;
    c = a + b;                          // Add two double numbers
    cout << c << '\n';
    complex  m(11.1, 13.3), n(20.6, 11.4);
    z = m.operator+(n);
    z.display();
}
```

——————— **Program's Output** ———————

3.7 + 4.7 i
3.3
31.7 + 24.7 i

The principle advantage of operator overloading is that you can make your user–defined classes have an interface that is similar to the interface of predefined data types by using operators to do the necessary work. Thus, user–defined types and operator overloading, the C++ language can be extended.

In our example, a user–defined class that handles complex numbers was defined. The class has two constructors that initialize data members, a display() function that displays the data members in a complex format, and an overloaded operator, **+,** which adds complex numbers in the same way that we would add together two floating–point numbers.

To overload an operator, a member function called *operator+( )* is used. The keyword, operator, along with the operator being overloaded (in this case, +) forms the function name. This function takes a complex as an argument (actually, because it is a member function, it takes two arguments: the first is the implicitly passed address of the complex object calling the member function, and the second is the explicitly passed–in by value object) and it returns a complex by value.

The definition of an overloaded operator provides the code that is executed when the operator is used in the program with objects of the appropriate data type. The real part of the object explicitly passed as an argument is added to the real part of the object calling the function and assigned to the real part of a locally declared temp object; the same holds true for the imag part of the complex object. The temp object is returned by value. Whenever we use the operator + to work with complex numbers, this is the code which is executed. Note that the use of the operator + within the function is for doubles and not for objects of type complex.

In the example, we declared three objects of type complex, **x, y,** and z. Objects x and y were initialized through calls to their constructor complex(double r, double i); z was initialized to nothing by its constructor complex(). Object z got its data members set when the overloaded operator + was used with the x and y objects. The data member values of **z** were then displayed.

Contrast this to the use of double to see the similarities in the user interface. The operator + used a member function. Two new complex objects were declared and values were passed to their constructors. However, this time the operator+() function was called through the z object.

This contrast brings up an important point in using binary operators such as +; the left operand of the operator is the object calling the overloaded operator function and the right operand is the argument passed as an argument. The astute reader will have probably noticed that we used the assignment operator, =, with complex numbers without overloading it. Assignment is one of the few operators that knows how to deal with user–defined objects.

When we say in our code

z = x + y;

the compiler sees

z = x.operator+(y);

The first argument to every overloaded binary operator is the left operand and the second argument is the right operand. The infix notation is only a syntactic convenience we can use instead of an actual function call.

3.9   Inheritance

Occasionally, you will be using a class that , although suitable, does not have all the functionality that you need to solve your problem. In languages such as C, you have the following options:

1)   You can use the function as it is written (usually these are functions and macros found in the C Standard Library);

2)   You can recode it; or,

3)   You can borrow some source code from someone else and use it.

C++ allows you the ability to use one class as the parent of another class. The original class is the *base class* and the child class is the *derived class*. The derived class inherits all the properties of the parent class. The derived class can also have properties not found in the parent class.

Inheritance provides you with the mechanism to reuse code that is already written and debugged and incorporate it into your program. The derived class inherits all the data members and functions of the parent class without having to rewrite the code. New data members and member functions can be added into the derived class that give that the class the functionality that is required. The derived class, then, can be differentiated from its base class by:

●   Adding data members

●   Redefining data members inherited from the base class

- Adding member functions
- Redefining member functions inherited from the base class.

A base class can have more than one derived class, and a derived class can have more than one base class (multiple inheritance). A derived class can be the base class for other derived classes, thus providing the potential to develop a hierarchy of classes.

The example below shows a *base class* being developed that contains information about a parent. The class contains a constructor that is used to initialize data members, a destructor that is used to de–allocate memory, and a display() function that is used to output data.

```
#include <iostream.h>
#include <string.h>

class parent {                          // Base class
     int age, mar_stat, no_child;
protected:
     char* name;
public:
     parent(int a, int b, int c, char* nm)
     {
         age=a;
         mar_stat=b;  no_child =c;
         name= new char[strlen(nm) +1];
         strcpy(name, nm);
         cout << "Parent constructor called" << '\n';
     }
     void display()    {cout << name << "\n " << age << '\n';}
     ~parent()         {cout << "Parent destructor called" <<'\n';
                        delete name;}
};

class child : public parent {            // Derived class
     int  school;
public:
     child(int sch, int a, int b, int c, char* nm)
     : parent (a, b, c, nm)              // Initialize parent
     {
         school = sch;
```

```
            cout << "Child constructor called" << '\n';
        }
        void display(void)
        {
            cout << parent::name << '\n'
                    << age << '\n' << school << '\n';
        }
        ~child() {cout << "Child destructor called" << '\n';}
};

main()
{
        parent  bill(47, 1, 0, "William ");      // Base object
        child  art(57, 45, 1, 0, "Bill");        // Derived object
        bill.display();                          // Use base's display
        art.display();                           // Use derived's display
}
```

In the example, a derived class is declared that inherits its properties from the parent class.
The derived class has a new data member(school) not present in the parent and also has a
recoded display() function. Each class has its own constructor (we will discuss later how to
initialize a base constructor from a derived constructor in Chapter 6). The derived class is
able to access the name data member from the parent class and use the school data member
from its own class.

Although this example is simple, it shows that you do not have to rewrite code if you need
new functionality; the code for copying in the string for the name was used for both classes,
but only defined in the base class. Note how the two objects of the different classes were
declared and initialized. Also note how the two display() functions were called.

In Figure 3.1, note that each object resides in its own data space (each has a unique memory
address). Also note how the memory is laid out (the derived class gets a template of the base
class's data members). The derived class does not inherit any data from the base class; it
inherits a template and is responsible for assigning the values to the template.

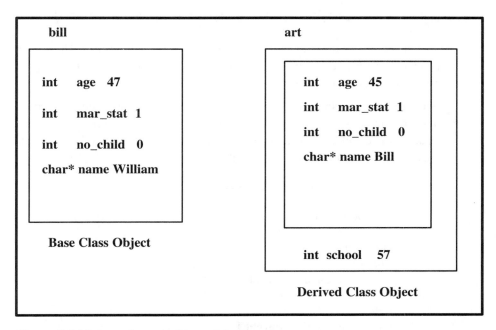

Figure 3.1 Memory layout of two objects.

3.10 Virtual Functions

C++ provides you with the ability to determine at run–time which function code to execute when using redefined functions. This is often desired when using redefined functions with derived classes.

Normally, at compile–time, the compiler selects the code which is to be executed when a redefined function is called. However, with inheritance, it is often necessary to delay until run–time the choice of just what code to execute when a redefined function is called.

In the next example, a base class called parent is defined which includes a member function called display(). An object called oscar is declared for the parent class. A derived class called child is created whose base class is parent. The derived class contains only one member function, also called display(), which has a different implementation. An object called mayer is declared for the child class.

In the global area, the objects oscar and mayer are declared. In the main() function, a pointer is declared of type parent and initialized to the address of the base class object oscar. The pointer is used to call the display() function defined in the base class. The pointer is reset to point to the derived class object mayer. The pointer is then used to call the display() function associated with the child class.

For both calls, the same code is executed — the code associated with the display() function in the parent class. This was determined at compile time by the pointer's type. The pointer changes value with the new assignment, but by that time the compiler has already selected what code to execute. This is not the desired behavior.

```
// Example without using a virtual function

#include <iostream.h>

class parent {
public:
        void  display() {cout  << " Parent\n"; }
};

class child : public parent {
public:
        void  display() {cout  << " Child\n"; }
};

parent  oscar;
child    mayer;

main()
{
        parent  *bp = & oscar;
        bp –> display();
        bp = &mayer;
        bp –> display();
}
```

——————— **Program's Output** ———————

Parent
Parent

In the above example, we did not get the result we wanted, which was *Child* to be printed out when we invoked display through a pointer to the child object. The compiler decided at compile time, based on the type of the bp pointer, which display() function to call. In both cases, *parent::display( )* was called. Also note that the base class pointer *bp* was assigned the address of the derived class object. This is acceptable because the system implicitly converted a derived class object, pointer, or reference to the corresponding base class object, pointer, or reference.

The next example shows how to obtain the desired behavior through the use of virtual functions:

```
// Example using virtual functions

#include <iostream.h>

class parent {
public:
    virtual void  display() {cout << "Parent\n"; } // virtual
};

class child : public parent {
public:
    void  display() {cout << "Child\n"; }          // virtual
};

parent  oscar;
child    mayer;

main()
{
    parent  *bp = & oscar;
    bp -> display();
    bp = &mayer;
    bp -> display();
}
```

──────────── **Program's Output** ────────────

Parent
Child

In the above example, the display() functions are virtual and a base class pointer points to different types of objects within the class hierarchy. The compiler decided at runtime what type of object to point to and which function to call.

As you have seen, if you use the keyword virtual in the base class, the choice of what code to execute is delayed until run–time. Virtual functions only have meaning when used within a class hierarchy (base class, derived class, etc.), the functions have the same identifier and argument list in the base and derived classes, and the function is called through a pointer, which is usually a base class pointer.

The only difference in this last example program and the preceding one is that the keyword virtual preceded the function declaration in the base class. Also note that the derived class function display() was virtual even though the keyword virtual was not explicitly used. This is because the "virtualness" of a function is inherited.

In the main() function, a pointer was declared of class parent and initialized to the address of oscar. The pointer was used to call the display() function for base. The pointer was reset to point to the object derived. The pointer was then used to call the display() function associated with mayer

The code that was executed is different for both calls to display(). When a pointer contains the address of a parent object, the display() function in the parent class is executed. When a pointer value is changed so that it contains the address of a child object, the display() function of the child class is executed. The system can do this because of additional information that it automatically puts in each object that has a virtual function. This is explained in detail in Chapter 9.

3.11   Stream I/O and User–defined Types

An iostream.h header file is provided with each C++ compiler that supports the stream I/O library. In an iostream.h header file, a class called ostream is defined. In this class, the left–shift operator (<<) is overloaded to handle I/O for all built–in data types. An object of ostream called cout is created when a program, which uses stream I/O, begins execution. In doing stream I/O we have used this object and the following member function:

```
cout << 57 << 'c' << 33.33 << "Tom";
```

C++ allows you to overload the >> and << operators to work with user–defined data types, such as

```
#include <iostream.h>

class complex {
    double real, imag;
public:
    complex(double r = 0.0, double i = 0.0)
                {real = r;  imag = i;}
    friend ostream& operator<<(ostream&, complex&);
};

ostream& operator<<(ostream& sout, complex& comp)
{
    sout << comp.real << " + " << comp.imag;
    sout << "i" << '\n';
    return sout;
}

main()
{
    char* name ="C++";
    complex  problem, type(1.1, 2.2);
    cout << problem << name << '\n';
    cout << type << name << problem << '\n';
}
```

The overloaded << functions must be friend functions (the reason for this will be discussed later in Chapter 7). They have the following characteristics:

- They return the appropriate stream reference value.

- They take an appropriate stream reference as their first argument.

- They take a complex reference as their second argument.

- The stream object is used as the I/O object in the body of the function.

- They use the complex object in their body.

- They can be used in user–defined data types.

Notice that the interface for sending output to your user–defined data type is the same as for a built–in data type. The iostream library will be covered in Chapter 11.

3.12 Example

The following comprehensive example defines an array class to create an abstract data type to work on arrays. It illustrates most of the concepts described in this chapter.

```
#include <iostream.h>
#include <stdlib.h>

const int ARRSIZE = 81;

class ArrayClass{
protected:
    int size;
    int *ip;
public:
    ArrayClass(int sz = ARRSIZE);
    ArrayClass(const  ArrayClass&);
    ~ArrayClass()   {delete ip;}
    int getSize()      {return size;}
    ArrayClass& operator=(const  ArrayClass&);
    virtual  int&    operator[](int);
};

ArrayClass::ArrayClass(int sz)
{
    size = sz;
    ip = new int[size];
    for(int i = 0; i < size; ++i)    {
        ip[i] = 0;
    }
}

ArrayClass::ArrayClass(const ArrayClass &IP)
{
    size = IP.size;
```

```
    ip = new int[size];
    for(int i = 0; i < size; ++i)    {
        ip[i] =  IP.ip[i];
    }
}

ArrayClass& ArrayClass::operator=(const ArrayClass &IP)
{
    delete ip;
    size = IP.size
    ip = new int[size];
    for(int i = 0; i < size; ++i)    {
        ip[i] =  IP.ip[i];
    }
    return *this;
}

int& ArrayClass::operator[](int  index)
{
    return ip[index];
}

class RangeCheck : public ArrayClass  {
    void  check(int);
public:
    RangeCheck(int = ArrSize);
    int&    operator[](int);
};

void  RangeCheck::check(int index)
{
    if(index < 0 || index >= size)  {
        cerr << "Index out of range\n"
        << "\tSize: " << size << '\n'
        << "\tIndex: " << index << '\n';
        exit(1);
    }
}
```

```
RangeCheck::RangeCheck(int sz)  : ArrayClass(sz)  {}

int& RangeCheck::operator[](int index)
{
    check(index);
    return ip[index];
}

const SIZE =12;

main()
{
    RangeCheck    array(SIZE);

    for(int i = 0; i < SIZE; ++i)  {
        array[i] = i;
        cout << array[i] << '\n';
    }

    cout << "\n\n";

    for(int j = 0; j <= SIZE; ++j)  {
        array[j] = j;
        cout << array[j] << '\n';
    }
}
```

A constant, ARRSIZE, is declared to provide a default size for arrays.

The class, ArrayClass, has two data members, size and a pointer ip, that are declared protected. These data members can only be accessed by the member functions of ArrayClass, and from any class derived from ArrayClass.

The class, ArrayClass, has six member functions that are public:

1) ArrayClass(int sz = ARRSIZE) is a constructor that passes in the maximum size of the array. The implementation of this constructor will be discussed shortly.

2) ArrayClass(const ArrayClass&) is a constructor that passes in a constant reference to the class. The implementation of this constructor will be discussed shortly.

3) ~ArrayClass() {delete ip;} is a destructor that frees the memory pointed to by ip. Note that when this function is declared within a class and its code body is given, the code is implicitly inlined.

4) int getSize() {return size} returns the size of the array. Note the implicit inlining of code.

5) ArrayClass& operator=(const ArrayClass&) is an overloaded = operator that takes ArrayClass& as an argument and returns ArrayClass& .

6) int& operator[](int) is an overloaded [] operator that takes int as an argument and returns a reference to int. This is a virtual function.

The first constructor receives as an argument the size of the array, sz, and sets the data member size to that argument. It then allocates memory for an array of that size and sets the data member pointer, ip, to that memory. Finally, it sets every member of the array to 0. If no argument is given, it defaults to ARRSIZE.

The second constructor receives as an argument the reference to another ArrayClass. It copies the size of the argument array into the new class. It then allocates enough memory for the new array and sets the pointer ip to that memory. Finally, it copies each element of the passed–in array into the new array.

The first function is an overloaded operator for =. It frees up any memory associated with ip. It then sets the size value to the size passed in the class reference. It allocates memory for the new array and assigns the pointer ip to that memory. It then copies the values of the passed in array into the new array. Finally, it returns a reference to the object under consideration through the dereferencing of the *this* pointer.

The second function is an overloaded operator for subscript notation, []. It takes an int value for an index and returns an int reference. This operator requires statements such as, gorp[22] = 57;. To use gorp[22] on the left–hand side of an assignment statement, it must be an lvalue. By returning a reference from this function we can use it as an lvalue.

The next step derives from the base class, ArrayClass, a class that does range checking.This class is a derived class from ArrayClass. It can directly access ArrayClass's protected data members. It has its own constructor and overloaded operator, []. It also contains a member function, check(), that checks the array's range to see if it is within bounds.

The function check(int index) is in the private part of the class and can only be called by the member function, operator[](int index). It takes the index and does a range check on it. If the index is out of bounds, an error message is generated and the program exits.

The second function is a constructor whose only purpose is to pass values back to the base class constructor.

The third function is an overloaded operator. There is a function in the base class with the same name, so this is a virtual function. If this function is called, it leads to range checking as well as passing a reference to the index.

The driver function declares the array to be an object of class RangeCheck and initializes its data member size to 12. It then goes through a for loop and initializes the array elements and prints them to the monitor.

Finally, the driver function goes through a second for loop, but this time, the last time through the loop, an out–of–bounds condition is generated. This is detected and an error message is generated and the program exits.

4

Fundamental Concepts and Building Blocks

4.1   A Logical C++ Data Model: UNIX Process Model

Figure 4.1 shows a C++ a conceptual model of a program and its corresponding run–time machine code at the point where main has called function f() and the program is currently executing inside f(). Knowing an underlying conceptual data model is necessary to clearly understand C++'s static, automatic, dynamic, and register storage classes for variables and objects.

A logical C++ data model describes how C++ source code is represented in a machine at run–time, and its ancestors, C and ANSI C, use the same model. Dennis Ritchie at Bell Labs invented C to implement UNIX in a high–level language. It is not surprising that the C++ model of an executing program, and the UNIX process model of an executing process are the same. A C++ source program is transformed into an executing process by the C++ compiler, linker, and operating system process–management software.

The text region is frequently a read–only fixed–size region of memory and contains all the machine code executed by the CPU. The data region is a read/write fixed–size region in memory and it corresponds to the static storage area for static variables and objects. Static data that have initial values are placed in the initialized data region. All static data that are not explicitly given initial values are placed in the uninitialized data region and always initialized to zero.

The heap is also known as the free store and its size dynamically grows and shrinks at run–time in response to explicit memory management requests (new and delete) by the program. The C++ memory management operator new allocates storage for dynamic objects at run–time in the heap. If there is not room in the heap for a new object, the size of the heap is expanded up into the hole between the heap and the stack to make room for the new object.

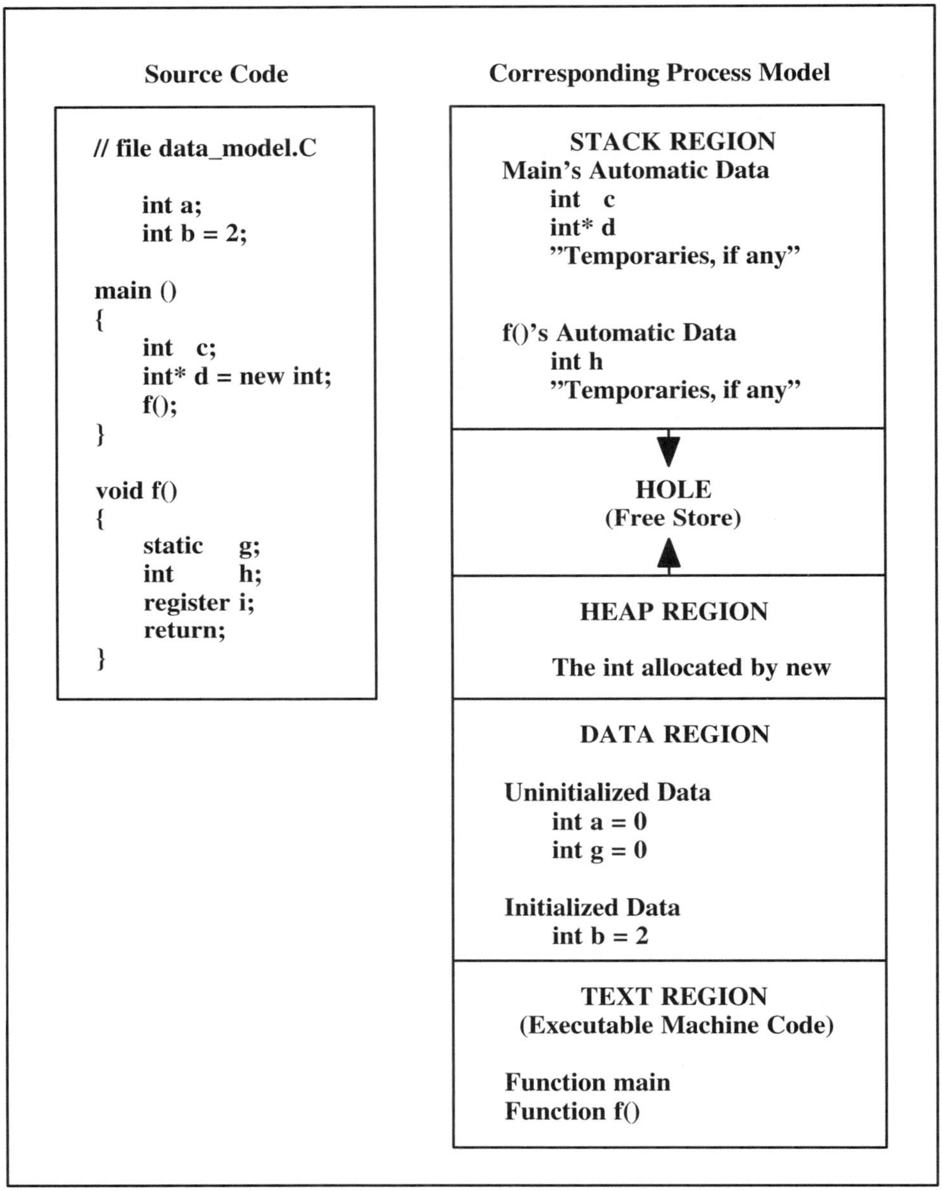

Source Code	Corresponding Process Model
| ```
// file data_model.C

    int a;
    int b = 2;

main ()
{
    int   c;
    int* d = new int;
    f();
}

void f()
{
    static    g;
    int       h;
    register i;
    return;
}
``` | **STACK REGION**<br>**Main's Automatic Data**<br>    **int   c**<br>    **int* d**<br>    **"Temporaries, if any"**<br><br>**f()'s Automatic Data**<br>    **int h**<br>    **"Temporaries, if any"**<br><br>▼<br>**HOLE**<br>**(Free Store)**<br>▲<br><br>**HEAP REGION**<br><br>**The int allocated by new**<br><br>**DATA REGION**<br><br>**Uninitialized Data**<br>    **int a = 0**<br>    **int g = 0**<br><br>**Initialized Data**<br>    **int b = 2**<br><br>**TEXT REGION**<br>**(Executable Machine Code)**<br><br>**Function main**<br>**Function f()** |

Figure 4–1 C++ source code and corresponding run–time process model
```

The C library routines malloc and realloc also allocate space from the heap. When an object in the heap is no longer needed by a program, the program can explicitly get rid of the object and the memory that was occupied by the object is returned back to the heap for reuse. This is done by using the C++ operator delete. The C library routine free performs a similar function.

The stack is typically the highest region in memory address space and its size dynamically grows and shrinks in response to function calls and returns. The stack grows downward into the hole between the stack and the heap. When a function is called, the stack is expanded to hold the function's data and information on how to get back to the calling function. This new stack area is called a stack frame. A copy of a function's parameters are copied onto the stack and the function begins execution. When an automatic variable or object definition statement is encountered, the data are dynamically created on the stack.

If this function calls a function, another stack frame is created and that function begins execution. When a function returns, its return value is returned by some compiler–dependent mechanism to the calling function, its stack frame is de–allocated from the stack (stack frame is popped), the size of the stack shrinks, and the hole increases into available space. At this point the calling function continues to execute. When it returns, its stack frame is popped. This process continues until main returns (exits) and then, the program terminates. There are additional details about variable and object initialization, destruction, and copying in Chapter 6.

A hole is available memory, or an available virtual memory address space between the stack and heap. It is used as a pool of dynamically available memory that is used by both the heap and stack, which both dynamically change in size at run–time. If the stack needs to expand and there is no more available memory in the hole, a run–time stack overflow error occurs. If this happens to the heap, a run–time heap overflow error occurs. A non–terminating recursive function call or a cycle of calls will result in a stack overflow.

Machine hardware registers are special memories that are integrated with or part of the central processing unit (CPU). Registers are much faster than memory, they typically hold data, and are used to perform computations, such as add, subtract, etc. The C++ register storage class keyword is advisef to the compiler to allocate a data variable or object in a computer register rather than in memory. What is done with the advice is compiler–dependent. One way to see the effect of a register definition and/or compiler flags that affect optimization is to inspect the assembly output of the compiler. A compiler flag is used to get assembly output, and an editor is the easiest way to look at the output.

Remember, figure 4.1 represents a conceptual model. The actual hardware and software physical implementation of the model is machine–dependent. Hardware characteristics of the stack(s), existence of memory segments, and the existence of virtual memory are some of the resources that affect the design of a data model's realization.

4.2   C++ Operators 'Precedence and Associativity

C++ has the familiar operators +, –, * and /. They are like their corresponding FORTRAN and Pascal operators, and two numbers are added using familiar notation.

> **a = 1 + 2;**

C++ also has operators that are very different from those used in FORTRAN and Pascal. In a C++ expression, just about everything is either an operator or an operand. This is a key characteristic and understanding this notion is fundamental to understanding C++. For example, the expression statement

> **a[1] = sin(x);**

has three operators, which are the operators subscripting [], assignment =, and function call (). The operator [] has the operands a and 1; the operator () has the operands sin and x; and the operator = has the operands a[1] and sin(x). The meaning of this statement, which is to assign the array element a[1] the value of sin(x), is determined by the precedence, associativity, and definition of the operators in it. This makes C++ expressions much more expressive and powerful than expressions in other languages such as Pascal, FORTRAN, and BASIC.

It is essential to know the C++ operators and their precedences and associativities in order to understand the language. Interpreting the following definition of the standard C library function getc() strongly emphasizes this point:

> **#define getc(p) (– –(p)–>cnt>=0?((int)*(p)–>ptr++):f(p))**

We will come back to the above expression later in this chapter and show that is not difficult to understand after you have acquired the skill to handle operator precedence and associativity.

Understanding C++ operators is important for another reason too. As discussed in later chapters on operator overloading and classes, almost all operators can be given new meanings for user–defined types, and this capability allows the language to be extended in a natural way. A good example of this is adding a complex number data type to the language and having the operators +, –, *, and / operate on the complex numbers.

Operator Terminology

The C++ operators are listed in Table 4.1 and operator terminology and characteristics are described here.

Each operator

- Takes a fixed number of operands (one or two or three operands).

- Performs some operation or computation using them and then yields or returns a result.

- Example:
  1 + 2;   // Operator + with operands 1 and 2. The result is 3.

A unary operator

- Takes one operand.

- Example:
  & buffer;   // Operator & with operand buffer

A binary operator

- Takes two operands.

- Example:
  a + b;   // Operator + with operands a and b

A ternary operator

- Takes three operands.

- Example:
  payday? cash_check() : dig_into_wallet();
  // The operator is ?: the operands are payday, cash_check()
  // and dig_into_wallet()

The C++ Operator Summary Table

The following operator summary table lists all of the C++ operators. For each operator, the columns show its associativity (right or left), symbolic token, and the name of the operator. The last column shows an example usage of the operator and illustrates whether the operator is unary, binary, or ternary. Operators grouped together in a box have the same precedence. Groups that are higher in the table have higher precedences. Parentheses, when used for grouping, has the highest precedence.

Table 4.1 C++ Operator Summary Table.		
Associativity and Operator	**Operator Description**	**Example**
R ::	Global Scope Resolution	::name
L ::	Class Scope Resolution	class_name::member
L .	Member Selection	class_object.member
L ->	Member Selection	expr->member
L []	Subscripting	expr[expr]
L ()	Function Call	expr(expr_list)
L ()	Type Construction	type(expr_list)
L sizeof	Size of Object	sizeof expr
L sizeof	Size of Type	sizeof(type)
R ++	Post Increment	lvalue++
R ++	Pre Increment	++lvalue
R – –	Post Decrement	lvalue– –
R – –	Pre Decrement	– –lvalue
R ~	Bitwise NOT	~expr
R !	Logical NOT	!expr
R –	Unary Minus	–expr
R +	Unary Plus	+expr
R &	Address of	& lvalue
R *	De–reference	* expr
R ()	Type Conversion (cast)	(type)expr
R new	Allocate Free Store	new type
R delete	De–allocate Free Store	delete pointer
R delete[]	De–allocate Free Store Array	delete [expr] ptr

Table 4.1 (*cont*)

L	.*	**Member Pointer Selection**	**class_obj.*member_ptr**
L	–>*	**Member Pointer Selection**	**class_ptr–>*member_ptr**
L	*	**Multiply**	**expr * expr**
L	/	**Divide**	**expr / expr**
L	%	**Modulo**	**expr % expr**
L	+	**Add (plus)**	**expr + expr**
L	–	**Subtract (minus)**	**expr – expr**
L	<<	**Shift Left**	**value << expr**
L	>>	**Shift Right**	**value >> expr**
L	<	**Less Than**	**expr < expr**
L	<=	**Less Than or Equal**	**expr <= expr**
L	>	**Greater Than**	**expr > expr**
L	>=	**Greater Than or Equal**	**expr >= expr**
L	==	**Equal**	**expr == expr**
L	!=	**Not Equal**	**expr != expr**
L	&	**Bitwise AND**	**expr & expr**
L	^	**Bitwise Exclusive OR (XOR)**	**expr ^ expr**
L	|	**Bitwise Inclusive OR**	**expr | expr**
L	&&	**Logical AND**	**expr && expr**
L	||	**Logical Inclusive OR**	**expr || expr**
L	? :	**Arithmetic If**	**expr ? expr : expr**

Table 4.1 (*cont*)

R	=	Simple Assignment	lvalue = expr
R	*=	Multiply and Assign	lvalue *= expr
R	/=	Divide and Assign	lvalue /= expr
R	%=	Modulo and Assign	lvalue %= expr
R	+=	Add and Assign	lvalue += expr
R	–=	Subtract and Assign	lvalue –= expr
R	<<=	Shift Left and Assign	lvalue <<= expr
R	>>=	Shift Right and Assign	lvalue >>= expr
R	&=	Bitwise AND and Assign	lvalue &= expr
R	|=	Bitwise OR and Assign	lvalue |= expr
R	^=	Bitwise XOR and Assign	lvalue ^= expr
L	,	Comma (sequencing)	expr, expr

An *lvalue* is an area in memory whose value may be changed, and the area consists of a starting memory location address and some specific number of consecutive bytes of memory. Non–constant variables that are ints, doubles, structs, etc. are lvalues. The term lvalue originates from its appearance on the left side of an assignment operator; likewise, the term *rvalue* originates from its occurring on the right side. Given a variable's name, its rvalue refers to the variable's value and its lvalue refers to the area where the variable's value lives (resides in memory). In the statement

   x = y + z;

x is used as an lvalue and y and z are used as rvalues. This statement means to add the value of the variable named y and the value of the variable named z and to store the results at the address in memory of the variable named x. In the statement

   *(age_pointer + 3) = 21;

the result from evaluating the expression

   *(age_pointer + 3)

is an lvalue and the assignment operator = causes the value 21 to be stored in that location in memory. If an operator that requires an lvalue operand is used with a non–lvalue operand, a compile error will catch the mistake. The following code fragment illustrates some non–lvalue errors:

```
int a[3];
*(a++) = 1;          // Illegal, an array name is a constant and a
                     // pointer and its value cannot be changed
const int c;
c++;                 // Illegal, cannot modify a constant
1 = 2;               // Illegal, 1 is a constant and not an lvalue
```

Expression Evaluation Order

C++ expressions are evaluated basically the same as they are in other computer languages such as BASIC, FORTRAN, and Pascal. Precedence determines what comes first; the expression

a + b * c

means multiply b and c and then add a.

Associativity is the tie–breaker when operators have the same precedence. The expression

a = b = c

means assign c to b and then assign b to a.

Parentheses override precedence and force a particular order of evaluation; the expression inside the parentheses is evaluated as a unit.

Operand Rule:

Unless the definition of an operator guarantees that its operands are evaluated in a particular order, the operands are evaluated in whatever order each compiler chooses, which could be their interleaved evaluation.

```
x = f() + g();       // f() may be evaluated before g() or
                     // g() may be evaluated before f() or
                     // f() and g() may be evaluated at the
                     // same time by some mechanism such as
                     // the interleaving of their partial evaluations
```

Only the operators

> && || ?:

guarantee that their operands are evaluated in a particular order, which is left to right.

> **(a+b) , (c+d);**   // Evaluates **a+b** and then evaluates **c+d**

Parentheses Rule:

Parentheses are used to override the natural order of evaluation that is determined by precedence and associativity. Parentheses can be viewed as having the highest possible precedence, and any expression inside parentheses is evaluated as a unit. When parentheses are nested, the innermost nested expression is evaluated first, then the next out, and so on.

There is a technical exception to this rule for fundamental types (char, short, int, long, float, double, and long double). In general, parentheses are not guaranteed to force an order of evaluation on multiply and divide, and do not force an order of evaluation on add and subtract. Basically the compiler is free to use the laws of mathematics (associative, commutative, distributive, etc.) and rearrange your expressions into equivalent expressions when generating code to evaluate them. Mathematically, the following three statements are equivalent:

> **a = b * c / d ;**
> **a = (b * c) / d ;**
> **a = b * (c / d);**

In this spirit, C++ and its ancestors are free to evaluate the multiplications and divisions in any order, even if the expression contains parentheses. If a particular order of evaluation is needed, for reasons such as side effects or numerical precision, you must store intermediate results in temporary variables:

> **t = c / d;**   // First **c** is divided by **d**
> **a = b * t;**   // then that result is multiplied by **b**

The same exception applies to the add and subtract operators.

Optimizing compilers take even more freedom in how they generate code that computes a correct mathematical answer. For example,

> **y = (a + i) + (a + i) + (a +i);**

with the common subexpression (a + i) could actually result in evaluating the statement as

y = 3 * (a + i);

because the two expressions are mathematically equivalent and produce the same correct answer.

Precedence Rule:

When evaluating an expression, do all the highest–precedence operators first, then do the next highest–precedence operators, and so on. For example,

a * b + c * d;   // Means **(a*b) + (c*d)**

Associativity Rule:

If adjacent operators have the same precedence, the associativity rule is the tie–breaker. The associativity of the operators is used to determine which one to do first.

If operators have left associativity, the operator on the left is done first, then the one on the right. For example,

a + b + c;   // Means **(a+b) + c**

If operators have right associativity, the operator on the right is done first, then the one on the left.

*++p;   // Means ***(++p)**

Expression Evaluation Order Examples

1 + 2 * 3   * has higher precedence than +
                              1 + (2 * 3)

3 * ++ a   ++ has higher precedence than the
                              multiply operator *
                              3 * (++a)

– 1 * 2 – 3   – unary minus, highest precedence
                              * multiply, next highest precedence
                              – subtract, lowest precedence

The following examples illustrate an underlining technique that helps analyze expressions:

– 1 * 2 – 3

___	Do first
_____	Do next
_____	Do last

((–1) * 2) – 3

1 * sin(2) + 3   Function call () has highest precedence
* multiply next highest precedence
+ addition has lowest precedence
1 * sin(2) + 3

_____	Do first
_____	Do next
_____	Do last

(1 * (sin(2))) + 3

1 + 2 + 3   The + operators have the same
precedence, thus associativity must be used
to determine which operator to do first.
+ is left associative, so the left
operator is first.
(1 + 2) + 3

a + b – c + d   Binary + and – have same precedence.
They are left associative, so do the
left–most one first.

a + b – c + d

_____
_____
_____

(((a + b) – c) + d)

a = b = c   Binary operators = and = have the same
precedence. There is not an assignment
statement in C++. It is an operator.
= is right–associative

a = b = c

_____   Do first

_____   Do next

(a = (b = c))

*ptr++   The unary operators, dereference * and
post increment **++,** have the same
precedence. All unary operators are
right–associative.
(* (ptr++))
Note: The post–increment operator ++
returns the current value of its operand
and at some time later, before the execution of
the current statement ends, its operand is
incremented (the compiler writer
decides exactly when incrementing occurs).

++*pt   The unary operators pre–increment and
dereference * have the same precedence.
All unary operators are right–associative.
(++ (*ptr))

*a[1]   Operator subscript [] has higher
precedence than * dereference.

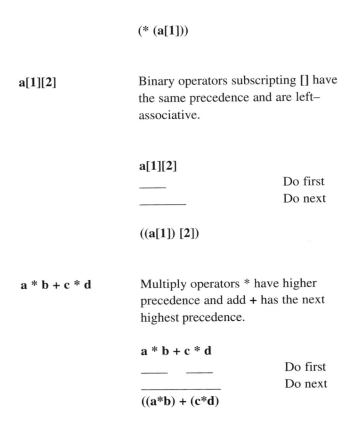

(* (a[1]))

a[1][2]   Binary operators subscripting [] have
               the same precedence and are left–
               associative.

a[1][2]
_____   Do first
_____   Do next

((a[1]) [2])

a * b + c * d   Multiply operators * have higher
               precedence and add **+** has the next
               highest precedence.

a * b + c * d
____   ____   Do first
_____   Do next
((a*b) + (c*d))

A Step–by–step Evaluation Example

The previous material explained how to evaluate expressions and showed an underlining technique to analyze expressions and fully parenthesize them. The following definition of the standard C library function getc(p):

#define getc(p) (– –(p)–>cnt>=0?((int)*(p)–>ptr++):f(p))

is a good challenge of your understanding of C++ expressions. Before reading any further, try to fully parenthesize the above expression on your own, and then compare your answer with the answer below. Note that the parentheses around the macro argument p in the expression are required to make sure that p is evaluated as a unit, because when getc is used, its argument may be an expression. The expression

(– –(p)–>cnt>=0?((int)*(p)–>ptr++):f(p))

is involved because it has several operators.

The following steps show how to fully parenthesize the expression.

1. Identify where parentheses are used to group expressions and control the order of evaluation. Note that (int) is a type–cast and not a use of parentheses to group expressions.

(– –(p)–>cnt>=0?((int)*(p)–>ptr++):f(p))

— —	Do first
——————	Do next
—————————————————	Do last

2. Identify the operators and their expected operands

Operators and Operands

– –	pre–decrement	– – lvalue
–>	member selection	pointer –> member
>=	greater than or equal	expr >= expr
?:	arithmetic if	expr ? expr : expr
(int)	cast	type (expr–list)
*	pointer dereference	* expr
–>	member selection	pointer –> member
++	post increment	lvalue ++
f(p)	function call	expr (expr–list)

3. Use the Operator Summary Table and order the operators in the expression into groups of equal precedence; put the groups of higher precedence before groups of lower precedence.

Operator Precedence Groups

–>	member selection	pointer –> member
f(p)	function call	expr (expr–list)

++	post increment	lvalue ++
– –	pre–decrement	– – lvalue
*	pointer dereference	* expr
(int)	cast	(type) expr
>=	greater than or equal	expr >= expr
?:	arithmetic if	expr ? expr : expr

4. Underline the matching balanced parentheses and then parenthesize each of the underlined segments.

(– –(p)–>cnt>=0?((int)*(p)–>ptr++):f(p))

            —   —   4A. first

                             _____   4B. next

_____   4C. last

4A. The (p) expressions are already fully parenthesized.

4B. Fully parenthesize the expression ((int)*(p)–>ptr++).

<u>Operator Precedence Groups</u>

–>	member selection	pointer –> member
++	post increment	lvalue ++
*	pointer dereference	* expr
(int)	cast	(type) expr

Note that the operators ++, * (int) are unary operators and therefore right–associative.

((int)*(p)–>ptr++)

Do first

Do next

Do next

Do next

_____

_____

_____

_____

((int)(*((p)–>ptr)++))

Now, change the original expression to include the above fully parenthesized subexpression:

(– –(p)–>cnt>=0?((int)(*((p)–>ptr)++)):f(p))

4C. Fully parenthesize the remaining part of it.

(– –(p)–>cnt>=0?((int)(*((p)–>ptr)++)):f(p))

—	_____	Done
— _____	_____	To Do

<u>The operators To Do</u>

–>	member selection	pointer –> member
f(p)	function call	expr (expr–list)
– –	pre decrement	– – lvalue
>=	greater than or equal	expr >= expr
?:	arithmetic if	expr ? expr : expr

(– –(p)–>cnt>=0?((int)(*(((p)–>ptr)++))):f(p))

Do First

Do Next

Do Next

Do Next

_____   _____

_____

_____

_____

Adding parentheses for each of the underlined sequences above gives
the following progression of expressions:

$$(--((p)\text{--}\textgreater cnt)\textgreater=0 \quad ? \quad ((int)(*(((p)\text{--}\textgreater ptr)++))) \quad : \quad (f(p)))$$
$$((--((p)\text{--}\textgreater cnt))\textgreater=0 \quad ? \quad ((int)(*(((p)\text{--}\textgreater ptr)++))) \quad : \quad (f(p)))$$
$$(((--((p)\text{--}\textgreater cnt))\textgreater=0)? \quad ((int)(*(((p)\text{--}\textgreater ptr)++))) \quad : \quad (f(p)))$$
$$(((--((p)\text{--}\textgreater cnt))\textgreater=0)? \quad ((int)(*(((p)\text{--}\textgreater ptr)++))) \quad : \quad (f(p)))$$

The last expression above is the final answer and it is the fully parenthesized version of the original expression. It has the same meaning as the original expression, but the order of evaluation is shown explicitly with parentheses. When all of the matching parentheses are connected with lines, it is easier to see the operand(s) of the operators in the expression. This is particularly true for the ?: operator as shown below, that has three operands, and each of them is composed of nested subexpressions.

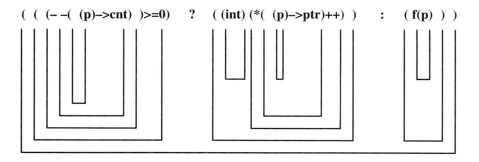

The value of p is the address of a standard I/O structure that is used to control files. (stdin is an example and is shown in Figure 4.2.)

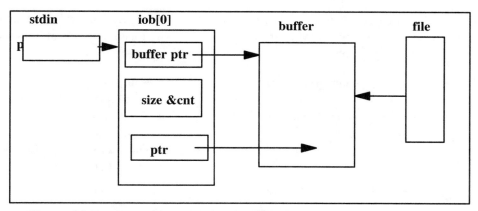

Figure 4.2 Standard I/O structures that control files.

4.3   Types

Introduction

Fundamental types (synonym: built–in types) are the data types that are provided by language. They correspond directly to computer–hardware representations of data, and the hardware's operations on those data: i.e., hardware data types. These types are a fundamental characteristic of computers.

User–defined types are types that are defined by programmers in the software; they are composed from fundamental types and/or other user–defined types. These types may represent concepts that are meaningful in the computing environment (e.g., lists, queues, trees, and windows) or concepts that are meaningful in an application program (problem domain) (e.g., paycheck, navigational system, line integral, surfing condition, fragrance, sea–state, galactic–coordinate, a_childs_first_word, etc.).

In object–oriented programming (OOP), a type (class) represents a specific category of things (objects), like guide dogs for the blind. A unique occurrence or instance of a class is called an object, like Twylas_dog_Sammy. The following code illustrates the creation of a guide_dog object, assuming that the class guide_dog was previously defined:

guide_dog Twylas_dog_Sammy;

A Type's Name

The C++ reserved word *typedef* is used to name a type definition, called a type name. A named type is defined by putting the word typedef in front of a statement. It looks like the definition of an object.

```
char* planet[9];            // Creates object named planet
                            // An array of 9 char* elements
typedef char* tree[20];     // Type's name is tree
                            // Tree is not an object
tree conifers;              // Create object named conifers that
                            // is an array of 20 char* elements
```

A typedef is not required to create named classes, structs and unions.

```
class book {                // This type's name is book
        char title[100];
        char author[50];
};

book K&R_C;                 // Using the type name book
book Stroustrup_Cpp;
book this_book;
```

Typedefs are a programming convenience and if a complicated or messy type specification is used repeatedly, naming the type with a typedef and then using the type name can improve code readability and avoid inadvertent specification errors. Using a typedef type name is equivalent to using the original type specification; a typedef does not create a new user–defined type. The following code example illustrates type names:

```
class {                     // Type has no name (anonymous)
        int a;
} obj1;

class name1 {               // Type name is name1
        int b;
} obj2;

name1 obj3, obj4;           // Create two objects of type name1
int obj5;                   // int is a built–in type name
```

```
typedef int counter;              // Type name counter, no object
                                  // created

counter obj6, obj7;               // Create two objects of type counter
                                  // which is an alias for int
                                  // counter and int are equivalent

typedef int* board [8][8];        // Type name board
board obj8, obj9, obj10;          // Create three objects that are
                                  // of type pointers to 8–by–8
                                  // arrays of ints
```

Type Void Semantics

Type void is built into the language, but it is fundamentally different from the above types. A void represents something that has no value. For example, the following function prototypes:

```
void f(int);
int  g();                 // A C++ style to say no arguments
int  h(void);
```

mean that function f takes an int argument and does not return a value (void); function g has no arguments and returns an int value; and function h has no arguments and returns an int. In these cases, void is a place–holder for nothing.

Type void* has a special meaning for pointers. It means that the pointer points to an object of unspecified type. A void pointer cannot be dereferenced; however, once a void pointer is either cast or converted to a particular type, it can then be dereferenced.

```
char* ocean_ptr= "Pacific", op;
void* vp;
vp = ocean_ptr;cout << vp;        // Illegal, cannot dereference a void pointer
op = (char*)vp;
cout << op;                       // Legal, op is type char* and points
                                  // to the string "Pacific"
```

When a function parameter can point to many different types of objects, it is typically declared as a void pointer.

Category Terminology

The type categories shown in Figure 4.3 are used when discussing a particular category as a whole:

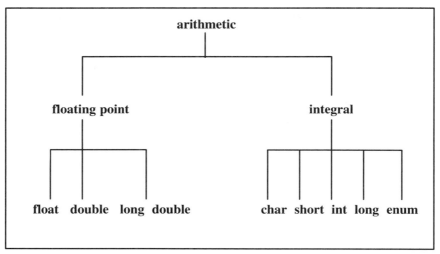

Figure 4.3 Terminology of type categories.

Figure 4.3 illustrates the two main types of data that are used in C++ for arithmetic operations: floating point and integral, which have different data representations. Collectively, these two data types are referred to as arithmetic types.

Anonymous User–defined Types and Objects

A user–defined class, struct, union, or enum may be defined without specifying a name for the type (no tag name). This is called an anonymous class, anonymous struct, anonymous union, and anonymous enum, respectively.

```
struct {                    // Anonymous struct
    int   a;                // It has no name
    double b;
} x, y, z;
```

An anonymous type is useful when a type definition is not going to be used or needed anywhere else. It also simplifies coding and keeps from unnecessarily cluttering up the namespace with names that are not needed.

When an anonymous type is defined, instances (objects) of it are only specifiable as part of the definition, like the objects x, y, and z in the struct example. If an anonymous struct or class definition does not specify any objects, a compile error will occur; however, both an anonymous union and anonymous enum can be defined without specifying an object. These objects are called anonymous objects. The following program illustrates anonymous user–defined type definitions and anonymous object definitions:

```
main()
{       // Anonymous type names

    class {
       char    x;
       int  y;
    } a;

    struct {
       char    x;
       int  y;
    } b;

    union {
       char    x;
       int  y;
    } c;

    enum   { red, green, blue  } d;

// Anonymous object of anonymous user–defined type

/* – – comments out the code that causes compile errors – –

    class {
       char    x;
       int  y;
    };                              // Error

*/
```

```
struct {
    char    x;
    int  y;
};                              // Error

union  {
    char    x;
    int  y;
};                              // OK
                                // Also, x and y are visible in
                                // the same scope as their union

}

enum   { sun, planet, moon, asteroid, comet };
                                // OK
                                // For enums the enumerators inside the braces
                                // are always visible in the same scope as their enum
```

The following program illustrates defining and using anonymous unions and anonymous objects:

```
#include <iostream.h>

main()
{               // Define a named union
    union U1 {
        char*       s;
        int         i;
        double      d;
    };

    // Create an object (instance) of the named union U1 and use it
    U1 a;
                    // Define an anonymous (unnamed) union
                    // Also must create
                    // all of its instances now, because it has no name
                     // to use its definition again anywhere else
```

```
union {
    char*   c;
    float   d;
} b;

b.c = "I'm the value of b.c \n";
cout << b.c;

        // Note that if an anonymous union definition does not
        // explicitly specify any instances (objects), one instance
        // is created and its members are directly referenced by
        // their member names.

union {        // Anonymous type name (no name)
    char*   s;
    float   d;
};             // Anonymous object name (no name)

s = "I'm the value of an object with the alias name s. \n";
cout << s;

d = 1.23;
cout << d << " is the number 1.23 \n";
cout << &s << " is the memory address of s.\n";
cout << &d << " is the memory address of d.\n";
cout << "They are the same, because they are members of "
        << "the same union. \n";

        // Named and anonymous unions that are class members
class C {
public:
    U1 data_member_1;      // First data member
    union {
        char*  s;
        float  d;
    } data_member_2;       // Second data member
```

```
        union {                    // Third data member
            char*  s;
            float  d;
        };
    };

        // Create an object of class C and then use it
        // Note how the union members are referenced

C obj;
obj.data_member_1.s = "A";
obj.data_member_2.s = "B";
obj.s           = "C";

cout << obj.data_member_1.s
        << obj.data_member_2.s
        << obj.s
        << " are the letters ABC \n";

}
```

———————— Program's Output ————————
I'm the value of b.c
I'm the value of an object with the alias name s.
1.23 is the number 1.23
1bdaffee is the memory address of s.
1bdaffee is the memory address of d.
They are the same, because they are members of the same union.
ABC are the letters ABC

4.4   Type Conversion

Data typing, strong type checking and type–safe linkage are very important in software engineering because they

- Support the development of reliable software.

- Make it much easier to detect and fix inadvertent, erroneous usage of variables, objects, and functions.

Data typing is done by the programmer when writing the source code of a program and involves defining new types (classes) from existing defined types and creating objects of defined types. Strong type checking is done at compile time by the compiler. If an object is used in a way that is erroneous (not defined for its type), the compiler notifies the programmer with a compile–time error message. The output of a successful compile is an object module. A program usually consists of many object modules that are produced by separate compiles. The linker combines the object modules into an executable program, which can be run on a computer. Type–safe linkage is done by the linker and it makes sure, based on type information, that functions and data (externals) used in one module are correctly linked to their definitions in other modules. If a link error occurs, the programmer is notified with a linker error message.

C++ is a typed language with strong type checking and type–safe linkage. Type conversion is an important operation in a typed language, because it is often desirable or necessary (e.g., for efficiency reasons) to convert an object of one type to an object of another type when the conversion is meaningful. This often occurs when two types have a common characteristic.

An everyday example of type conversion is converting inches to centimeters. The number 10 of type inches converts to the number 25.4 of type centimeters, and vice–versa. Converting between inches and centimeters is meaningful because they both represent a measure of distance. While there is always an exact conversion between inches and centimeters, this is not true in general for conversions between dissimilar types.

An example of type conversion in C++ is converting ints to doubles and vice versa. Both ints and doubles represent a common thing: numbers. Some numbers, like 2001, are representable precisely by both ints and doubles and in these cases, there is an exact conversion between ints and doubles. Other numbers, like the number of atoms in a mole of an element (6.022E23), or pi (3.14159 ...), are represented by doubles but poorly, or not at all, representable by ints. Likewise, on some very large machines, ints are not exactly representable by doubles. In these cases, the meaning of the conversions (semantics) must be specified, and it is. A pragmatic way to find out the meaning of ints and doubles on your system is to run a program similar to the following code:

```
// Sample conversions between ints and doubles
#include <iostream.h>          // For cout <<
#include <math.h>              // For constant M_PI

main()
{
    double  year = 2300.0;
```

```
double  pi = M_PI;
double  avogadro = 6.022E23;
int            y, p, a;
double  Y, P, A;

// Type conversion occurs implicitly when a variable of
// one type is assigned to a variable of another type

Y = y = year;
cout << Y << '\t' << y << '\t' << year    << '\n';

P = p = pi;
cout << P << '\t' << p << '\t' << pi      << '\n';

// 6.022E23 is too big to represent as an int
// Is converting it to an int meaningful?
A = a = avogadro;
cout << A << '\t' << a << '\t' << avogadro << '\n';

return 0;
}
```

──────────── Program's Output ────────────

```
2300    2300    2300
3   3   3.141593
Floating Point Error:  Overflow
Abnormal program termination
```

Explicit Type Conversions

An explicit type conversion, which is also called casting, is an explicit expression made by a programmer to convert an object of one type to an object of another type. In C++ there are two styles of explicit type conversion and they produce equivalent results. The following program shows both the C style of casting and the new functional notation style:

```
#include <iostream.h>
main()
{
    int    i1, i2;
    double d = 5.6;
    i1 = (int) d;                        // Using casting operator
    i2 = int(d);                         // Using function notation
    cout << i1 << '\t' << i2 << '\t' << d << "\t\n";
}
```

───────────── **Program's Output** ─────────────

    5   5   5.6

The casting style uses the casting operator and it has the form

        (type) object_to_convert

This style is typically used when a left operand specifies a conversion to a derived type using the declarative operators

*	pointer
&	reference
[]	subscripting
()	function
void*	pointer to void
::*	pointer to member

The functional style has the form

        type_name(arguments)

This style is a more readable syntax and is typically used in preference to the casting style. The left operand is the name of the resulting conversion type and it is typically either a fundamental type name (like int or double) or a user–defined class name. The right operand is an argument list, which may contain zero or more arguments, depending on the conversion type. (Note that casting is limited and takes exactly one argument as its right operand.)

The following code fragment illustrates these two forms:

```
int         i = 7;
double d1, d2;
char*       a0;

d1 = (double)i;              // Casting operator
d2 = double(i);              // Function notation
a0 = (char*) 0;              // Cast int to char*

// Converting ints to objects of user–defined class complex
// Some C++ products provide this user–defined class

complex c1, c2, c3;
c1 = complex();      // Function notation with no arguments
c2 = complex(1);     // Function notation with one argument
c3 = complex(3,4);   // Function notation with two arguments
```

Implicit Type Conversion

Implicit type conversion is the automatic conversion of an object from one type to another. A benefit of this automatic feature is increased programmer productivity. The implicit type conversions that occur for built–in types are defined by the C++ language. The implicit type conversions that occur for user–defined types (classes) are defined when class definitions are coded. Chapter 6 on constructors and destructors covers this topic in detail. Implicit type conversion occurs when

- An object of one type is used but an object of another type is required.

- There is either a direct or indirect way to convert a used object into the required object.

The following program contains several implicit type conversions:

```
// Example of some implicit type conversions
#include <math.h>                      // for sin(x)

main()
{
    double a, b;
    int    c;
    a = 1;                             // 1 converts to 1.0
    b = a + 2;                         // 2 converts to 2.0
    c = sin(1) + 23;                   // 1 to 1.0 and 23 to 23.0
                                       // Answer converted to int

}
```

If the above program, with the comments changed to the form /* */, were run using C (not ANSI C), it would run and produce the wrong answers, without any hint of a problem. In C, the int is not implicitly converted to a double, but the called routine interprets the value of its argument as if it were a double: a run–time bug. In this situation the programmer frequently debugs the problem(s) at run–time, which can be both difficult and time–consuming. In general, a program that is not type checked is sensitive to run–time data and may run most of the time, but crash on occasion because of particular data values.

The Causes of Implicit Conversions

Implicit type conversions of built–in types occur in the following situations:

- Using the assignment operator = converts its right operand to the type of its left operand if their types differ, and then assignment is done.

- Using the arithmetic binary operators with built–in types requires that both of their operands are of the same type. A complete list of implicit type conversions is given in the next subsection.

- Using function parameters that are typed requires an argument of that type when the function is called.

- Using a function that is declared to return a particular type will return a value of that type.

In these situations, implicit type conversion of an operand or argument occurs if it is needed and if it is also possible (the conversion is defined either directly or indirectly). If a required conversion is not possible, an error will be diagnosed at compile–time. If there is more than one way to do a conversion, which may inadvertently happen when user–defined conversions are defined, an ambiguity error will occur at compile–time. This case is discussed in later chapters.

The following program illustrates some implicit type conversions that occur for binary operators and function arguments:

```
// Example of some implicit type conversions
#include <math.h>                    // for sin(x)

main()
{
    double a, b;
    int    c;
    a = 1;                           // 1 converts to 1.0
    b = a + 2;                       // 2 converts to 2.0
    c = sin(1) + 23;                 // 1 to 1.0 and 23 to 23.0
                                     // Answer converted to int

}
```

The following simple program has a return value that is implicitly converted to the function's defined return type. When the sizes of types differ, sizeof will give a hint of an expression's resulting type.

```
#include <iostream.h>

main()
{
    double  f(char);                 // Function prototype
    char        c = 1;

    if (sizeof(f(c)) == sizeof(double))
        cout << "OK  \n";
    else
        cout << "BAD \n";
}
```

```
double f(char x)
{
    return x;                           // x is implicitly converted to double
}
```

———————— **Program's Output** ————————
OK

Many binary operators do not cause implicit conversion of their operands. The bitwise operators (&, |, <<, etc.) and logical operators (&&, ||, etc.) require integral operands (char, short, unsigned, etc.) and do not implicitly convert their operands.

```
1 &  2.0;                 // Illegal
1 << 2.0;                 // Illegal
1 && 2.0;                 // Illegal
```

The square brackets ([]) operator also does not cause any implicit type conversions of its operands. For example,

```
int a[3];
a[1.0] = 386;             // Error, operand is of incompatible type
                          // 1.0 is not converted to 1
```

What is the quickest way to find out what will happen in a particular situation? The answer is that there is always an expert at your fingertips — your C++ compiler. It only takes a minute to write a 10–line program that asks the compiler your question and it will quickly respond with the answer.

Implicit Conversion of Built–in Types

As mentioned above, the arithmetic binary operators with built–in operand types cause implicit type conversion if their operands are not of the same type. While the actual conversions that occur are system–dependent, the rules that follow give the principles behind the conversions:

Arithmetic Binary Operators

*	/	%	+	−
*=	/=	%=	+=	−=
==	!=	<=	>=	< >

Built–in Types

long	double
	double
	float
unsigned	long
	long
unsigned	int
	int
unsigned	short
	short
unsigned	char
	char

Implicit Type Conversion Rule:

- If both operands are the same type, no conversion occurs.

- Otherwise, locate the two operand types in the subsequent built–in types list; the one that is lower in the list is implicitly converted (promoted) to the one that is higher in the list. While this rule in not always true, it is true with the following modifications:

  - If the operand highest in the list is long double, double, or float, the rule above is true.

  - Otherwise, if the operands have different sizeof values, convert the smaller sized operand to the type of the larger sized operand.

  - Otherwise, if both operands have the same sizeof and one of them is unsigned, convert the other one to the type of the unsigned operand.

  - Otherwise, if the operands have the same size, either one can be converted to the other's type: the choice made is system dependent. Typically the conversion will occur to the one highest in the list.

To determine the implicit type conversions that occur on your system, enter and run the program in Appendix B. This is a good example of having the computer provide real answers to tough questions. Table 4.2 summarizes the program's output on the authors' systems:

Table 4.2 Implicit type conversion table.

sizeof	Left Operand		Right Operand										
			c	uc	s	i	us	ui	l	ul	f	d	ld
10	long double	ld	<	<	<	<	<	<	<	<	<	<	*
8	double	d	<	<	<	<	<	<	<	<	<	*	^
4	float	f	<	<	<	<	<	<	<	<	*	^	^
4	unsigned long	ul	<	<	<	<	<	<	<	*	^	^	^
4	long	l	<	<	<	<	<	<	*	^	^	^	^
2	unsigned int	ui	<	<	<	<	<	*	^	^	^	^	^
2	unsigned short	us	<	<	<	<	*	^	^	^	^	^	^
2	int	i	<	<	<	*	^	^	^	^	^	^	^
2	short	s	<	<	*	^	^	^	^	^	^	^	^
1	unsigned char	uc	<	*	^	^	^	^	^	^	^	^	^
1	char	c	*	^	^	^	^	^	^	^	^	^	^

Legend:

< means that the right operand is converted to the type of the left operand, which is at the left on the row (symbol < points left).

^ means that the left operand is converted to the type of the right operand, which is at the top of the column (symbol ^ points up).

* means that no implicit type conversion occurs.

Note: The above one– and two–letter abbreviations, like ld and d, are only used in this table. They are not related in any way to the printf format specifications.

The following annotated code fragment illustrates how to use Table 4.2:

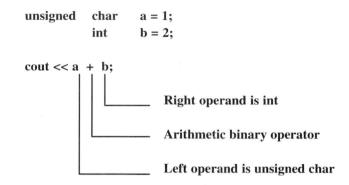

Locate in the above table, the row labeled unsigned char and the column labeled int; they intersect at a box with the symbol ^ in it. This means that the left operand, a, is converted to the right operand's type (int). Then, the variables a and b are added and the resulting expression has a type of int and a value of 3.

5

Classes and Abstract Data Types

The power of C++ stems from its notion of a class. It is the class and its extremely efficient implementation that distinguishes C++ from all other computer programming languages, including its ancestors C and ANSI C. A class encompasses an extensive number of features and concepts. This chapter covers class basics; the succeeding chapters cover class concepts and features, which include the following:

- Constructors — guaranteed initialization when an object is created by a definition or type conversion (casting), or by proper handling of the copying of an object during assignment, argument passing, and function value returning.

- Destructors — guaranteed cleanup when an object is destroyed.

- Casting — casting user–defined class objects to built–in type objects and other user–defined types of objects.

- Derived classes — using inheritance to make a new class from an existing class or classes.

- Virtual functions — run–time selection of a function based on the class of object.

- Others — like a data member that is shared by all the objects of a class.

5.1   Introduction

The C++ language allows you to create *user–defined data types* (*abstract data types*) that can be used in the same way as language–defined data types. The name of class or struct is the specifier for the abstract data type. An abstract data type specifier can be used anywhere in a program that a predefined type specifier can appear.

```
#include <iostream.h>

class adt  {
      int          x;
      char         *y;
public:
      adt()              {x = 57;  y = "b";}
      ~adt()             {x = 0;   y = 0;}
      void display()   {cout << y << x << '\n';}
};

main()
{
      char * title = "example";
      cout << title << endl;
      adtcpp_class;
      cpp_class.display();
}
```

space ——————→

Every operation a user–defined type must carry out is to be provided by you. Therefore much care must go into the design of a class. A class should have its data representations (data members) in the private or protected region of the class unless there is a specific reason for including them in the public region. A class should have its *member functions* (*methods*) in the public region of the class unless there is a specific reason for including them in the private or protected region. This is the interface of the abstract data type. *Encapsulation* occurs when you have data and functions together in the same unit, but restrict the access to data. A class should have its implementations of the member functions included in another file. This second file should be compiled to object code and the user should get only the object code for that module, and not the source code. This is referred to as *information hiding*.

5.2   Class, Struct, and Union Relationships

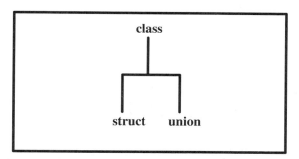

Figure 5.1 Relationship of class, struct, and union.

Figure 5.1 implies that both a struct and a union are classes. In fact, they have the same syntax but some differences in semantics. A struct is identical to a class, except a struct has public default member access; a class has private default member access. Users (clients) of a class can only access public members. A union is similar to a class, but a union has public default member access; also, a union's object contains at most one of its members at any one time and a union lacks many of the capabilities of a class. These capabilities will discussed in later chapters.

In the following program, the class, struct, and union definitions are equivalent:

```
#include <iostream.h>
main()
{                          // Beginning of main block
                           // The class, struct and union are in sepa-
                           // rate blocks and each is local to only its
                           // own block. This avoids duplicate defini-
                           // tion problems.

    {                      // Beginning of class block
        class z {          // Class's name is z
        public:            // Makes what follows public
            int a;         // Data member
        } obj;             // Create object obj of type z

        obj.a = 123;       // Obj's data member a = 123
        cout << obj.a << '\n';
    }                      // End of class block
```

```
{    // Beginning of struct block
     struct z {
          int a;
     } obj;

     obj.a = 456;
     cout << obj.a << '\n';
}    // End of struct block
{    // Beginning of union block
     union z {
          int a;
          float b;
     } obj;

     obj.a = 789;
     cout << obj.a << '\n';
}    // End of union block
}    // End of main block
```

———— **Program's Output** ————
123
456
789

The following program illustrates the differences between classes and unions:

```
// Example of class and union differences

#include <iostream.h>

main()
{
// Use local blocks so that same names can be used

     {
          class z {
          public:    // Make what follows public
               int       a;
               double   b;
          } obj;
          obj.a = 12;
          obj.b = 34;
```

```
        cout << obj.a << " " << obj.b << '\n';

        cout << "sizeof(obj) = "<< sizeof(obj)  << '\n';
        cout << "sizeof(int) + sizeof(double) = "
                << sizeof(int) + sizeof(double)<< "\n\n";
    }

    {
        union z {
            int    a;
            double b;
        } obj;
        obj.a = 56;
        obj.b = 78;
        cout << obj.a << " " << obj.b << '\n';
        cout << "sizeof(obj) = " << sizeof(obj)<< '\n';
        cout << "sizeof(double) = "<<sizeof(double) << '\n';
    }
}
```

——— **Program's Output** ———
12 34
sizeof(obj) = 10
sizeof(int) + sizeof(double) = 10

0 78
sizeof(obj) = 8
sizeof(double) = 8

The above program shows that a class object is sized exactly to hold its int and double data members only. Note that the sizes of int, double, c, etc. are machine dependent.

The size of the union object is smaller and it is sized to hold its largest member. Because it holds only one of its data members at any single time. When the statement

obj.a = 56;

is executed, object obj contains the data member a, which has a value of 56. When the statement

obj.b = 78;

is executed, the data member a is overwritten and the union object contains the data member b which has the value of 78. At this time, printing obj.a the int is meaningless because the obj contains only data member b.

Going back to the relationship between a class and a struct, the following fact is restated because it takes awhile to truly think of them as the same thing. In C++ a class and a struct are identical, except a class has default private access and a struct has default public access. For the remainder of this book, whatever is said about classes also applies to structs. When a distinction is important, it will be clearly noted.

A Class Defines a User–defined Data Type

The C++ language class construct allows you to create user–defined data types that are used in the same way as built–in types, like int and double. C++, user–defined types are first–class citizens. They look and feel like built–in types.

The name of a class is the name of its type. A class type is used to create an instance of a class, called an **object**. In C++ terminology, a variable is not called an object. The members of a class are referenced using the following notations:

> **class_name.member_name**
> **class_name.*member_pointer_name**
> **class_name_pointer–>member_name**
> **class_name_pointer–>*member_pointer_name**

and the member operators are

.	(dot)
.*	(dot star)
–>	(arrow)
–>*	(arrow star)

Classes (synonym: user–defined types) are easy to use. The following code is an overview of how an object is created and how its members are used:

```
car heaths_car;                 // Create a car object
heaths_car.driver = "HEA";      // Assign "HEA" to data member
                                // driver

heaths_car.start_engine();      // Call member function
                                // start_engine
```

In the first statement above, car is a class (synonym: user–defined type) that is assumed to be already defined. It is used to create a car object, named heaths_car. In the next statement, the data member driver of the object heaths_car is referenced with the dot operator and then assigned the value HEA. In the last statement, the member function start_engine() is called with the argument heaths_car. This chapter explains classes, data members, and member functions in detail.

Classes Have Data Members and Member Functions

Both data and functions may be class members and they have class scope; in other words, they only have meaning within the scope of their class. Data members are used to represent the value (state) of objects of the class. Each object of a class contains its own copy of all the data members (excludes static members), which are declared in its class definition. Member functions implement the *behavior* of objects and they are used primarily to reference and/or change the value of objects of their class. They are also used for their side effects: input, output, etc. Member functions always have access to all the members of their class, while clients can access only the public members of a class. While there are typically many objects of a class, there is only a single copy of a class's member functions and it resides in the process's text segment. Figure 5.2 shows the memory layout of an object with a single data member that is an int named x:

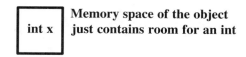

Figure 5.2 An object's memory layout.

The following program defines a user–defined type named trivial and then uses the type to define objects with storage classes of static, automatic, and dynamic. The storage class register was skipped because objects are rarely, if ever, put into a register; remember, register is just advice to the compiler. This example also shows a member function, how it is defined, and how it is used. The whole idea of functions as members is often hard to grasp at first; fortunately, it quickly becomes second nature after some practice. Objects of class trivial in the following program look like the diagram above:

```
// Example of objects with storage classes of
//         static, automatic, and dynamic
//
//
// Example of a function that is a member of the class

#include <iostream.h>

class trivial {                 // Class definition begins
public:                         // What follows is public to clients
      int x;                    // Data member of the class
                                // Typically data are kept private
      int f();                  // Function member of the class
};                              // Class definition ends

int trivial::f()                // Member function definition
{                               //    class_name::member_function_name
      return x;                 // Reference to member variable x
}

trivial a;                      // Create static object a

main()
{
      trivial  b;               // Create automatic object b
      trivial* c;               // Create automatic pointer c
      trivial* d = new trivial; // New creates a dynamic
                                //    trivial object on the heap and d
                                //    points to it

      trivial e[3];             // Creates automatic array
                                //    of 3 trivial objects

      // Use the created trivial objects

      a.x  = 1;
      b.x  = 2;
      c    = &b;                // c points to object b
      c->x = 3;                 // b.x is now 3
      d->x = 4;
      for (int i = 0; i < 3 ; i++)
         e[i].x = i + 5;
```

```
            cout << a.x    << '\t';
            cout << b.f()  << '\t';          // Object b does f()
            cout << c->x   << '\t';
            cout << d->x   << '\t';
            cout << d->f() << '\t';          // Object *d does f()
         for (i = 0; i < 3; i++)
            cout << e[i].f() << '\t';        // Object.member_function()
     }
```

──────────────── **Program's Output** ─────────────────
          1   3   3   4   4   5   6   7

Notice that using the trivial type is very much like using a built–in type. Also, there is a new usage. The C++ notation

b.f()

to execute function f() on object b (procedural–oriented viewpoint) might look unusual at first; however, it is a natural extension of C's member selection notation and function f() is a member of b's class. Additionally, it reflects the way one thinks when doing object–oriented programming (OOP). This style involves thinking about objects and the actions that they perform. Only an object knows how to perform the actions that it can do (change its state, etc.). From an object–oriented viewpoint, the object named b is requested to do the action f().

The function f() is a member of the class trivial and its full name is

trivial::f()

When a member function is defined outside of its class's definition, the function's full name must be used. The reason for this is explained in Subsection 5.

An existing class definition can be used in two different ways. One usage is to create objects (instances) of the class, and in this case, the user of the class is called the *client* and the code that is using it is called the client code. The other usage is to create a new class (a new user–defined type) that is derived (also called inherited) from an existing class; derived classes are explained in Chapter 9.

Control over Member Access

A class also has control over access to its members. Part of a class can be public and the general public (*clients*) can use members; another part can disallow access to its members, and this is called the private part. This capability to hide data (disallow access to it) is necessary to safely implement abstract data types (ADTs), which are covered in the next chapter. There is another access called protected that is discussed in Chapter 9.

Classes have default private access and the keywords private, protected, and public are used inside a class definition to define the access category of the code that follows the keyword. Keywords can be used any number of times. The following example illustrates using member access controls:

```
// Example of controlling access to class members

access_example {           // Default access is private
        char a;            // Private data member
        void f();          // Private member function
      public:              // Change access to public
        char  b;           // Public data member
        void g();          // Public member function
      private:             // Change access to private
        char c;            // Private member
        void h();          // Private member
};

void access_example::f() { }    // A do nothing function

void access_example::g()        // Define access_example's
  {                             // Member function g()
      a = 'W';                  // A member function can
      b = 'X';                  // Access all of its class's
      c = 'Y';                  // Data members
      f(), g(), h();            // Note: All member names
  }                             //    are visible inside a
                                //    member definition

void access_example::h() { }    // A do nothing function

main()
{
      access_example x;         // Create object x
      x.a = 'A';                // Illegal, private member
      x.f();                    // Illegal, private member

      x.b = 'B';                // OK, public member
      x.g();                    // OK, public member
```

```
        x.c = 'C';                  // Illegal, private member
        x.h();                      // Illegal, private member
}
```

5.3   Class Declarations and Definitions

A class has two parts:

1. Class head

2. Class body.

```
class tag            /* This is the class head */

{
                     /* Everything between braces is the body */
};
```

A *class head* consists of the keyword *class,* a *tag name,* and ends at the opening brace. The tag name is the name of the *user–defined* data type and can be used as a data type in the language (the language has been extended to include a user–defined data type). The class head comprises the class declaration and registers with the system the fact that there is a new data type. At this time you can only declare pointers or references to a class ,but a class cannot have an object.

The *class body* consists of everything that is included within the class braces. It would include, both *data members* and *member functions*. By default, everything within a class body is private (contrast this to the struct in C++ in which everything is public). By using the keywords *public*, *protected*, and *private*, the body can be divided into *access regions*. The class body must be terminated with a semicolon or a declaration list followed by a semicolon.

```
class adt  {             // Now adt is declared as a class
    int     x;           // Private region by default
public:
    adt();               // Public region
    void display();
private:
    float   y;           // Private region
protected:
    double  z;           // Protected region
```

```
        public:
            ~adt();                    // Public region
        protected:
            int     a;                 // Protected region
        };                             // Class adt is now defined


        adt     alpha, beta, gamma;
```

A class is not considered defined until the closing brace of the class body is seen. A class which has been declared , however, can have references and pointers to itself which can be included inside the class body (self–referencing pointers and references). If this were not possible, you could not make linked lists, queues, and stacks of class objects.

```
        class list_element {
            int             x;
            list_element    *next;        // Self–referencing pointer
            list_element    *previous;    // Self–referencing pointer
            list_element    *beginning;   // Self–referencing pointer
        public:
            list_element();
            void display(void);
        };
```

You cannot declare an object of a class which has not been defined. Therefore, you cannot declare a data member to be an object of its own type because you cannot use an object as a data member until it is defined. Objects are not defined until the closing brace is reached. If you try to use an object of a type within that type, the compiler will give an error message:

error: class tag–name undefined, size not known

This prevents you from getting into a recursive loop from which you cannot exit.

5.4   Data Members

The declarations of data members of a class are similar to the declarations of data variables outside a class. However, class data members cannot be explicitly initialized. This is true even though you are the designer of the class. You should remember that only member functions and friend functions of a class should be able to read or write to the private data. Therefore, only member functions can set or change the values of **x** and **nm** in the example below.

```
class hello  {
    int     x;               // Valid – not initialized
    char    nm = 'b';        // Invalid
public:
    set(int xx, char aa) {x = xx; nm = aa;}
    void display(void);
};
```

The declaration of variables within a class follow the same format as the declaration of variables outside a class: the variable type is given, followed by the variable identifier, followed by a semicolon. If a class has multiple variables of the same type, they can be declared as a comma–separated list or listed on separate lines.

```
class multiple {
    int         x, y, z;
    float    a, b, c;
public:
    multiple();
};
```

The class can also be written as

```
class multiple  {
    int         x;
    int         y;
    int         z;
    float       a;
    float       b;
    float       c;
public:
    multiple();
};
```

You can declare an object of one class to be a data member of another class if the object has been previously defined. Such an object is referred to as an *embedded object*.

```
#include <iostream.h>

class world {
    int         x;
public:
    world() {x = 57;}
    void display(void)    {cout << x << '\n';}
};
```

```
class hello  {
     float          y;
     world   view;                        // Object of  type world
public:
     hello() {y = 57.57;}
     void display(void)   {cout << y << '\n';}
};
```

You cannot declare a data member to be an object of another class unless the other class has first been defined. If you do so, the compiler will give an error message similar to the following:

error: class tag–name undefined, size not known

The compiler must know the size of an object so that it can lay out enough memory to hold its data members. A forward declaration of a class is not adequate, it must be defined. You can, however, declare pointers to objects of a class's type and include them inside the class body. If this were not possible, as you have seen, you could not make linked lists, queues, and stacks. As a general rule, anything that you can do with structs in C, you can do with structs and classes in C++.

Typically, class definitions are kept in header files. The following example assumes that the definition for the class world is in the header file world.h, so that you can use that header file when you are defining class hello.

```
#include "world.h"

class hello {
     float          y;
     world   view;                        // Object of world
public:
     hello() {y = 57.57;}
     void display(void)   {cout << y << '\n';}
};
```

If an enclosed class object (world view;) has a constructor that requires an argument, it is the responsibility of the enclosing class (hello) to provide the value which is used. This is a simple example of good etiquette. We say *the host (enclosing class) must take care of of its guest (embedded object).*

```
#include <iostream.h>

class world {
    int        x;
public:
    world(int xx)    {x = xx;}                    // Constructor requires
                                                  //    a value
    void display(void) {cout << x << '\n';}
};

class hello  {
    float        y;
    world   view;                                 // Object of world
public:
    hello(int x) : view(x)      {y = 57.57;}      // Note view(x)
    void display(void)          {cout << y << '\n';}
};
```

In the example above, the constructor of the enclosing class, hello, passes a value to the constructor of the enclosed class object, world. The value is used to initialize the enclosed object, view. Syntactically, the region after the function's arguments list closing parenthesis and up to the code body's opening brace is called the *constructor initialization list*. It is where the constructor does *initialization*.

An enclosing class can also call a member function of an enclosed class object through one of its member functions. However, member functions of the enclosing class do not have any special access to the private and protected data members of the enclosed class object just because there is an enclosed class object.

In the following example, a member function of class hello wants to display the value of x in the view object. Notice that the display() function of class world was called through the view object from a member function of class hello. This is the same as calling display using a non–embedded object. The point to be seen here is that having embedded class objects is a way of organizing (a hello object *has a* world view), but it does not give the enclosing object any special visibility into the private or protected access regions of an enclosed object.

```
#include <iostream.h>

class world {
    int     x;
public:
    world(int a)            {x = a;}
```

```
        void set(int xx)        {x = xx;}
        void display()          {cout << x << '\n';}
};

class hello {
        int          x;
        world   view;
public:
        void set(int x)         {view.set(x);}
        int          y;
        hello(int z):view(z)  {x = 57; y = 66;}
        void display()          {cout << x << " " << y << '\n';
                                    view.display();}
};

main()
{
        hello    peace(55);
        peace.display();
}
```

In the example, the object peace is created and the constructor hello(55) executes to initialize it. The constructor first executes its constructor initialization list (this will be discussed later), which initializes the embedded view object with the value 55. This initialization is done by executing world(55). Then the code body of the hello constructor executes. The code assigns a fixed value to the x and y data members and completes execution. At this point, the peace object is completely initialized.

The hello member function display() is called through object peace. This display() function directly prints out the x and y data members of peace. It then displays the view data member by calling view's display() function, which outputs view's data member x. This function was used because the hello class's member functions have no direct visibility into the private part of the world object.

As long as you use a forward declaration, you can declare pointers and references to a class object, even to the object of an enclosing class.

```
        class link_list;                        // Forward declaration

        class list_item  {
                list_item     *next;
```

```
        link_list     *ptr;                    // Pointer to link_list
        int           value;
public:
        list_item(int val = 0)      {value = val; next = 0;}
};

class link_list {
        list_item     *listptr;               // Pointer to list_item
public:
        link_list()   {listptr = 0;}
        link_list(int val)  {listptr = new list_item(val);}
};
```

Note that each class above contains a data member that is a pointer type of the other class. Because each class needs the other class declared before it, there is no way to order the class definitions to eliminate a compile error. The solution is to forward–declare one class before the other and then define them later.

Type, Member, and Object Names

The following programs have comments that explain both legal and illegal uses of user–defined type names, class member names, and object names:

```
main()
{                       // A member name is always local to its class
                        // and a member may use any (legal) name, including
                        // its class's name.

        class a {
        public:
            int a;      // OK for a member and its class
        } x;            // to have the same name

        x.a = 1;
}

main()
{                       // User–defined type names and object names share
                        // the same name space; therefore, they should
                        // not be the same.

        class a {
```

```
            public:
                int a;      // OK
            } a;            // OK, but don't. It introduces
        }                   // subtle coding problems.

        main()
        {                   // When a class name is anonymous, its objects
                            // may have any (legal) name, because they will
                            // never clash with the (unspecified) class name.

            class {
            public:
                int a;
            } a;

            a.a = 1;        // OK, no type is named a
        }
```

A good C++ style to adopt for type names is to use a upper–case letter for the first character, lower–case for the rest of the characters and to separate the parts of the name with the under–score character; a compatible style for objects is to use all lower–case letters and the under–score character as an in–word separator. For example,

```
    Eminent_scientist       albert_einstein;
    Cat                     cat;
```

This style automatically avoids clashes between user–defined type names and object.

Static Data Members

A class's static data member is shared among all of its objects and its value is common to the entire class. This is analogous to static variables in a function definition. A static data member is called a class variable because there is only one copy of its variable that is shared by all the objects of the class.

```
        // Example of a static data member

        #include <iostream.h>
        class A {
        public:
            static char* greeting;          // A static data member
        };
```

→
```
        char *A::greeting = "";                    // Explained below

main()
{
    A obj1;                              // Define two objects
    A obj2;

    obj1.greeting = "Good morning. \n";
    cout << obj1.greeting;
    cout << obj2.greeting;
    cout <<  A::greeting;                // Explained below

    obj2.greeting = "Good afternoon. \n";
    cout << obj1.greeting;
    cout << obj2.greeting;
    cout <<  A::greeting;

    A::greeting = "Good evening. \n";
    cout << obj1.greeting;
    cout << obj2.greeting;
    cout <<  A::greeting;
}
```

——— Program's Output ———

Good morning.
Good morning.
Good morning.
Good afternoon.
Good afternoon.
Good afternoon.
Good evening.
Good evening.
Good evening.

When an object (excluding unions) is defined, its memory space contains a copy of all of its class's data members except static data members. There is only a single copy of a static data member and it is shared by all classes. If a member is private, it can be accessed only by its class members. If it is public, it can be accessed also by clients of the class, as shown in the previous program.

It is not necessary to create an object of a class to cause its static data member(s) to exist. A static data member's full name has the form

Its_class_name::its_data_member_name

In code that is not defining its class, it is necessary to reference a static data member either typically by its full name, or less commonly by one of the member selection operators, like obj1.greeting in the previous program.

Each static member in a class must have a corresponding definition outside the class. It is this definition that actually allocates and optionally initializes memory for the static data member. Note that static data members are never initialized by constructors. This method is used even when a static data member is in the private access region of a class. If initialization by constructors were legal, it would result in the resetting of the value of the shared variable every time another object was created.

Static Data Member Scope

A static data member exists when its class's definition is in scope. It becomes non–existent when its class's definition is no longer in scope. The following program has one class definition that has global scope (the definition occurs at a global place, which is not inside of any block) and another class definition that has local scope (the definition occurs inside a block). You do not need to have an object of a class when working with static data members. For example,

```
// Example showing when a static data member exists

#include <iostream.h>

class G {                        // This definition has global scope
public:
    static char* loner;
    };

char*  G::loner;                 // This statement is required because
                                 // it allocates memory for the static variable
```

```
main()
{
    G::loner =  "G::loner is alive. \n";

    cout << "A static data member exists when its class "
         << "definition is in scope. \n";

    cout << G::loner;
    {
       // —— A local block ——

       class L {                      // This definition has local scope
       public:
           static char* local_loner;
       };

       char*  L::local_loner;
       L::local_loner = "L::local_loner is now alive. \n";

       cout << "\nClass L is in scope inside of its "
               "block."; \n";
       cout << L::local_loner;
    }

    cout << "\nClass L is not in scope here, "
            "which is outside of its block. \n";

            // Removing the comment on the next code line causes
            // a compile error, because class L is not in scope and
            // it no longer exists.

    // cout << L::local_loner;     // Illegal, out of scope
    cout <<   "L::local_loner no longer exists, "
            "because it is out of scope. \n";


       G::loner =  "\nG::loner is still alive. \n";
       cout << G::loner;
}
```

――――――― **Program's Output** ―――――――

A static data member exists when its class definition is in scope.
G::loner is alive.

Class L is in scope inside of its block.
L::local_loner is now alive.

Class L is not in scope here, which is outside of its block.
L::local_loner no longer exists, because it is out of scope.

G::loner is still alive.

The above program output shows that the static data G::loner of the globally–scoped class G exists for the entire life of main. The static data member L::local_loner of locally–scoped class L only exists in its block and in the code that is after its class definition.

Typically, class definitions are put in a header file, which has a .h suffix. The header file is typically included in a globally–scoped place in C++ source code files , which usually have .cc, .C, or .cpp suffixes. Consequently, programmers usually deal with globally–scoped class definitions and their globally–scoped static data members.

5.5   Memory Allocation for Objects

When a class is defined, no memory is set aside for the class; instead, the class serves as a template, letting the system know how much memory is required for an object of the class and how the memory within an object is laid out. In describing an object's memory, three issues must be discussed: where is the memory allocated for non–static data members, where is memory allocated for static data members, and where is memory allocated for member functions. Another issue to be discussed is where in the process memory space can objects be created, how are they created, and how are they destroyed.

Memory Allocation for Class Objects

Memory allocation for non–static data members of a class or struct occurs in an object's memory space (either in the stack, heap, or data segments). The compilation system knows how much memory is required for an object of a class and allocates that amount of memory when the object is declared. An important fact that you should realize is that the layout of an object's data members in the memory space is determined by the order in which they are declared in the class definition (see Figure 5.3). For example,

```
class memory {
    int         x;
    float       y;
    char        c;
    char        *cp;
    int             *ip
    float       *fp;
public:
    memory();
    void display();
};

memory     location;
```

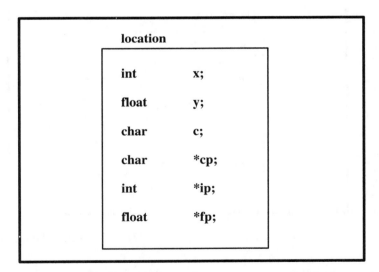

Figure 5.3 Name and contents of an object in memory.

Name, address, and contents of a memory object

Memory allocation for static data members of a class or struct does not occur in an object's memory space. All static data reside in the data segment and not in the object's memory space (see Figure 5.4). For example,

```
class memory {
      static int    x;
      float         y;
      char          c;
      char          *cp;
      int           *ip
      float         *fp;
public:
      memory();
      void display();
};

int          x;
memory       location;
```

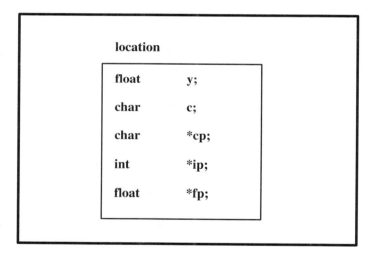

Figure 5.4 Memory layout of an object with a static data member.

Figure 5.4 shows the memory layout for the object named location. The memory is laid out in the object's memory space first for a float, then a char, then a char*, etc. The static data member resides separately in the data segment of the process.

Memory allocation for all member functions is made in the text segment of a process space. That is where all executable code resides. Only one copy of a member function is made for a class and this function is shared by all objects of the class, but is not in the object's memory space. Also, all member functions are invoked through objects.

> **location.display();**

All member function are implicitly passed a first argument, which is the address of the object calling them (the *this* pointer). In the above code statement, the member function display() knows to display the data found in the memory space associated with the location object.

Memory allocation for different objects of the same class occur at different memory locations. In the following example, assume that the header file memory.h contains the definition of class memory:

```
#include "memory.h"

memory      area;                        // Data segment object

main()
{
     memory     location;                // Stack object
     memory *mp = new memory;            // Heap object

     area.display();
     location.display();
     mp –> display();

     return 0;
}
```

In this program, the objects area, location, and the object pointed at by the memory pointer, mp, all reside at different memory locations. The display function that is shared by all of them is called through an object or pointer, providing the address of memory that the display function will use. Figure 5.5 shows where the objects, pointer and member functions reside within a process executing the program.

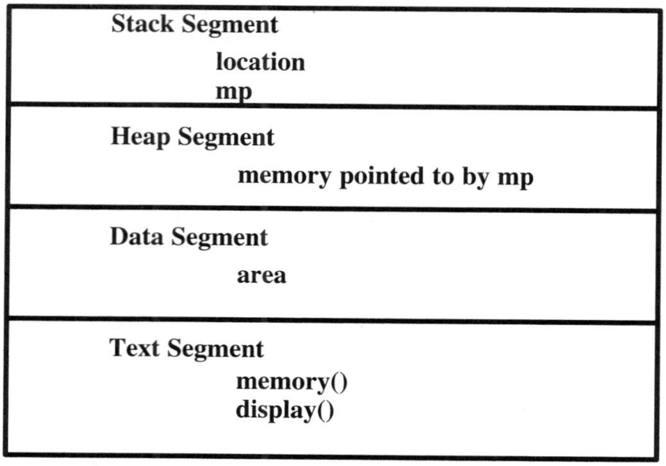

```
Stack Segment
        location
        mp

Heap Segment
        memory pointed to by mp

Data Segment
        area

Text Segment
        memory()
        display()
```

Figure 5.5 C++ Process model showing object storage.

Memory Allocation in the Process Space

An object can be created in any of three process segments. The scope and lifetime of an object is determined by where and how it is created. This also determines who is responsible for the destruction of the object.

When you declare objects inside a function block or sub–block, the objects are local to that block and they are created on the stack when the block is entered and their corresponding declarations are executed. They are popped from the stack and destroyed when the block is exited.

```
class stack_object {
      int          x;
public:
      stack_object(int xx)       { x = xx;}
};
```

```
main()                              (57)
{
     stack_object        local ≠(57;

          {   // This is a nested block within the main function block
              stack_object      sub_local(33);
          }
}
```

The object local is declared and created on the stack when the main() function block is entered. This object can be referenced anywhere within main(), within any sub–block within main() (after the point where it was declared), and within any function as an argument that main() calls. When the main() function returns, this object will be automatically destroyed by the system when the stack frame that contains it is popped from the stack.

The object sub_local is created on the stack when the sub–block inside main() is entered and its statement executed. This object can only be referenced within this sub–block and will be automatically destroyed when the stack frame that contains it is popped off the stack. This occurs when the sub–block is exited. Local objects tend to be short–lived and their creation and destruction are controlled by the compilation system.

When you declare objects outside a function, the objects are global and memory is allocated for them in the data segment of your process. These objects are created before the main() function is called and they are destroyed after the main() function returns. Global objects have program scope and can be referenced anywhere within a program, even if the program consists of separate files. Global objects are by definition long–lived.

```
class global_object {
     int       x;
public:
     global_object() { x = 57;}
};

global_object      global;

main()
{
     // ...
}
```

When you declare objects outside a function, but precede them by the keyword *static*, the objects are static and memory is allocated for them in the data segment of your process.

These objects are created before the main() function is called and are destroyed after the main() function returns. These static objects have file scope and can be referenced anywhere within the file, after the point at which they are declared. Static objects are by definition long–lived.

When objects are declared within a block and preceded by the keyword *static*, the objects are again static and memory is allocated for them in the data segment and, in many ways, they behave like file statics; however, they can only be referenced within the block in which they are declared, any sub–block of that block, or in any function that is called within the block, passing them as arguments.

```
class data_object {
    int         x;
public:
    data_object() { x = 57;}
};

static  data_object     file;                    // File scope

main()
{
            static  data_object     local;      // Local scope
}
```

You can also declare objects on the heap (free store). You can use the new operator to do this. These objects are created explicitly by you and persist for the duration of the process or until you explicitly destroy them by using the operator delete on their pointers.

```
class heap_object {
    int         x;
public:
    heap_object(int xx = 57) { x = xx;}
};

main()
{
    heap_object *ptr = new heap_object;     // Heap object
    // ...
    delete ptr;                             // Explicitly destroy it
}
```

Nested Class Definitions

Class definitions can be nested and they are treated as nested definitions. Nested classes can be used to avoid potential class name conflicts, which often occur when independent programming groups develop class libraries. Nested classes are also useful to hide class definitions that are not part of the external interface of a class library.

When a class is defined inside another class, the nested class is scoped inside the enclosing class. Outside of its enclosing scope, a nested class is referenced using its fully qualified name, which has the form

enclosing_class_name::nested_class_name

In versions of C++ prior to version 2.1, class definitions could be nested, but these class definitions were actually defined as if they were not nested.

This example illustrates a nested class.

```
// Example of nested class definitions

#include <iostream.h>

class A {
public:
    class B {
    public:
        int z;
    } obj_b;                          // Data member of class A

    class   {                         // Anonymous class has same
    public:                           // scope as class A
        int z;
    } obj_c;                          // Data member of class A

    void display();                   // Member function of class A
};

void A::display()
{
    cout << obj_b.z << '\t' << obj_c.z << '\n';
}
```

```
main()
{
    A x;
    x.obj_b.z = 123;
    x.obj_c.z = 456;
    x.display();

    A::B y;                        // Use notation A::B to refer
                                   // to class B defined inside of A

    y.z = 2;                       // Note z is in public region of B
    // y.display();                // Illegal, A::display is not a
                                   // member of object y's class,
}                                  // which is B
```

——— Program's Output ———
123   456

The above program's output shows that the objects, obj_b and obj_c, that are declared by the nested class definitions are data members of the enclosing class (class A).

Nested structs and unions that only contain data members are very useful and can enhance the readability and maintainability of code. In particular, this feature is useful when FOR-TRAN code that uses labeled common blocks is converted to C++. Anonymous structs, unions, and references are also extremely useful in code conversion.

Classes can be nested to several levels, and a locally scoped class hides a globally scoped class. For example,

```
#include <iostream.h>

class A {
    class AA {
        class AAA {
          public:
            void describe() { cout << "Class A::AA::AAA \n"; }
        };
        AAA aaa;
      public:
        void describe() { cout << "Class A::AA \n ";
                    aaa.describe(); }
    };
```

```
        AA aa;
        AA::AAA aaa;
      public:
        void describe() { cout << "Class A \n  ";
                aa.describe(); }

};
class AA {
   public:
      void describe() { cout << "Class AA \n"; }
};
void f()
{
      // A locally scoped class definition
      class A { public: void describe() { cout << "f()'s A \n"; } };

      A a;                            // An object of the local class A
      a.describe();
}
main()
{
      cout << '\n';

      A              a;      a.describe();
      A::AA          aa;     aa.describe();
      A::AA::AAA     aaa;    aaa.describe();
      AA             b;      b.describe();

      f();

      return 0;
}
```
————————— Program's Output —————————
```
Class A
  Class A::AA
  Class A::AA::AAA
Class A::AA
  Class A::AA::AAA
Class A::AA::AAA
Class AA
f()'s A
```

A nested class definition is not affected by the access region where it is defined. If a class is defined in the private region of another class, the nested class definition is public. For example,

```
#include <iostream.h>

class A {
    // This is the private access region class A
    // Define class B
    class B {
      public:
            void  display()    { cout << "Hi from class A::B::display(). \n"; }
            void  f()          { display(); }
    };
};

main()
{
    A::B    x;                          // Use nested class A::B, which is defined
                                        // in the private region of class A

    x.display();
    x.A::B::display();
    x.f();

    return 0;
}
```

————————— Program's Output —————————
Hi from class A::B::display().
Hi from class A::B::display().
Hi from class A::B::display().

Nested Class Definitions in Pre–2.1

In pre–2.1 versions of C++, a class defined inside another class has the same scope as its enclosing class; this is contrary to other languages, like Pascal and Lisp that support nested definitions. This is one of the many reasons why nested definitions can lead to confusion in pre–2.1 versions of C++. Nested classes are a programming convenience and in general they should not be used on pre– 2.1 versions of C++.

In the following example, you may think that class beta is scoped inside class alpha. However, in version 2.0 and earlier C++ versions, the compilation system treats these as two separate definitions of their respective classes. In version 2.0 and earlier versions, they each have their own scope and the enclosing class has no special visibility into the private access region of the enclosed class.

```
// Beware, pre–2.1 example

#include <iostream.h>

class alpha {
    int         x;
    class beta {
        float       y;
    public:
        beta()          {y = 57.57;}
        void display()  {cout << y << '\n';}
    } bitter;
public:
    alpha()         {x = 57;}
    void display()  {cout << x << '\n';}
};

beta    beware;
```

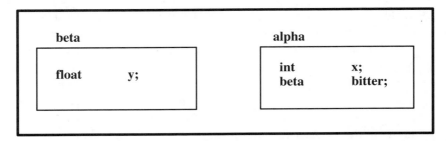

Figure 5.6 Memory layout for classes alpha and beta.

You may think that class beta is nested inside class alpha and that you can only declare objects of beta within class alpha (this is true in version 2.1, but not in earlier versions). In pre–2.1 versions however, objects of type beta can be declared anywhere within the program even though the class was defined within alpha. The compilation system treats these as two separate definitions of their respective classes (see Figure 5.6). They each have their own scope and the enclosing class has no special visibility into the private access region of the enclosed class. Because nesting classes and structs this way often leads to confusion, it is strongly suggested that you do not nest classes or structs when using pre–2.1 versions of C++. Instead, define your classes separately as follows:

```
#include <iostream.h>
class beta {
    float    y;
public:
    beta()              {y = 57.57;}
    void display()   {cout << y << '\n';}
};
class alpha {
    int      x;
    beta     bitter;
public:
    alpha()             {x = 57;}
    void display()   {cout << x << '\n';}
};
```

5.6   Unions in Classes

You can save memory when creating data members by using a union to use the same memory location for more than one variable. However, an instance of a union can only represent one of its data members at any point in time. When a union is nested inside a class, it is often written as an *anonymous union*: it has no tag name or instance declared of it. Also, if there is only one instance of a union, it is often written as an anonymous union. This makes its members defined at the enclosing scope. All members of a union are public by default, and a union cannot contain either a static data member or a class object that contains a constructor or destructor. When using unions inside a class, it is a good idea to provide a set of access functions to get values from the union.

```
#include <iostream.h>

class screen;
```

```
class canvas {
    union {
        char    *str;
        int     a;
    };
    screen    *ptr;
public:
    canvas(char*);
    canvas(int);
    const char * get_string(){return str;}
    int get_int()            {return a;}
};
```

5.7   Accessing Class Members

There are different methods of accessing class members, depending on whether a member is in the private, protected, or public access region of the class.

```
#include <stdlib.h>

class access_example  {
    char* str;
    void error_routine() { exit(1); }
public:
    int x;
    access_example() {}
    access_example(int, char*);
    ~access_example();
    int get_value();                // Access function
    const char* get_string();
    int count _characters(char*);
};

inline int   access_example::get_value() {return x;}

int access_example::count_characters(char* str)
{
    int temp;
    temp = strlen(str);
    if(temp == 0)
        error_routine();
```

```
        return(temp);
}
main()
{
    int temp, temp1;
    access_example   today;
    temp = today.x;
    temp1 = today.count_characters("William J. Heinze");
    cout << "Number of characters = " << temp1;
}
```

Members of a class have access to all other members of a class and can access data members and make member function calls directly. Non–members of a class (users of the class) have direct access to public data members and member functions of a class and can access them through a class object. In the example the member function error_routine() was made private because users of the class were not supposed to call it; it was only for the class's personal use.

5.8   Member Functions

A unique feature of structs and classes in C++ is their ability to declare functions within aggregates. These member functions can see everything which is declared within a class; that is, they have visibility into the private, protected, and public access regions of a class and/or struct. A unique feature of member functions is that the system implicitly passes the address of an object (the *this* pointer) as the hidden first argument of all member function calls. More will be said about the this pointer later in Section 5.10.

Single–argument Member Functions

Ordinary functions and member functions are both defined differently and used differently. The following program highlights their differences:

```
// Example of regular and member function differences

#include <iostream.h>

class Int {
public:
    int a;                      // Data member
    int times_3();              // Member function
};
```

```
int Int::times_3()              // Member function definition
{                               // Note Int::
     return a * 3;              // a is the data member a
}

int times_3(int a)              // Regular function definition
{
     return a * 3;              // a is the parameter a
}

main()
{
     int five = 5;

     Int seven;
     seven.a  = 7;

     cout << times_3(five);        // Use regular function

     cout << " is the value of times_3(five) \n";


     cout << seven.times_3();      // Use member function

     cout << " is the value of seven.times_3() \n";
}
```

──────────── **Program's Output** ────────────
15 is the value of times_3(five)
21 is the value of seven.times_3()

The regular function just described is defined with one parameter in its formal parameter list. It is called with one argument in its argument list.

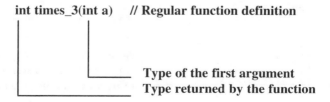

int times_3(int a)   // Regular function definition

                                          Type of the first argument
                                          Type returned by the function

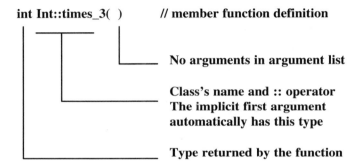

The following member function below is defined with no arguments in its formal parameter list:

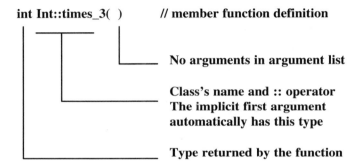

All member function definitions (excludes statics) automatically have an implicit (you do not specify it) formal first parameter, and the parameter is always a pointer of the class's type. Also, functions are always called with an object of their class using a member selection operator.

The following member function is called with no arguments in its argument list. The member function is invoked on object seven, and the address of seven (*this* pointer) is passed implicitly as the first argument of the function.

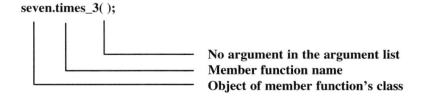

A non–static member function always has at least one argument (an object of its class), implicitly passed as the *this* pointer. In a member function definition, all of the members of a class are directly referenceable. When a member function is invoked on an object, such as

seven.times_3()

the function operates on the object's data members that are referenced in the function's definition. In the expression above, the function Int::times_3 accesses object seven's data member a, which contains the integer 7, multiplies it by 3, and returns the result 21.

When the member function times_3 is defined, Int:: is placed in front of the function's name. Int:: is the class name and scope resolution operator.

Multi–argument Member Functions

A member function with two or more parameters handles the first argument exactly like a member function with a single implicit argument. The remaining arguments are specified like regular functions. The following program illustrates a member with three parameters:

```
// Example of a member function with 3 parameters:
// one implicit parameter and two explicit parameters

#include <iostream.h>

class Int {
public:
    int a;
    int max(Int b, int c);          // Int and int are
                                    // different types
};

int Int::max(Int b, int c)
{
    if (a   > b.a && a > c)
        return a;
    if (b.a > c)
        return b.a;
    return c;
}
```

```
main()
{
    Int x;  x.a = 10;
    Int y;  y.a = 30;
    int z;  z   = 25;

    cout << x.max(y, z);
}
```

————— **Program's Output** —————
30

The class Int has a single integer data member named a,

int a;

and a member function with three parameters.

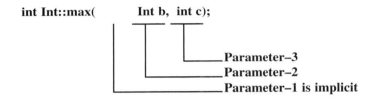

The first parameter is never declared (it is implicitly declared) and its type is always a pointer to the class's name. Parameter–2 is an object of class Int and Parameter–3 is an integer. Except for the first argument, a member's argument may be any type.

In a member function definition, like Int::max in the previous program, the members of the first parameter are referenced by their names. Static data and static member function, which are not contained in any object, are also directly referenceable by name. The other arguments are used just like regular function arguments. The following extracted statement illustrates these points:

if (a > b.a && a > c) return a;

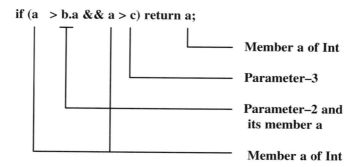

Member a of Int

Parameter–3

Parameter–2 and
its member a

Member a of Int

Calling a member function was illustrated in the statement

cout << x.max(y, z);

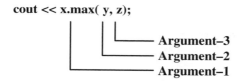

Argument–3
Argument–2
Argument–1

A Member Function Programming Pitfall

Avoid the pitfall of returning a pointer or reference to an automatic object. This applies to non–member functions too. The reason is that when a function terminates, its automatic objects also terminate (become non–existent) and the memory space that they occupied is reclaimed and used for something else. The following program illustrates this pitfall and the code is intentionally oversimplified to keep the point clear:

```
// Example of the pitfall of using a nonexistent object

#include <iostream.h>int* sum1(int i, int j)
{
    int a;                 // a is an automatic variable
    a = i + j;
    return &a;             // BUG
}
```

```
int sum2(int i, int j)
{
    int a;
    a = i + j;
    return a;                        // OK, returns a copy
}

main()
{
    int *x, y;

    x  =  sum1(1,2);
    y  =  sum2(1,2);

    cout << *x  << '\t'
            << y << '\n';
}
```

——— **Program's Output** ———
–72 3

The desired program output was

3   3

but the first number printed was –72, which is unpredictable garbage and could be anything; its output could even crash the program. If the correct answer did happen to appear, it would be a happenstance and a misleading indication of the program's correctness. The program is buggy and not reliable. The fix to this problem in sum1() is to allocate dynamic storage rather than use an automatic variable.

```
int* a = new int;      // replaces "int a;"
```

Coding the function sum using references rather than pointers is also wrong, and if the compiler does not produce a compile–time error, the same run–time error exists. The following code illustrates this pitfall and the two versions are equivalent:

```
int& sum3(int i, int j)
{
    int a;
    a = i + j;
    return a;                        // BUG or compile error
}
```

```
int& sum4(int i, int j)
{
    return i + j;                    // BUG or compile error
}
```

In sum4 the expression i + j is evaluated and the result is stored in a temporary automatic variable that the compiler creates. The return statement returns a reference to the temporary variable. Beware of this pitfall when using functions with a return type of reference.

Constant Member Functions

If an object is a constant, such as

x is an object of class A::Bconst   Constant   beta = 48;

the object's value cannot be changed. To enforce this rule, the compiler restricts how a constant object can be used. For member functions, only const member functions can be called with a constant object because the compiler knows it cannot change an object's value; using non–const member functions causes a compile error.

To create a constant member function, place the keyword *const* after the argument list and before the opening brace of the function. In the code body of the function, it is a compile error to change the value of a data member or call a non–const member function. By enforcing these restrictions, the compiler knows that constant member functions of a class are safe to use with constant objects, because they do not change an object's value, either directly or indirectly. Note that it is legal and safe to call a const member function through a non–const object.

You can declare objects of user–defined data types to be constants. If you do, only member functions that are declared constant can use them. For example,

```
#include <iostream.h>

class Constant {
    int  integer;
public:
    Constant(int a)      {integer = a;}
    void increment()     {++integer;}
    void display() const {cout << integer << '\n';}
};
```

```
main() {
    Constant alpha(57);
    const Constant beta = 48;
    alpha.increment();
    beta.increment();                        // Compile error
    alpha.display();
    beta.display();
}
```

In this example, the member function increment changes the value of the object by incrementing its data member named integer.

The member function display() is declared a const member function. It outputs the value of a data member named integer. It does not change the value of the object; it treats the object as a constant. The compiler will not allow you to change the value of a class data member through a const member function, or allow you to call another member function that would change the value of a data member.

In main(), the object alpha of type Constant is created and initialized to the value 57. The object beta of type const Constant is created and initialized to the value 48. As will be described later, the following statement has the same meaning:

const Constant beta(48);

The increment function is invoked on the alpha object and alpha's value is changed to 58. In the next line, a compile error occurs because you can only use constant member functions with const objects. The last two lines call the constant member function on alpha (a non–const object) and beta (a const object). This illustrates that a constant member function can be used wherever a non–const member function can be used; however, only const member functions can be used on const objects.

If you want any function, including the copy constructor and the operator=() function to accept a constant object as an argument, you must declare that parameter to be a constant.

void example(const X&);

Constructors and destructors cannot be declared as constant member functions.

Pre–2.0 versions of C++ did not include const member functions.

Inline and Non–inline Member Functions

An *inline* member function is a member function whose complete code body is placed inline at each point in the program where the function is called. The compiler may place additional code inline to handle a function's parameter(s) and return value so that the semantics of the function is not changed by making it inlined.

When a function is very small and simple, the time spent executing the body of the function is minuscule compared to the function's call/return time. The call/return time is the time required to set up the call to the function (putting the caller's return address and parameters on the stack and jumping to the function) and then to clean up after the function completes execution.

If a very small function is heavily used, inlining it can significantly improve the program's run–time performance; alternatively, without an inline capability, using many small functions can result in degraded system performance. The disadvantage of inlining is an increase in a program's code size.

Inlining is particularly important for class member functions because member functions are frequently only one or two statements long. Thus, inlining allows a programmer to exploit the power of member functions and to preserve the high performance of the C language.

Inlining is only advice to the compiler and the compiler may decide not to inline a particular function because of its complexity or some other reason.

There are two different ways to inline a member function:

- Implicit inlining

- Explicit inlining.

If a member function is defined inside its class definition, the function is *implicitly inlined*.

```
// Example of "implicitly" inlined member functions

#include <iostream.h>

class Coffee_cup {
public:
    double percent_full;

    void fill()                      // Defined here, so it's inline
    {
        percent_full = 90;           // Don't overfill it
    }

    void  drink()
```

```
    {
        percent_full -= 10;
        if (percent_full < 0)
            percent_full = 0;
    }

    void describe()
    {
        cout << "The cup is "
                << percent_full << " percent full. \n";
    }
};
main()
{
    Coffee_cup  blue_cup;

    blue_cup.fill();

    for (int i = 0; i < 6; i++)
        blue_cup.drink();

    blue_cup.describe();
}
```

———— Program's Output ————
The cup is 30 percent full.

In the above program, the Coffee_cup member functions fill(), drink(), and describe() are inline functions because they are defined inside their class definition.

The functions above were written with a common coding style. Another style is frequently used for single–statement inline member functions and the following code illustrates this style:

void fill() { percent_full = 90; }   // fill a cup

While this style is very easy to read, mixing two styles of defining functions in a program makes it harder for the eye to quickly discriminate a program's parts from its appearance. Programmers unaccustomed to one–liner function definitions often have difficulty reading code that uses them.

The second way to define inline member functions is to declare member function in its class definition and to define member function outside of its class definition with the reserved word inline preceding its definition. The following program is the same as the previous program except the functions drink() and describe() are *explicitly inlined*:

// Example of implicitly and explicitly inlined member functions

```
#include <iostream.h>

class Coffee_cup {
public:
    double percent_full;

    void fill()  { percent_full = 90; }        // Implicit inline
    void drink();
    void describe();
};

inline void  Coffee_cup::drink()               // Explicit inline
{
    percent_full -= 10;
    if (percent_full < 0)
        percent_full = 0;
}

inline void  Coffee_cup::describe()            // Explicit inline
{
    cout << "The cup is "
         << percent_full << " percent full. \n";
}

main()
{
    Coffee_cup  blue_cup;

    blue_cup.fill();

    for (int i = 0; i < 6; i++)
        blue_cup.drink();

    blue_cup.describe();
}
```

——— Program's Output ———
The cup is 30 percent full.

When inline functions are explicitly defined outside of their class's definition, the class definition is easier to read. In the example, it is easy to see that the class has one data member and three function members. This style promotes readability. It also makes it easier to change a function between inlined and non–inlined during an application's performance–tuning phase, which typically occurs after program coding and before the program is put into operation (completed). If the word inline were removed from a definition, the function would be a non–inline member function. If the keyword inline were then added back, the function would again become an inline member function. To change an implicitly inlined function between inlined and non–inlined requires considerably more code changes.

The following code is extracted from the previous program and it points out the parts of an explicitly defined member function header:

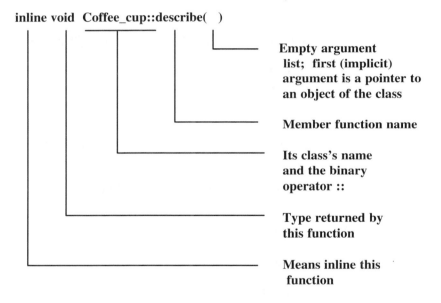

inline void Coffee_cup::describe(   )

Empty argument list; first (implicit) argument is a pointer to an object of the class

Member function name

Its class's name and the binary operator ::

Type returned by this function

Means inline this function

There is a usage restriction on inline functions: Whenever a file is compiled that uses an inlined function, the inlined function's definition source code must be part of the compiled code and available whenever the function is called.

A typical practice is to put class definitions and function declarations in a header file (.h file) and class member function definitions in a source code file (. cc, .C, or .cpp file) that is separate from the code which calls the inline function. If this practice is followed with an inline function, a linker error will occur because when the class's header file is included, the required source code of the inline function will not be available. A straightforward solution to this problem is to always put the inline member function definitions inside of their class's header file. Then, whenever a class is used (its header file is included) the required inline member function definitions (if there are any) are available as required at compile time.

Static Class Functions

A static class function is a class function that is callable without any reference to a particular object. Static class functions do not have a *this* pointer, no implicit first argument, and they cannot access member functions and member data within a class object.

A static function member's name has the form

Its_class_name::its_member_function_name(its_arguments)

The following program illustrates keeping class data private and allowing clients (the public) read–only access to information about the class. This is accomplished by using a private static data member and a public static member function.

```
// Example of static member functions and data

#include <iostream.h>

class Apple_box {
     static int  large_apples_in_all_boxes;
     static int  small_apples_in_all_boxes;

     int         large_apples_in_this_box;
     int         small_apples_in_this_box;

public:
     void        put_large_apple();
     void        put_small_apple();
     static int  total_number_of_apples();
};

int Apple_box::large_apples_in_all_boxes;
int Apple_box::small_apples_in_all_boxes;

void Apple_box::put_large_apple()
{
```

```
        large_apples_in_this_box++;
        large_apples_in_all_boxes++;
}

void Apple_box::put_small_apple()
{
        small_apples_in_this_box++;
        small_apples_in_all_boxes++;
}

int Apple_box::total_number_of_apples()
{
        return large_apples_in_all_boxes
            + small_apples_in_all_boxes;
}

main()
{
        Apple_box arts_box;                    // Create some boxes
        Apple_box bills_box;

        arts_box  .put_large_apple();          // Collect 5 apples
        bills_box .put_small_apple();
        bills_box .put_small_apple();
        arts_box  .put_large_apple();
        bills_box .put_large_apple();

        cout << "The apple pickers collected "
            << Apple_box::total_number_of_apples()
             << " apples today. \n";
}
```

———————— Program's Output ————————
The apple pickers collected 5 apples today.

In the above program, the class Apple_box has global scope because it was defined in its file and outside of all blocks (not enclosed by { and }). Static data and function members have external scope when their class is defined with global scope; otherwise, they have the same scope as their class's definition.

If you declare static class data, you might want to change their values. Although you can do this through a specific object of a class, you can also do it through a static class function.

```
#include <iostream.h>

class Stat {
    static int integer;
public:
    static void increment() {integer++;}
    void display() {cout << integer << '\n';}
};

int Stat::integer = 57;

main()
{
    Stat alpha;
    alpha.display();
    Stat::increment();
    alpha.display();
}
```

A static class function is analogous to static data: it belongs to the class rather than to an object of the class. Therefore, a static class function can be called for the class as a whole without specifying an object of the class. It is an error to try and use it on a non–static data member; it can, however, be used on global data. Because there is no *this* pointer associated with a static member function, you cannot call non–static member functions and you cannot manipulate non–static data members. You cannot create static constructors and destructors because they require a *this* pointer.

Volatile Member Functions

There are situations in which every time you read or write a particular variable, you want the variable referenced. Volatile data have this semantics and the compiler enforces the semantics. An example of this is a clock variable that resides in the memory where a system's hardware clock resides. The hardware continually updates this clock's value (external to the program). Reading the clock's memory location gets the current value; writing to this clock's memory location resets the clock to a new value.

Because the compiler can, and frequently does, optimize away references to variables which it knows it has not changed, your program loses the capability to have explicit control over memory references. Using the keyword *volatile* gives you this control back. Whenever you access or change a volatile's value, the compiler will always do it; it can never optimize away volatile data accesses.

You can declare objects of user–defined data types to be volatiles. If you do, only member functions that are declared volatile can be called through them.

```
#include <iostream.h>

class Volatile {
    int  integer;
public:
    Volatile(int a) {integer = a;}
    void increment() volatile {++integer;}
    void display() {cout << integer << '\n';}
};

main()
{
    Volatile alpha(57);
    volatile Volatile beta = 48;
    alpha.increment();
    beta.increment();
    alpha.display();
    beta.display();                          // Compile error
}
```

If you declare a member function volatile, that member function can be used to change the value of a data member which is part of a volatile object. The volatile member function can also be used to change the value of a non–volatile object. To create a volatile member function, place volatile after the argument list and before the opening brace of the function. When you are defining a volatile member function, you can only call other volatile member functions. Constructors and destructors cannot be declared volatile member functions. Pre–2.0 versions of C++ did not support volatiles. However, those versions of the language supported using const volatile (or equivalently, volatile const) together for functions and data.

Template Functions

In C, the math function max() is typically written as a preprocessor macro. Using this technique, a single function definition accepts many different types of arguments, and the appropriate code is generated. If a macro was not used, it would be necessary to define a distinct function for each type of argument that was needed. For example, three function definitions would be necessary to handle arguments of ints, longs, and doubles. This macro technique is available in C++, but this approach undesirable because it defeats type checking.

Implementing the max() function with templates in C++ is a better approach, because strong type checking is enforced. A single template max() function definition is used to define max() for specific parameters.

To define a template function, precede the function definition by the keyword *template* and a comma–separated list of one or more type declarations, which are enclosed in angle brackets < >.

A template function provides code sharing at the source code level. Therefore, when a template function is used in a source code file, the corresponding template definition must also be available for the compiler to generate the function's code. A template function definition is typically placed in a header file and included in source code files that use them.

When a template function is used with actual arguments (i.e., ints, doubles, etc.), the compiler generates corresponding function definitions using the template. The following example illustrates a simple usage of function templates:

```
// Using templates with a function.

#include <iostream.h>


template<class X>                      // Define template function max
                                       // X is a parameter name
                                       // X is not a defined class

X max(X a, X b)
{
     return a >= b ? a : b;            // Operator >= must be defined for
                                       // every particular type that is used
                                       // with this max function

}

main()

{
  {
     int a = 33, b = 55;
     cout << "max(" << a << ',' << b << ") is "
          << max(a,b) << endl;         // Use template max
                                       // with ints
  }
```

```
    {
        double a = 3.14159, b = -77.66;
        cout << "max(" << a << ',' << b << ") is "
            << max(a,b) << endl;              // Use template max
                                             // with doubles
    }


    {
        char a = 'z', b = 'H';
        cout << "max(" << a << ',' << b << ") is "
            << max(a,b) << endl;              // Using template max
                                             // with chars
    }


    return 0;
}
```

——— Program's Output ———
```
max(33,55) is 55
max(3.14159,-77.66) is 3.14159
max(z,H) is z
```

This program defines the template function max() that takes two arguments, and returns the argument that satisfies the relationship >=. The max() function is then used with ints, doubles, and chars. A compile error will result if max() is used with a data type that does not have the operation >= defined. No error occurs, because >= is defined for ints, doubles, and chars.

Template function can be overloaded. Like other overloaded functions, they must have distinguishable argument lists.

Template Classes

When several class definitions only differ by a single data member, writing the definitions duplicates a lot of code. If templates are used, the duplication is eliminated.

A template class is defined by preceding a class definition with the keyword *template* and a comma–separated list of one or more type declarations, which are enclosed in angle brackets < >. A template class definition cannot be nested within other classes, which is a restriction that ordinary classes do not have.

A template class's name is formed by concatenating the name in the class definition with the template's parameter list enclosed in angle brackets < >. The name of the template class in the next example is

> container<T>

When a template class is used with actual arguments (i.e., ints, doubles, etc.), the compiler generates corresponding class definitions and member function definitions. A template argument can also be a constant or constant expression. Constant arguments are often used to specify the size of an object's data member.

A template class provides code sharing at the source code level. Therefore, when a template class is used in a source code file, the corresponding template definition and all of its member function definitions must be available for the compiler's use. A template class definition and all of its member function definitions are typically placed in a header file and included in source code files that use them.

Templates are very useful for defining container classes, such as a linked list. The following example illustrates a simple container class using templates:

```
// Using templates with a class.
#include <iostream.h>

template<class T> class container {    // T is a parameter to this class
                                       // T is not a defined class
    public:
        container(const T&);           // Copy constructor
        T get_value() const;           // Access the contained data
    private:
        T value;                       // The contained data
};

template<class T>                      // A template member function
container<T>::container(const T& a)
: value(a)
{}

template<class T>
T container<T>::get_value() const
{
        return value;
}
```

```
main()
{
    container<int>       a(1);                  // Class container<int>
    container<double>  b(1.23);                 // Class container<double>
    container<char>     c('z');                 // Class container<char>
    container<char*>   d("This is a string.");//Class container<char*>


    cout << a.get_value() << endl;   // Uses int container<int>::get_value()
    cout << b.get_value() << endl;
    cout << c.get_value() << endl;
    cout << d.get_value() << endl;


    return 0;
}
```

——— **Program's Output** ———
1
2.34
z
This is a string.

This program defines a template class that has a single parameter. The class has a data member and three member functions that use the template parameter. The member functions defined outside of the class definition are preceded by the same template specification that the class uses. In main, the container template class is used to define four container classes and their associated member functions, which use ints, doubles, chars, and char*s. Objects of each of these classes are defined and used to access the contained data, which are printed.

The following example illustrates defining member functions inside a template class definition:

```
#include <iostream.h>

template<class X>
class C {
  public:
    C(X a) : value(a) {}              // Implicitly inlined member
    X get_value()    { return value; } // functions that use the template
                                       // parameter
  private:
```

```
        X value;
};
main()
{
    cout << endl;

    C<int>    a(1);
    cout <<   a.get_value() << endl;

    C<double> b(2.3456);
    cout <<   b.get_value() << endl;

    C<char*>  c("This is a string.");
    cout <<   c.get_value() << endl;

    return 0;
}
```

——— Program's Output ———
1
2.3456
This is a string.

A template can have several parameters, and one template class can use another template class. For example,

```
#include <iostream.h>
#include <stdio.h>

template<class X>              // Define a template class
class U {
    friend class A<T,Y>;      // Declare a friend of a template class
    X value;
  public:
    U() : value(57) {}        // Default constructor
};
template<class T, class Y>     // Define a template class
class A {                      // with two parameters
    T    t;                    // A data member of type T
    U<Y> u;                   // A data member of type U<Y>
  public:
    void display();
};
```

```
template <class T, class Y>          // A member function definition
void A<T,Y>::display()
{
    cout << "A<T,V>::display(), value = " << u.value << endl;
}

main()
{
    A<double, int> a;                // Use template<class T, class Y> class A
    a.display();

    return 0;
}
```

——————— Program's Output ———————
A<T,V>::display(), value = 57

5.9   Pointers to Class Members

C++ has two distinct types of pointers:

- Regular pointers, which are the addresses of data variables

- Member pointers, which are relative offsets into objects of a class.

Member pointers have their own operators of

.*

->*

Pre–2.0 versions of C++ did not have these operators.

Class Data Member Pointer

You can declare pointers to a class data member.

```
#include <iostream.h>

class Pointer {
public:
    int  integer;
```

```
        Pointer(int a = 0) {integer = a;}
};
main()
{
    int Pointer::*p;
    p = &Pointer::integer;
    Pointer alpha = 57;
    Pointer *beta = new Pointer(48);
    int a, b;
    a = alpha.*p;
    b = beta->*p;
    cout << a << '\t' << b << '\n';
}
```

The syntax for declaring a pointer to a class data member is slightly different. In that case, you must declare what class the pointer points to.

int Pointer::*p

p is a pointer to an int, but the int referred to is a data member of class Pointer. When assigning pointer the address of a class data member, you must include the class's tag name.

p = &Pointer::integer;

Now, the member pointer p can be used to reference the integer data member in any Pointer object. It is a relative position within objects.

Dereferencing pointers to class data members uses the two new operators.

- .*

- ->*

To dereference a member pointer, you must also include the object of a class.

a = alpha.*p;
b = beta->*p;

Pointers to static class data members use the same syntax as pointers to non–class variables; therefore, do not use member pointers with static data members because static data members do not reside in the object's memory space.

While a practical use of data member pointers is very uncommon, they are useful in rare situations. For both regular pointers and member pointers, the value of 0 is treated as a NULL pointer. If a member pointer points to some class member, its value will never be 0.

Class Member Function Pointer

You can declare pointers to a class's member functions, such as

```
#include <iostream.h>

class Pointer {
public:
     int  integer;
     Pointer(int a = 0) {integer = a;}
     void display() {cout << integer << '\n';}
};

main()
{
     void (Pointer::*pf) ();
     pf = &Pointer::display;
     Pointer alpha(57);
     Pointer *beta = new Pointer(48);
     (alpha.*pf)();
     (beta->*pf)();
}
```

The syntax for declaring a pointer to a class member function is slightly different than just declaring a pointer to a function. You must declare what class the pointer points to.

void (Pointer::*pf)()

pf is a pointer to a member function of class Pointer that takes no arguments and returns no value. When assigning a pointer to the address of a class member function, you must include the class tag name.

pf = &Pointer::display;

Dereferencing pointers to class member functions uses the two new operators.

- .*

- ->*

To dereference a pointer, you must also include the object of a class.

```
(alpha.*pf)();
(beta->*pf)();
```

If the above class had additional member functions that also had the same argument type and return value as pf (no argument and no return value), pf could be assigned to point to one of them and that function could be called through the pf pointer.

5.10   The this Pointer

We have seen that each class object maintains its own copies of class data members, but not member functions. When a member function is called that reads class data members or writes class data members, it must know which class object to use. This is accomplished by using an implicit pointer called *this*. The *this* pointer contains the address of a class object. Whenever a member function is called, the *this* pointer is the first argument to the function. Therefore, the function knows with which object it is dealing.

The *this* pointer is implemented as follows:

```
class this_example  {
     int x;
public:
     this_example() {x = 57;}
     void display(void);
};
void this_example::display(void) {
{
     cout << x << '\n';
}
```

When the compiler processes the above program, it generates code that logically looks like the following:

```
void display__this_example(this_example* this) {
     cout << this->x << '\n';
}
```

If obj is an object of the class this_example

```
this_example  obj;
```

the call

```
obj.display();
```

is translated into

```
display__this_example(&obj);
```

Most of the time, you do not use the *this* pointer explicitly, although on occasion, you must. In the following example, we are use this to create the ability to cascade function calls:

```
class screen {
      int  x,  y;
      char back;
public:
      screen()                     {x = y = 0; back = '*';}
      screen(int a, int b, char c)  {x=a; y=b; back=c;}
      screen& home()               {x = 0;  y = 0; return *this;}
      screen& move(int a, int b)   {x = a;  y = b;  return *this;}
      screen& set_back(char c)     {back = c;  return *this;}
};

main()
{
      screen   computer;
      computer.home().set_back('#').move(35, 57);
}
```

The member function home() takes no arguments and returns a screen object by reference. How can a function return the object through which it was called? If you look at the return statement

return *this;

you will see the answer. Whenever a function is called, the system–supplied local variable *this* always points to the object which called the function. If we dereference the *this* pointer, we will get back the object, which is then returned. The same return statement would be used for a return–by–value function too.

The first function call is made (computer.home()) and then computer is returned. computer is used to make the second call (computer.set_back('#')), and computer is returned again. computer is then used to make the third call (computer.move(35, 57)) and computer is returned the third time. By using the *this* pointer explicitly, each function call returns the appropriate class object. As a rule of thumb, if a function is going to be used for cascading, always return its value by reference. Chapter 8 explains cascading of functions in detail.

The word *this* is a reserved word and it is only available inside the body of a (non–static) member function definition. The variable *this* which points to the first argument is the object upon which the function is acting.

The *this* pointer is typically used in two situations. The first situation is when a member function's parameter name and a member of its class have the same identifier; using name references, the parameter and the name of the member are masked. The member may be accessed either by its full name, using the form

class_name::member_name

or by using the this pointer

this–>member_name

```
// Example of using the this pointer

#include <iostream.h>
class  A {
     int x;
public:
     A() {x = 0;}
     void set(int);
     void display() {cout << x << endl;}
};
void set(int x)
{
     this–>x = x;            // The this pointer allows us to use A::x
}
main()
{
     A   object;
     object.set(123);
     object.display();
}
```

In this example, the member function set() has a formal parameter named x and the class has a data member named x. Whenever x is referred to inside the set function, the formal argument is used; this local parameter hides the data member with the same name. We can reference the data member in one of two ways:

- Using this–>x

- Using A::x.

The second situation is when the type returned by a member function is a reference to an object of the class. If it is necessary to return the object that the function was invoked on, dereferencing the *this* pointer returns the needed object.

> **return *this;**

5.11 Class Scope

Every class maintains its own scope. A variable name within a class hides the variable with the same name that is at global/file scope, such as

```
#include <iostream.h>


const int integer = 57;

class scope_example  {
      int integer;
public:
      scope_example() {integer = 9999;}
      void display(void)
      {cout << integer << " \n"              // Prints 9999
          << ::integer << '\n';}            // Prints 57
};

main()
{
      int  integer = 3333;
      scope_example   test;
      test.display();
      cout << integer << '\n';               // Prints 3333
}
```

Data members and member functions are local to a class and are not visible until there is an object of that class. When the object test goes out of scope, the members also go out of scope. In the previous example, the integer inside the main function masks the global integer and the integer inside the class scope masks the object inside main(). When the program is executed, the following output is seen:

> **9999**
> **57**
> **3333**

The first value comes from the class definition value. The second value is the global variable which was obtained using the scope resolution operator. The third value is the result of accessing the variable integer local to the main function, not through a member function of the class scope.

Member functions maintain their own scopes that can mask variables declared within a class. For example,

```
#include <iostream.h>

const int integer = 57;

class scope_example {
    int integer;
public:
    scope_example()     {integer = 9999;}
    void display(void)
        {int integer 1234;  cout << integer        // Prints 1234
            << " \n"  << this ->integer              // Prints 9999
            << " \n" << ::integer << '\n';}          // Prints 57
};

main()
{
    int  integer = 3333;
    scope_example   test;
    test.display();
    cout << integer << '\n';                          // Prints 3333
}
```

In the example, the integer inside the main() function masks the global variable and the integer inside the class scope_example masks the variable inside main(). The variable inside the display() member function masks the variable within the class. When the program is executed, the following output is seen:

> **1234**
> **9999**
> **57**
> **3333**

The first value comes from the member function declaration. The second value is the integer from the class that was accessed through the *this* pointer. The third value is the global variable which was obtained using the scope resolution operator. The fourth value is the result of printing main's local variable integer.

The following algorithm is used by the compiler to resolve identifiers:

- Search the immediate block containing the identifier for a declaration of the identifier. If found, the identifier is resolved; otherwise, search the enclosing block.

- If the immediate block is a nested block within a member function, search the enclosing scope's member function. If found, the identifier is resolved; otherwise, search the enclosing block.

- If the immediate block is a member function, search the enclosing space's class. If found, the identifier is resolved; otherwise, search the enclosing block.

- If the immediate block is a class, search the file/program for an identifier. If a declaration is found, the identifier is resolved; otherwise, flag the identifier as an illegal reference to an undeclared identifier.

5.12   Class – A Better Module

A C++ class is a much better module than a C module (a file)! By just using C++'s class construct as a better module, software development and maintenance productivity is significantly improved. This is because the compiler enforces a discipline that very experienced programmers practice, and at the same time makes it easier for all programmers to use this methodology. It creates software with Abstract Data Types (ADTs), where data and the only functions that operate on the data are packaged together. This formalized closeness makes it easy to find the list of functions that are possible bug candidates when a data item gets corrupted. There are additional significant benefits to be gained by using C++'s object–oriented programming (OOP) features, which are discussed in later chapters.

The concept of a class is only superficially like a module in that it contains both data and functions that operate on the data; also, the functions are made available to clients through a formalized external interface. Then, the similarity stops. There are typically many instances of class objects, but only a single instance of a module.

In C++, a user–defined class is a user–defined type and it is used like a built–in type. Also, a user–defined class instance (object), like a defined variable of a built–in type, is a first–class citizen in the language and it has all the characteristics and privileges of built–in type instances (variables). For example, a locally–scoped object is automatically destroyed when it goes out of scope. C++ operators can be used with an object if its class definition includes operator definitions. Additionally, all well–designed class objects are automatically initialized when they are created and automatically cleaned up (de–initialized) when they are destroyed.

Thus, the C++ language with its built–in types is extended with user–defined types and, if properly designed, the new types will appear as if they were built into the language. This means that the C++ language is an *extensible language*, and extensibility is a very powerful feature. However, C++ is not mutable; you cannot change the meaning of what the compiler provides, such as redefining the meaning of the + operator for double.

Abstract Data Type Concepts

A C++ class is both a module (packaging mechanism) and a data type and it is used to implement *ADTs* (Abstract Data Types). Abstract data types are common and some of them are probably familiar to you. They are

- **Integer**

- **Double**

- **Complex number**

- **Point**

- **Line**

- **Polygon**

- **Stack**

- **Queue**

An ADT is a data type that specifies a data structure (also called data representation) and the collection of functions and operators that access and modify an instance of the data structure.

Data Representation

The data structure or data format that an ADT uses to represent its type is used by the ADT's functions and operators. An ADT data representation is not used by client programmers.

In C++, an ADT's data definition resides in its class's header file.

Functions and Operators

An ADT's functions and operators are used by a client programmer to indirectly access and modify the data representation. In C++ this source code is typically separated into two parts:

1) **Implementation of an ADT** The implementation is the source code definition (.cc, .C, or .cpp file) of the functions and operators, and it is usually unavailable to clients. The corresponding object code and/or executable code is available for clients to use.

2) **Interface of an ADT** The interface is the source code declarations (.h header file) of the function/operator prototypes that client programmers include in their programs that use the ADT's functions and/or operators.

The Built–in Double as an ADT

The familiar C++ built–in data type double is a good example of an ADT. A double has an internal data representation and functions and operators that operate on the double.

Most programmers know that a double (binary floating–point number) is represented in a machine's memory by a data format that has an exponent part and a mantissa part. This representation, while not strictly hidden, is usually of little concern to the programmer, and most programmers cannot tell you off the top of their heads how the number $-1.2E-3$ is really represented in their machine, let alone in our machine. Also, how is the result of $-1.0 / 0.0$ represented? Do infinity and not a number have double representations? While it is usually unknown how doubles are internally represented in a machine, virtually every programmer knows how to create doubles and operate on them:

```
double a = 1.0;
double b;
b = a * 3;
cout << b;
```

Knowing a double's internal representation is unnecessary because operators (=, +, −, *, etc.) and functions (printf, scanf, sin, etc.) are predefined for the programmer to use. Only the provided operators and functions themselves need to know the internal representation because they must create, access, modify, and interpret the internally represented data — that is their job. In C++, each user–defined ADT is coded as a class.

An ADT Example: Date

A date is a very common data structure and there is a set of typical operations (functions) to use and manipulate dates. A C programmer would probably implement a date as a structure and all of the functions that operate on it as a C module: a source code file (.c file) of definitions and an associated header file (.h file) of corresponding declarations.

A C++ programmer would implement date as a class (a user–defined type). The header file date.h would contain the class's definition and the member function definitions would be put in the file date.cpp (or date.C depending on the compiler's preference), and would be compiled into an object code file (.o or .obj file). A client's program that uses the Date class would include the header file in its source code and link its object code with the class's object file date.o or date.obj.

The following comprehensive program uses many of the features described in this chapter. It defines the class Date in files date.h and date.cpp and tests the class with the code in file datetest.cpp.

```
// File date.h — interface of class Date
#ifndef DATE_H
#define DATE_H
#include <stdio.h>

class Date {
    int month;                  // 1 .. 12
    int day;                    // 1 .. 31
    int year;                   // 0 .. 2001 .. a big number
public:
    void  set_date(int month, int day, int year  /* like 1998 */);
    const char* display_date();
    const char* display_time_span();
    Date  time_span(Date, Date);
};

#endif  /* DATE_H */

// File date.cpp — implementation of class Date
#include <iostream.h>
#include <stdlib.h>                 // For exit(1)
#include <stdio.h>                  // For sprintf()
#include "date.h"
```

```
static int month_days[13] = {
    0, 31,28,31,30,31,30,31,31,30,31,30,31
};

static char* month_name[13] = { "",
    "January",      "February",      "March",        "April",
    "May",          "June",          "July",         "August",
    "September",     "October",       "November",     "December"
};

void Date::set_date(int mm, int dd, int yyyy)
{
    // Domain check all arguments

    if (mm < 1 || mm > 12) {
        cerr << "Date::set_date   Bad month. \n";
        exit(1);
    }
    else
        month = mm;

    if (dd < 1 || dd  > 31) {
        cerr << "Date::set_date   Bad day. \n";
        exit(1);
    }
    else
        day = dd;

    if (yyyy < 0) {
        cerr << "Date::set_date   Bad year. \n";
        exit(1);
    }
    else
        year = yyyy;
}
```

[handwritten annotation: error! →]

[handwritten annotation: month_days [mm] ←]

```
char* Date::display_date()
{
    char* s = new char[30];
    sprintf(s, "%s %d, %d", month_name[month], day,  year);
    return s;
}

char* Date::display_time_span()
{
    char* s = new char[80];
    sprintf(s, "%d year%s, %d month%s and %d day%s",
            year,    (year   > 1)  ? "s" : "",
            month,  ( month > 1)  ? "s" : "",
            day,    (day    > 1)  ? "s" : "" );
    return s;
}


Date Date::time_span(Date a, Date b)
{
    Date d;

        // do the date arithmetic borrowing
    if (a.day < b.day) {
        a.day += month_days[a.month];
        if ( month == 2 &&
            ( (a.year % 4) == 0 && (a.year % 100) != 0
            || (a.year % 400) == 0))
                a.day += 1;                 // Feb had 29 days
        a.month -= 1;
    }
    if (a.month < b.month) {
        a.month += 12;
        a.year  -= 1;
    }

    d.day       = a.day      - b.day;
    d.month     = a.month    - b.month;
    d.year         = a.year      - b.year;
    return d;
}
```

```
// File datetest.cpp — test the date class
#include <iostream.h>
#include "date.h"

// Note:  link with date.obj

main()
{
    Date first_moon_walk;
    first_moon_walk.set_date(7, 21, 1969);

    Date century21, dd;
    century21.set_date(1,1,2000);

    cout << "On the date "
            << century21.display_date()
            << " it will be "
            << (dd.time_span(century21,first_moon_walk))
                .display_time_span()
            << "\nsince the first moon walk by Neil Armstrong.\n";
}
```

———————————————— Program's Output————————————————
**On the date January 1, 2000 it will be 30 years, 5 months and 11days since the
first moon walk by Neil Armstrong.**

The client program (datetest.cpp) that uses the Date class is discussed first, then the Date
class code is discussed in detail.

The program datetest.cpp includes the interface specification (date.h) of the class Date so
that the program can define Date objects and use them. The program's object code is linked
with the class's object code (date) that contains the member functions of the Date class. The
statements

```
Date first_moon_walk;
first_moon_walk.set_date(7, 21, 1969);
```

define the Date object first_moon_walk and set its value to the date July 21, 1969.   The
statements

Date century21, dd;
century21.set_date(1,1,2000); *dd*

create the objects century21 and d; the first one is set to the date January 1, 2000.

In the multi–line output statement, the line

<< century21.display_date()

formats the century21's date to a string with the member function display_date() and the string is printed by the output stream operator <<. The first line of

<< (dd.time_span(century21,first_moon_walk))
.display_time_span()

uses the member function time_span(Date, Date) to determine the span of time from the Date first_moon_walk to the Date century21 and the result is put into object dd. The time_span function then returns the object dd. The member function display_time_span() formats the object d's data members into a years, months, days formatted string and the stream operator << on the above line outputs the string. The program's output shows the complete effect of executing the multi–line output statement.

The class Date is useful to represent dates, to represent durations of time, to perform date calculations, and to format represented data. The class is an ADT and client code can operate on a date object only with the provided date functions; the data members are private and not accessible by client code.

The class's date.h header file specifies the client's interface to use the Date class. A header file often contains enough information for a programmer to determine how to use a particular class.

The files date.h and date.cpp completely define the ADT Date. They define its data representation and functions (no operators are used).

A date is represented by the private data members

month
day
year

These same data are used to represent a duration of time in years, months, and days.

The operations on a date are declared in the public section of the class so that clients can use them. The operations are

```
void      set_date(int, int, int = 0);
char*     display_date();
char*     display_time_span();
Date      time_span(Date, Date);
```

The member functions are defined in the file date.cpp and there they have

Date::

appended to their member function names. This is because other classes may use the same member function names for their classes and the compiler needs to know to which class a member function belongs.

The member function set_date(int, int, int = 0) is used to give a Date object a date. The function validates the date for legal arguments, and if an error occurs, an error message is output and the program is terminated with an exit(1) which signals an error at the command interpreter level. Chapter 6 covers a much better way to initialize objects than using a member function like set_date.

The member function display_date() uses the standard C output function sprintf() to format a date into a month name, day, and year format. Chapter 11 describes how to do this without using sprintf().

The member function display_time_span() is similar to display_date() except that it returns a string with the date formatted into years, months, and days. The following code:

(year > 1) ? "s" : ""

is used to print the correct singular/plural form of the word year; it prints an "s" if the value of year is greater than 1 and it prints nothing "" if the year is 1 or less.

The member function time_span(Date, Date) returns the difference of two dates and the difference is the span of time between two dates. The function's return type is Date and this means that the statement

return d;

returns a copy of the value of the automatic Date object d; the parameter is returned by value.

The date.cpp file also contains data that the member functions require: the number of days in each month and the name of each month. The data are defined as "static" so that they have only file scope and are kept local to the member functions. Because only the ADT has access to them, the data could be changed in the future without affecting the operation of client code that uses the ADT. An alternative way to provide these data is by using static class data members inside of class Date.

Summary

In summary, an ADT is a very disciplined packaging of a user–defined type and it keeps the interface to an ADT distinct and separate from its implementation. An ADT's enforced interface makes it straightforward for a client to determine how to use the ADT and it also bulletproofs the ADT objects from the client's code and all other non–date–class code. If a bug exists, it is most likely isolated to the ADT itself. Code implemented as ADTs is easier to develop and maintain and its use will reduce software development costs. Another benefit in using ADTs is that there is a natural progression from programming with ADTs to programming with objects (OOP).

6

Constructors and Destructors
Class Initialization

6.1 Introduction

When you declare a variable of a built–in data type, such as a float or a char, the compiler automatically allocates enough space for the variable. If you initialize the variable (remember initialization is not the same as assignment), the compiler will initialize the variable with the appropriate data.

```
float    x = 57.57;
char     y = 'B';
```

The compiler *constructs* the variable by allocating the required memory and initializing the variable with a value.

When a variable of a built–in data type goes out of scope, the compiler automatically returns the memory associated with the variable. Another way of saying this is that the compiler *destroys* the variable.

When creating new objects, data members are uninitialized. If you forget to initialize them before using them, the results could be disastrous. It would be useful to have a mechanism that automatically initializes your data members to known values. Then, using them would be safe. Although the system takes care of destroying an object for you (when a stack frame is popped, all automatic objects are destroyed), it does no special cleanup on an object. If an object contains a pointer through which you are controlling dynamically allocated memory on the heap, when the object is destroyed by the system, the memory for the pointer will be reclaimed but the memory on the heap will remain as garbage (and C++ does not provide garbage collection). It would be nice to have a mechanism that automatically does any required cleanup for your objects just when they go out of scope.

C++ provides two special member functions to automatically initialize an object when it is created and destroy objects just before they go out of scope. They are the

- Constructor

- Destructor

It should be pointed out that the compiler will automatically allocate memory for an object but not necessarily initialize the data members of the object. The compiler will also automatically return the memory for an object when it goes out of scope, but it will not return any extra resources associated with the object.

6.2   Class Initializer

Because class data members cannot be explicitly initialized when they are declared inside of class definition, the class must provide a member function that will initialize them. The following example provides the member function set() that the user must explicitly call after creating each object of a class to initialize the data members and also when changing their values.

```
#include <iostream.h>

class initExample  {
     int x;
     char  y;
public:
     void set(int a =57, char b = 'b') {x = a;  y = b;}
     void display(void) {cout << y << '\t' << x << '\n';}
};

main()
({
     initExample    value, term;
     value.set();
     value.display();
     term.display();
}
──────────── Program's Output ────────────
b        57
         249570336
```

A problem with this approach is that you have to remember to explicitly assign an object's data member values just after the object is created; otherwise, when you try to access the data members you will get whatever values (garbage) that are in those memory locations. Notice that we did not explicitly call the set() function for the term object and therefore, when term.display() was called, we got garbage printed out.

If all data members are in the public access region, they can be initialized using a comma–separated list enclosed in braces just like a C struct.

```
#include <iostream.h>

class initExample  {
public:
    int x;
    char y;
    void display(void) {cout << y << '\t' << x << '\n';}
};

main()
{
    static initExample   value = {57, 'b'};
    value.display();
}
```

───────── **Program's Output** ─────────
b   57

However, this method of initialization does not work if there is at least one data member in the protected or private access region of a class, and it is a very rare class that does not have at least one data member in the protected or private access region.

6.3   Constructor Initialization

C++ provides a mechanism for the automatic initialization of class objects. It is a special class member function called the *constructor*.

The constructor is a user–coded member function that has the same function identifier as the tag name of its class. The constructor cannot specify a return type (not even the return type void) or explicitly return a value. The constructor cannot be explicitly invoked; it is invoked implicitly by the compiler whenever an object of a class is declared or copied. A constructor is always called when an object is created, if a constructor is defined for the class.

```
#include <iostream.h>

class initExample  {
     int x;
     float  y;
public:
     initExample(int a = 57, float b = 1.1) {x = a;  y = b;}
     void display(void) {cout << x << '\t' << y << '\n';}
};

main()
{
     initExample   value(9966, 14.14), term = 33, price;
     value.display();
     term.display();
     price.display();
}
```

——————— Program's Output ———————

```
9966    14.14
33      1.1
57      1.1
```

In this example, the constructor takes two arguments: an int which is defaulted to 57 and a float which is defaulted to 1.1. The value of the int is used to initialize x and the value for the float is used to initialize y.

Three objects are declared of type initExample: value, term, and price. We will discuss the methods of passing arguments to constructors later in this chapter. For now, value is initialized with 9966 and 14.14, term is initialized with 33 and 1.1, and price is initialized with 57 and 1.1. The output shows the results of the initialization.

6.4   Constructor Overloading

It is rare to have a class that contains only one constructor. Because constructors are basically C++ functions, they can be overloaded. When an object is created, the compiler will look at the arguments that are passed to the constructor and will choose the appropriate version of the constructor. In the next example, the declaration of value results in having the constructor initExample(int a, float b) invoked. The declaration of retail results in having the constructor initExample() invoked, which results in garbage being left in the object's data members. The declaration of wholesale results in having the constructor in-itExample(int a) invoked. If the constructor initExample() were not present, the declaration of retail would cause a compiler error. *If a class has a constructor, a constructor must be called when an object is create.* The remaining two constructors in the example require arguments and none are passed.

```cpp
#include <iostream.h>

class initExample {
    int x;
    float  y;
public:
    initExample(void) {}
    initExample(int a)  {x = a; y = 0;}
    initExample(int a, float b) {x = a;  y = b;}
    void display(void) {cout << y << '\t' << x << '\n';}
};

main()
{
    initExample  value(9966, 57.57);
    initExample  retail;
    initExample  wholesale(33);
    value.display();
    retail.display();
    wholesale.display();
}
```

─────────── **Program's Output** ───────────
57.57   9966
334567   12464
0.0   33

Overloaded constructors allow you flexibility when declaring objects of a class type.

A constructor that requires no arguments or takes no arguments is called a default constructor. In this case, the constructor also does nothing when it executes, because its body is empty.

```cpp
initExample() {}
```

This constructor is useful when you want to declare an object but not assign any values to its data members or declare arrays of objects on the heap. An array of objects is only initialized by a default constructor.

> **initExample value;**

> **initExample *p = new initExample[10];**

The default constructor is called ten times for the above heap array.

Calling a member function for a class object that has not been initialized can produce spurious results. In the previous example, *retail* used the default constructor and we did not know what values were in the memory locations of its data members.

6.5   Constructors and Information Hiding

Constructors assume the level of accessibility of the access region in which they are declared. If you declare all constructors in the private region of a class, the class becomes an unusable class.

```
#include <iostream.h>

class initExample  {
    int x;
    float  y;
    initExample() {}
public:
    void set(int a, float b) {x = a; y = b;}
    void display(void) {cout << y << '\t' << x << '\n';}
};

main()
{
    initExample  value;
    value.set(5, 13.44);
    value.display();
}
```

——————— Program's Output ———————
Error: main() cannot access A::A() private member

As you can see, the constructor initExample(void) is in the private part of class initExample. When we tried to declare an object of the class, initExample value;, we got a compile error. Let us rewrite our example and try to use a constructor that is in the private part of the class.

```
#include <iostream.h>

class initExample  {
    int x;
    float  y;
    initExample(void) {}
public:
    initExample(int a)  {x = a; y = 0; initExample  z;}
    initExample(int a, float b) {x = a;  y = b;}
    void display(void) {cout << y << '\t' << x << '\n';}
    friend initExample  create(initExample);
};

initExample  create(initExample  alpha)
{
    initExample  beta;
    return beta;                 // Return a copy of beta
}

main()
{
    initExample  value(9966, 57.57);
    initExample  wholesale(33);
    value.display();
    wholesale.display();
    initExample  retail = create(wholesale);
    retail.display();
}
```

In the above contrived example, a private constructor initExample(void) was defined that could create an object whose constructor took no values. Also, a friend function of class initExample was declared; this friend function also declared an object whose constructor took no values. The friend function was called, allowing the retail object to be created. This shows that only friend functions or member functions of this class can declare objects that take no arguments because they are the only ones who could use the private constructor that took no arguments. There is no restriction on the declarations of objects that take one or two arguments.

6.6   Passing Arguments to Constructors

There are four ways that arguments can be passed to a constructor They are

1. Explicit form (constructor acts as a type converter)

2. Parenthesized list

3. Apparent assignment

4. Dynamic allocation.

```
class initExample {
    int x;
    float  y;
public:
    initExample(int a)  {x = a; y = 0;}
    initExample(int a, float b) {x = a; y = b;}
};

main()
{
    initExample  retail = initExample(33,99.66);          // Way 1
    initExample  wholesale(33, 99.66);                    // Way 2
    initExample  gross = 33.33;                           // Way 3
    initExample *ptr = new initExample(9966, 33.66);      // Way 4
}
```

To fully understand these initialization forms, it is necessary to understand the copy constructor and temporary objects, which are explained later. In the above example, we use the casting method initExample retail = initExample(9966); to pass values to the constructor, which initializes retail by invoking the constructor on line 5. The object value of type init_example is created and its initial value is the value produced by calling the constructor init_example(9966). Technically, how this occurs is compiler–dependent. Most optimizing compilers will directly apply the constructor to value object; however, it is acceptable for a compiler to create a temporary init_example object with the constructor and then to call the copy constructor (a special constructor described later) to give the retail object the value of the temporary object. You will find this form of initialization (Way 1) useful when initializing an array of objects by using a comma–separated list of values. This method can also be used to handle multiple arguments.

We used the standard method of passing multiple values to a constructor initExample wholesale(33, 99.66);. When an object is declared, the values that are passed to the object's constructor are placed in a parenthesized, comma–separated, list, in the order that they were passed to the constructor, and they are placed immediately after the object identifier. This method can also be used when passing in a single value and is the method that we prefer.

We passed in a single value to the constructor initExample gross = 33.33;. This looks like the notation we would use when initializing a double.

> **double**   **alpha = 57.57;**
> **initExample**   **gross = 33.33;**

In the example, 33.33 is implicitly cast to an init_example object

> **initExample(33.33)**

and the object gross gets this value.

We created a block of memory on the heap to hold an object of type initExample with the statement

> **initExample *ptr = new initExample(9966, 33.66);**

Because initExample contained a constructor, one had to be called to initialize this heap memory. Our example shows that two values are passed.

It is very useful to be able to declare an object without having to pass any arguments to its constructors. This can be done in two ways, and both use a default constructor.

    1. Give all arguments default values:

> **initExample(int a = 0, float b = 0);**

    2. Provide a constructor with no arguments:

> **initExample() {}**

or

> **initExample() {x=0; y=0;}**

Although defaulting all values for a constructor and passing no values to a constructor may at first appear to have the same effect, they are not the same. A constructor that defaults all its arguments is a constructor that *requires no arguments*. A constructor that has no arguments is a constructor *that takes no arguments*. In release 2.1, both of the above constructors are called default constructors. In previous releases, these two constructors were not treated the same when dealing with arrays of objects on the heap (next section) and also with constructors in a multiple inheritance situation (Chapter 9).

You may want to declare an object that takes no arguments. This is done properly as follows:

> **initExample goodTry;**

The following is not the proper way to declare an object that passes no values to its constructor:

> **initExample but_no_cigar();**

In C and C++, this declares but_no_cigar to be a function that takes no arguments and returns an initExample object.

6.7   Class Object Arrays and Constructors

An array of class objects is defined in the same way as an array of built–in types.

```
class initExample  {
    int x;
    float  y;
public:
    initExample() {}
    initExample(int a)  {x = a; y = 0;}
    initExample(int a, float b) {x = a; y = b;}
};

main()
{
    initExample  my_array[20];
    initExample* ptr = new initExample[20];
}
```

In the above example, the default constructor is called 20 times for each array. Because each array element is an object that is being created and its class has a constructor, the constructor is called for each element.In general, if the default constructor were not available, but the class had one or more other constructors, a compile error would occur.

If a class has no constructors, you can create an array of objects, but you must explicitly call the necessary member functions to assign values to its private data members if you want them to have known values.

Deleting Dynamic Arrays of Objects

Before ptr goes out of scope, an explicit delete is required to de–allocate the dynamically allocated memory that was allocated on the heap (the system can remove the memory for my_array as it was created on the stack). However, the array created by initExample* ptr = new initExample[20]; was created on the heap and only its pointer, ptr, was created on the stack. If you do not explicitly free up the heap memory, the array will remain as garbage when ptr goes out of scope.   Writing

> **delete ptr;**

is not always satisfactory because, although the array memory in the heap will be de–allocated, if the class has a destructor, you should write delete [] ptr. The effect of not using the delete[] syntax is undefined. Although this is sufficient in many cases, it gets you into trouble when you have a class that dynamically allocates memory itself. By using the delete [] ptr syntax, you guarantee that the destructors for each object in the array are invoked. The syntax is as follows:

> **delete [] ptr;**

In earlier versions of C++, you had to use

> **delete [20] ptr;**

If you are deleting an array of class objects, use the syntax delete[]; otherwise, use delete. In C++ version 2.0, when you used the syntax delete[] ptr; you had to specify the number of elements deleted; for example delete[20]. Although this syntax was not elegant, it is required by the compiler. Look at the following two examples:

```
#include <iostream.h>

class A {
     int   x;
public:
     A() { x = 57;}
```

```
    ~A() { cout << "Destructor called" << endl;}
    void display() {cout << x << endl;}
};

main()
{
    A  *ptr = new A[5];
    for (int i = 0; i < 5; i++)
        ptr[i] . display();
    delete ptr;                   // Error: should be delete[]ptr;
}
```

——————— Program's Output —————

```
57
57
57
57
57
Destructor called
```

We created an array of 5 A objects on the heap. The constructor was called 5 times, once for each object. The system reclaimed the heap memory (it did for the entire array), but only the destructor in the first object was called (in general, the effect was undetermined). Although this was not a serious problem here, consider the following example:

```
#include <iostream.h>
#include <string.h>

class A {
    char*   x;
public:
    A() { x = new char[strlen("Bill") + 1];
        strcpy(x, "Bill");}
    ~A() { cout << "Destructor called" << endl; delete x;}
    void display() {cout << x << endl;}
};

main()
{
    A  *ptr = new A[5];
    for (int i = 0; i < 5; i++)
        ptr[i] . display();
```

        delete ptr;   **// Error: should be delete[]ptr;**

}

————————— **Program's Output** —————————
Bill
Bill
Bill
Bill
Bill
Destructor called

In this example, each object on the heap contained a pointer to another block of memory on the heap. When we called a delete on ptr, the array was de–allocated and the destructor in the first object was called (effect is implementation–dependent), de–initializing its memory, but the destructors for the remaining four objects were not called, which left four Bills on the heap as garbage. Look at Figure 6.1 to see what happened:

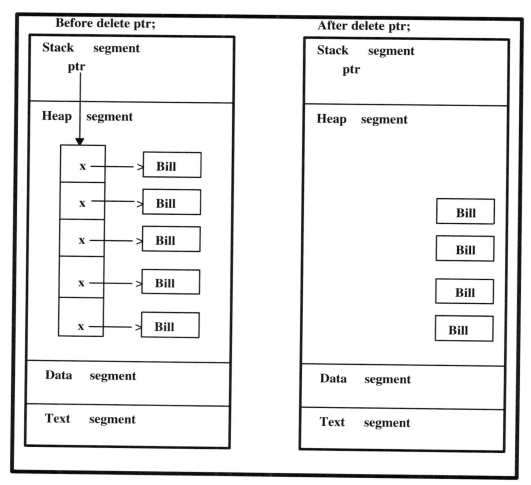

Figure 6.1 Memory layout for the example.

Had we called delete [] ptr; (or delete[5] ptr; on pre–2.1 systems) all of the objects would have been de–initialized by destructor calls and all of the memory would have been re-claimed from the heap.

Non–dynamic Arrays

Non–dynamic arrays of objects can be created in the same way as non–dynamic arrays of built–in data types. However, the use of constructors makes their declarations seem a little strange. In the next example, four arrays are created: one integer array and three initExample arrays.

An array of a built–in type, such as an int, can be initialized by specifying a list of initial values, such as

```
int a[3] = {1, 2, 3};
```

You can initialize the individual elements of the initExample arrays by causing their constructors to be invoked.

```
class initExample  {
      int x;
      float y;
public:
      initExample() {}
      initExample(int a)  {x = a; y = 0.0;}
      initExample(int a, float b) {x = a; y = b;}
      void display(void) {cout << x <<  \t  << y << ’\n’;}
};

main()
{
      initExample  array[20] = {9999, 1};
      initExample  barray[3] = {333, 5555, 66};
      initExample  carray[10] = {  initExample(33, 13.3),
                                   5555,
                                   initExample(66, 44.44)};
      int          darray[5] = {1, 2, 3, 4, 5};
}
```

In this example

- **array[0]** and **array[1]** have their respective values set by invoking the constructor initExample(int a) for the first two elements. The remaining elements call on the default constructor. If there were no default constructor, a compile error would result.

- **barray** has its respective elements set by invoking the constructor initExample(int a) for all elements.

- **carray** shows different ways to call constructors for the array by invoking the constructor initExample(int a, float b) for the first element; the constructor initExample(int a) for the second element; the constructor initExample(int a, float b) for the third element; and the default constructor initExample() for the remaining elements.

- **darray** is a standard integer array that has its elements initialized.

Whenever there are not enough explicit elements in a list to initialize all of an array's elements, the remaining array elements are implicitly initialized by a default constructor. Also, no empty elements can be left in a list.

> **initExample darray[3] = {1,,3}; // Error**

6.8   **Member Class Objects and Constructors**

When a class contains an object of another class and the enclosed object's class contains a constructor but has no default constructor, the enclosing class object must provide the argument value required by the enclosed class constructor. Another way of looking at this is to recognize that class initExample is the host and that an object of class obj is the guest. *It is always good social behavior for the host to attend to the needs of its guest.*

```
class  obj {
    float  y;
public:
    obj() {}
    obj(float a) {y = a;}
};

class initExample  {
    int x;
    obj  y;                          // Data member object
public:
    initExample() {}
    initExample(int a, float b) : x(a), y(b) {}
};
```

```
main()
{
    initExample  classObject(57, 57.57);
}
```

In this example, the constructor for the enclosed class obj is called before the constructor for the enclosing class initExample. The constructor in the enclosing class passes back its arguments through a *constructor initialization list.* The constructor initialization is placed between the closing parentheses of the argument list and the opening brace of the constructor code block. The list begins with a colon and contains a comma–separated list of elements, each of which initializes something.

```
initExample(int a, float b) : x(a), y(b) {}
```

The x(a) passes a value to the x data member of initExample and the y(b) passes a value back to the obj constructor to initialize y. If more than one object is a data member of a class, they will be included in the list as name/argument pairs. However, regardless of an element's position within the list, constructors (initializers) are called in an order that is compiler–dependent.

It should be noted that there are two ways that a constructor can pass values to a built–in data type:

- **initExample(int a, float b) : x(a), y(b) {}**

- **intExample(int a, float b) : y(b) {x = a;}**

The first method initializes x with the value a; whereas the second method assigns x the value a.

6.9   Constructors Execution

You should be clear about the distinction between initialization and assignment. In initialization, when you first create a variable, you also give it its initial value, such as

```
int x = 57;
```

In assignment, you create a variable in one statement and then in some future statement you assign it a value.

```
int x;
// ...
x = 57;
```

Constructors are executed in two phases:

1. Initialization

2. Assignment.

The initialization phase occurs if the constructor must pass values to an enclosed class constructor, to a base class constructor (more will be said of this in Chapter 9), to constants declared in the class, or to references declared in the object. In these cases, the argument list of the constructor is followed by a colon; between the colon and the opening brace of the function, a comma–separated list specifies the initializations.

```
class  obj {
     float  y;
public:
     obj() {}
     obj(float a) {y = a;}
};

class initExample  {
     int x;
     obj  y;
public:
     initExample() {}
     initExample(int a, float b);
};

initExample::initExample(int a, float b) : x(a), y(b) {}
```

If the body of a constructor is empty, there is no assignment phase.

```
obj() {}
```

If the class constructor for initExample takes no argument, implicit initialization occurs for object y of class obj (the constructor in obj that takes no argument is called). This is equivalent to having written.

```
obj() : y() {}
```

The assignment phase begins with the execution of the constructor's body.

```
obj(float a) {y = a;}
```

The following constructor initialization list shows explicit initialization:

initExample(int a, float b) : x(a), y(b) {}

The distinction between initialization and assignment becomes important when data members are constants or references.

```
int    alpha = 55;

class  obj {
      int  y;
      const int x;                    // Constant data member
      int& xx;                        // Reference data member
public:
      obj(int a);
};

obj::obj(int a) : x(a), xx(alpha)     // Initialization
{
      y = a;                          // Assignment
}
```

You are not allowed to assign a value to a constant or reference. Instead, both of these must be initialized. How do you do this when the constant or reference is a data member of a class? You can only use member functions to assign values to private data members. However, if you try to use a member function to assign a value to a constant or reference data member, you would get a compile error. The only way that you can *initialize* a value is to use a constructor initialization list of a constructor member function (constructor functions can be used to *initialize* a class's data members as well as assign to them). The previous example shows how to use a constructor initialization list to initialize constant and reference data members. If you had written your constructor as follows, you would get compile-time errors:

```
obj::obj(int a)
{
      y = a;                   // Valid assignment
      x = a;                   // Error: a constant cannot be an lvalue
      xx = alpha;              // Error: the reference is uninitialized
}
```

Initialization arguments can be complex expressions, such as

```
#include <math.h>

class obj {
     int x;
public:
     obj(int a) : x(rand(a)) {}
};
```

6.10 Memberwise Initialization (Copy Constructor)

When one class object is initialized with another object of the same class, as is the case in the following example, user–defined constructors may or may not be called:

```
int    alpha = 55;

class  obj {
     int  y;
     const int x;
     int& xx;
public:
     obj() {}
     obj(int a);
};

obj::obj(int a) : x(a), xx(alpha)          // Initialization
{
     y = a;   // assignment
}

main()
{
     obj      lesson(57);
     obj      plan = lesson;                // Note this line
}
```

The object lesson of type obj is created and initialized with the user–defined constructor obj(int). The object plan of type obj is created and initialized to the value of object lesson of the same type. In this example, no user–defined constructor is called; when the code is executed, the compiler implicitly creates and calls the following member function, which is the default copy constructor:

obj::obj(const obj& lesson) : y(lesson.y) {}

There are three situations in which this memberwise initialization function is created and called:

1.   The explicit initialization of one object with another

obj lesson = plan;

2.   Passing a class object by value as an argument to a function

extern int get_value(obj lesson);
// ...
int value = get_value(lesson);

3.   Returning a class object by value from a function call

#include <iostream.h>

extern obj object_ return(obj);

main() {
**   obj lesson = 66;**
**   cout << object_return(lesson) << '\n';**
}

There are occasions where using a compiler–generated copy constructor is not a good idea.

#include <iostream.h>
#include <string.h>

class member {
**   char* str;**
public:
**   member() {}**
**   member(char* s) { str = new char[strlen(s) +1];**
**   strcpy(str, s);**
**   cout << str << '\n';}**

```
        ~member() {cout << "destructor called\t"
                         << (void *)str  << endl; delete str;}
};

member  pass(member x)
{
    return x;
}

main() {
    member  nation("Bill"), home;
    home = pass(nation);
}
```

Using the default copy constructor is not a good idea when the object being copied contains a pointer to memory allocated from the free store (synonym heap) and a destructor.

Passing values by reference and returning values by reference does not lead to a copy of an object being made, and therefore, memberwise initialization does not occur.

The destructor above is called for every class object, even those created by memberwise initialization. This means that two different pointers point to the same area of memory in the free store. When one destructor is called, the memory is de–allocated and the remaining pointer is dangling. Trying to de–allocate through that pointer could lead to an error.

The output for the previous program is

> **Bill**
> **destructor called0x2022c**
> **destructor called0x2022c**

In the following example, it is a good idea to provide a special constructor to provide the initialization that you need. This is called a copy constructor.

```
#include <iostream.h>
#include <string.h>

class member  {
    char* str;
public:
    member() {}
```

```
member(char* s)
{
    str = new char[strlen(s) +1];
    strcpy(str, s);
     cout << str << (void *)str << '\n';
}
member(const member&);        // Copy constructor
~member()
{
    cout << "Destructor called\t" << (void *)str << endl;
     delete str;
}
void display(void) {cout << (void *)str << endl;}
};

member::member(const member&  x)
{
    str = new char[strlen(x.str) +1];
    strcpy(str, x.str);
}
```

Instead of having str pointers in the two classes point to the same block of memory in the heap (see the following figure), each object has its str pointer pointing at its own block of memory in the heap.

```
member  pass(member  x)
{
    return x;
}

main()
{
    member  nation("Bill"), home;
    nation.display();
    home.display();
    home = pass(nation);
    nation.display();
    home.display();
}
```

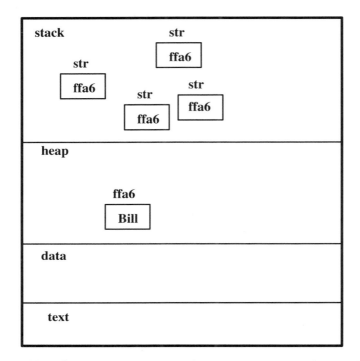

Figure 6.2 Default copy constructor in a class that dynamically allocates memory.

In the above program, in the main() function, four objects were created: two temporary objects were created when we passed and returned objects by value to the pass() function; one was created when nation was created; and the last was created when home was created.

In Figure 6.2, when the default copy constructor was used, there was only one block of data in the heap and all the str pointers in the objects pointed to that block. This is dangerous because not all objects go out of scope at the same time. When the first object goes out of scope, its destructor is called and the system is free to use that heap area again. Then, another object goes out of scope and its destructor is called, telling the system that the same memory area is free to be allocated again. Next, the third object goes out of scope, once again telling the system that the memory area is free to be allocated. Eventually, another variable, which really owns the memory, will try to use it and a bug will result. This type of bug is intermittent and each time it occurs, the behavior can be different. We need to prevent this situation, which is a normal result from using the default copy constructor, which has a pointer data member through which it dynamically allocates memory and a destructor that does a delete on that pointer.

Figure 6.3 illustrates the use of a user–defined copy constructor. Each time a new object is initialized with an object of the same type, the object creates its own block of memory in the heap and assigns the address to the object's pointer. Then, the strcpy() routine is used to copy the data into that heap area. When an object goes out of scope, it frees the memory that it exclusively controlled.

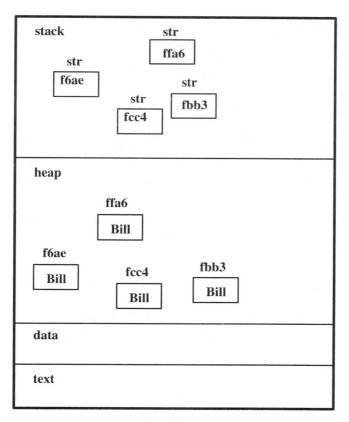

Figure 6.3 Memberwise copy in a class that uses a user–defined copy constructor.

6.11   Destructors

A second important member function is the destructor, which is automatically called when an object goes out of scope.

```
#include <iostream.h>
#include <string.h>

class member  {
    char* str;
public:
    member() {}
    member(char* s)  { str = new char[strlen(s) +1];
                          strcpy(str, s);
                          cout << str << '\n';}
    member(const member&);
    ~member() {delete str;}
};
```

A destructor has the same tag name as its class, but the name is preceded by a tilde. Destructors take no arguments and can return no values; it is an error to specify the return type void. Therefore, destructors cannot be overloaded.

Destructors do not actually de–allocate storage, the system does that. Destructors de–initialize a class object (clean up) prior to an object going out of scope. If memory was allocated using the operator new, the delete operator must be explicitly called to free the memory. All other values require no special treatment.

6.12   Static Objects

A static object has storage class static: an object that is declared outside of a function or an object declared inside a function must be preceded by the keyword *static*.

```
#include <iostream.h>
#include <string.h>

class member  {
    char* str;
public:
    member() {}
```

```
member(char* s)  { str = new char[strlen(s) +1];
                       strcpy(str, s);
                       cout << str << '\n';}
~member() {delete str;}
char* get_string() {return str;}
};

member   obj("getchar");

main()
{
    char* string;
    string = obj.get_string();
    cout << string << '\n';
}
```

Objects that are declared outside of a function will have their constructors executed before the main() function is called and their destructors executed after the main() function returns.

There are some interesting implications of this. Consider the following program:

```
#include <stdio.h>
#include <string.h>

class Stat{
    char* str;
public:
    Stat()  {printf("Enter  a  string\t");
            char  string[80];
            scanf("%s", string);
            str = new char[strlen(string) + 1];
            strcpy(str, string); }
    ~Stat() {printf("The string entered was: %s\n", str);
            delete str;}
}

main() {}
```

The class Stat has a constructor and destructor. The constructor prompts the user for information, stores the information in a buffer, does some dynamic memory allocation, and ends. The destructor prints out the information gained by the constructor and then does a delete on the pointer. The interesting thing is that the main() function is empty. Before main() is executes, the constructor interacted with the user, getting information, writing into a buffer, allocating memory, etc. After the main() function returns, the program continues to run; a string is printed out and memory is de–allocated.

A little warning: *when using I/O with constructors and destructors, use standard I/O and not stream I/O*, because there is no guarantee that the stream objects *cin* and *cout* will be built when the Stat object is built. If they are not, you will get an execution error.

7

Friend Functions and Operator Overloading

7.1 Friend Functions

We have seen that an important feature of C++ is the ability to restrict access to members of a class. If we put data members and member functions in the private or protected region of a class, only functions declared in the class can access them. To protect these private data, we essentially build a firewall around them. Engineers often build firewalls when they wish to protect something. For example, there is a firewall between the engine and passenger compartments of an automobile which protects the passengers from an engine fire. At first glance, this seems like an excellent engineering decision. However, when you wish to start a car, you find the gas pedal on the passenger side of the firewall and the carburetor on the engine side. Although lamentable, it is necessary to put a hole through the firewall for the accelerator linkage. This problem comes up again when you wish to turn the car; the steering wheel is on one side of the firewall and the wheels that must be turned are on the engine side. Once again, we are forced to drill a hole through the firewall for the steering column. Need we even discuss the brakes?

The point we are trying to make is that although it is very useful to restrict access to data declared in the private part of a class to member functions, sometimes this behavior is too restrictive. There are a few instances in which we want a non–member function to have access to the private members of a class. The mechanism to accomplish this is the use of *friend functions*.

Declaring Friend Functions

The following code shows a class with two data members and two member functions:

```
#include <iostream.h>

class init_exam  {
    int     x;
    char    y;
```

```
public:
    init_exam(int a = 57, char b = 'b') {x = a;  y = b;}
    void display(void) {cout << y << x << "\n";}
};

main()
{
    init_exam   value;
    value.display();
}
```

———————————— **Program's Output** ————————————
b57

The code is fairly simple. A point to remember is that the compiler implicitly passes the address of the object calling the function as the first argument (the argument is the *this* pointer). Using this address, the location of x and y in the process's memory space can be determined and init_exam() can write to these memory locations, while display() can read from them.

In the next program, two other functions are declared inside the class init_exam. They are

set()

get()

These functions are not member functions but are declared inside the ~~function~~ *class*.

```
#include <iostream.h>

class init_exam  {
    int      x;
    char     y;
public:
    init_exam(int a = 57, char b = 'b');
    void display(void);
    friend void  set(init_exam&, int, char);
    friend char get(init_exam&);
};

main()
{
    init_exam   value;
    value.display();
```

```
        set(value, 57, 'B');
        char y = get(value);
        cout << y << "\n";
}

init_exam::init_exam(int a , char b)
{
    x = a;
    y = b;
}

void init_exam::display(void)
{
    cout << y << x << "\n";
}

void set(init_exam&  frnd, int a, char b)
{
    frnd.x = a;
    frnd.y = b;
}

char get(init_exam&  frnd)
{
    return  frnd.y;
}
```

————————————— **Program's Output** —————————————

b57
B

Notice that two of the function declarations within this class are preceded by the keyword *friend*. These two functions are not member functions and therefore do not implicitly have the *this* pointer passed as their first argument. These functions are not scoped within the class but have the same scope as any normal function declared in C or C++ (the outermost scope of the module in which they reside). However, these functions have access into all access regions of the class just like member functions. A big difference between member functions and friend functions is how the function gets the address of the object it will read from or write to; in friend functions, we must explicitly pass the object of interest or a reference to the object.

Notice also that the keyword friend was is with the function declaration within the class but not with the function definition. The keyword friend can only be used inside a class definition and will generate a compiler error if used elsewhere. Why? Only a class can say who its friends are. If any function could declare itself a friend of a particular class, that function could access the private, protected, and public data without going through the class interface. If we let our friends use our cars, we want to be able to choose who our friends are. No stranger should be able to say that he is our friend and drive away in our car. C++ feels the same way.

Where in a class are friend functions declared? They can be declared in any access region of a class without restricting their use (this is different from member functions which take on the access attributes of the region in where they are declared).

Because friend functions are not member functions, their definitions look a little different. For function definitions, any member function must precede its identifier by the class name and the double colon operator. A friend function however is like any function in C++ that is not a member function and is defined as such (no class name an no double colon preceding the function identifier). Member functions use the *this* pointer to find an object and then can directly access data members; however, friend functions must use an explicitly passed object with the dot membership operator to access data. We know that this appears to violate the mechanism for accessing private data, but then friend functions are given special dispensation (no non–friend function could access private data using the dot membership operator).

When we call a member function, we use the object, dot membership operator, and function identifier, but when we call friend functions, we call them like any other C++ function.

Friend Functions and Operator Overloading

There are times when we wish to have a function with the ability to access all regions of a class but we wish the first argument to be something other than the *this* pointer. This is not possible with member functions which always pass the *this* pointer as the first argument. Why would this be important? Look at the following code:

```
#include <iostream.h>

class init_exam  {
    int     x;
    char    y;
public:
    init_exam(int a = 57, char b = 'b') {x = a;  y = b;}
    void operator<<(ostream& s) {s << y <<x << "\n"; }
};
```

```
main()  {
    init_exam   value;
    value << cout;
}
```

———————— **Program's Output** ————————
  b57

What is wrong with this example? When doing output for built–in data types, we have always written code similar to the following:

```
int x = 49;
cout << x;
```

Yet for this user–defined data type, our output interface is reversed and this is irksome (at least to us). How did this come about? Because all member functions pass the *this* pointer as the first argument, the left operand of << is always an init_exam object .

We can get around this by making our overloaded operator a friend function. Other friend functions will still be able to access the data members of class init_exam while passing in an ostream object as the first argument; this will make cout the left operand of <<, and value the right operand, which is what we want. The example can now be rewritten as follows:

```
#include <iostream.h>

class init_exam  {
    int      x;
    char     y;
public:
(    init_exam(int a = 57, char b = 'b') {x = a;  y = b;}
    friend ostream& operator<<(ostream&, init_exam&);
};

ostream& operator<<(ostream& s, init_exam& a)
{
    s << a.y <<a.x << "\n";
    return s;
}

void init_exam::init_exam(int a = 57, char b = 'b')
{
    x = a;
    y = b;
}
```

```
main()
{
    init_exam   value;
    cout << value;
}
```

———————— **Program's Output** ————————

   b57

Now our overloaded operator << is a friend function. To access the x and y data members of class init_exam, we used the *value.x* notation. When we called the function, we use the same interface with the user–defined data type that we did with the built–in data type. Thus, Friend functions find their most common use with operator overloading.

Friend Functions and Data Conversion

In the following example, we have overloaded the + operator as a member function. We have also provided a constructor that can convert a double to a complex object when required:

```
#include <iostream.h>

class complex {
    double  real, imag;
public:
    complex() {}                                            // Constructor
    complex(double r, double i = 0.0 ) {real=r; imag=i;}  // Another
    friend ostream& operator<<(ostream&, complex&);
    complex  operator+(complex);
};

complex  complex::operator+(complex a)
{
    complextemp;
    temp.real = this–>real +  a.real;
    temp.imag = this–>imag + a.imag;
    return temp;
}

ostream& operator<<(ostream& sout, complex& alpha)
{
    sout << alpha.real << " + " << alpha.imag << " i";
}
```

```
main()
{
    complex  x(1.1, 3.3), y(2.6, 1.4),  z;
    z = x + y;                    // Add two complex numbers
    z.display();
    double  a = 1.1;
    z = x + a;                    // Add a complex and a double
    z.display();
    z = 13.13 + y;               // Add a double and a complex
    z.display();
}
```

Because of the line **z = 13.13 + y;**, this program will not compile. We can add two complex numbers because we overloaded the + operator. We can add a complex and a double because we called operator+ through the complex object. The line **z = x + a;** is equivalent to

```
    z = x.operator+(a);
```

and the constructor **complex(double r, double i = 0.0)** will convert a to a temporary complex object so the function can execute. However, the line **z = 13.13 + y;** is equivalent to

```
    z = 13.13.operator+(y);
```

and there is no way that C++ can execute this function because we cannot call this function through a double. Does this mean that the program can never compile? Let us make operator+ a friend function instead of a member function.

```
#include <iostream.h>

class complex {
    double  real, imag;
public:
    complex() {}                                              // Constructor
    complex(double r, double i = 0.0 ) {real=r; imag=i;}  // Another
    friend ostream& operator<<(ostream&, complex&);
    friend complex  operator+(complex, complex);
};
```

```
complex  operator+(complex a, complex b)
{
    complextemp;
    temp.real = a.real +  b.real;
    temp.imag = a.imag + b.imag;
    return temp;
}

ostream& operator<<(ostream& sout, complex& alpha)
{
    sout << alpha.real << " + " << alpha.imag << " i";
}

main()
{
    complex  x(1.1, 3.3), y(2.6, 1.4),  z;
    z = x + y;                    // Add two complex numbers
    z.display();
    double  a = 1.1;
    z = x + a;                    // Add a complex and a double
    z.display();
    z = 13.13 + y;               // Add a double and a complex
    z.display();
}
```

The program now works because operator+ is a friend. The following calls are equivalent:

z = x + y;	z = operator+(x, y);
z = x + a;	z = operator+(x, a);
z = 13.13 + y;	z = operator+(13.13, y);

 a is converted to a temporary complex object and this function call works. 13.13 is also converted to a temporary complex object and this function call also works.

In this example, we did not want operator+() to be a member function because that would have precluded having any non–complex object as the first argument to the function call. When double was the first argument, we had a constructor that could convert the double to a complex, which was very useful.

Friend Functions that Bridge Two Classes

There will be times when you will want a function to access the private regions of two separate classes. Friend functions can do this. In the following examples, a function named display() can see in to both class employee and class date.

A common use of friend functions is to have them extract information from two separate classes. The following example shows a friend function that is declared in two separate classes but is a member of neither. It is allowed to read private data from both classes.

```
#include <iostream.h>
#include <string.h>

class employee;

class date {
    char* day;
public:
    date(char *d) {day = new char[strlen(d) + 1];
                        strcpy(day, d); }
    ~date() {delete day;}
friend void display(date&, employee&);
};

class employee  {
    char* name;
public:
    employee(char* nm)
        {name = new char[strlen(nm) + 1];
         strcpy(name, nm);  }
    ~employee() {delete name;}
friend void display(date&, employee&);
};

void display(date& today, employee& model)
{
    cout << model.name << "\n"
        << today.day  << "\n";
}
```

```
main()
{
    date  today = "October 24, 1990";
    employee model = "William J. Heinze";
    display(today, model);
}
```

─────────────── **Program's Output** ───────────────
William J. Heinze
October 24, 1990

Features to notice in this example include the forward declaration of class employee. This was necessary because a reference to employee was used as an argument to display().

The function display() was declared as a friend of both class date and class employee and was passed arguments of both classes. Therefore, it can access the private parts of objects of either class.

The keyword friend was not used with the function definition; nor was the :: operator used. How would we attempt to use member function notation for a function that was a member of two classes? The following code is not correct, but tries to show you why you would not want to use this notation:

```
void date::employee::display(date& today, employee& model)
{ // ... }
```

This form of syntax is used in C++ Version 2.1 to handle another problem and is not available for friend functions. Instead, friend functions are just normal functions, are defined like normal functions, and are called like normal functions.

It is possible to have all the member functions of one class potentially be friend functions of another class. In this case, we would declare the other class a friend. However, for any particular member function of the friend class to be able to access the private part of the class to which it is a friend, that member function would have to pass an object of the class to which the function is a friend. The following example should make this discussion more clear:

```
#include <iostream.h>
#include <string.h>

class employee;

class date {
    char* day;
```

```
public:
    date(char *d) {day = new char[strlen(d) + 1];
                      strcpy(day, d); }
    ~date() {delete day;}
    friend class employee;
};

class employee  {
    char* name;
public:
    employee(char* nm)
            {name = new char[strlen(nm) + 1];
             strcpy(name, nm);  }
    ~employee() {delete name;}
    void display(date&);
};

void employee::display(date& today) {
    cout << this->name << "\n"
        << today.day  << "\n";
}

main()
{
    date  today = "October 24, 1990";
    employee model = "William J. Heinze";
    model.display(today);
}
```

———————— Program's Output ————————

William J. Heinze
October 24, 1990

In this example, we declare class employee to be a friend of class date. However, the only member function of class employee that can access the private part of class date is display(). Notice that this function only passes an object of date as an argument. Because it is a member function of employee, the *this* pointer gives it the address of an employee object.

When display() is defined, it is defined as a member function of employee and the name field can be accessed directly because it was in the employee object, whereas the date field requires an object to be passed in explicitly as an argument.

When display() is invoked, it is called through an object of type employee because it is an employee member function.

For completeness, we will show you how to declare just one member function of one class to be a friend function of another class; however we prefer to declare classes as friends of other classes, as we did in the previous example.

```
#include <iostream.h>
#include <string.h>

class employee;

class date {
    char* day;
public:
    date(char *d) {day = new char[strlen(d) + 1];
                        strcpy(day, d); }
    ~date() {delete day;}
    void display(employee&);
};

class employee  {
    char* name;
public:
    employee(char* nm)
        {name = new char[strlen(nm) + 1];
         strcpy(name, nm);  }
    ~employee() {delete name;}
    friend void date::display(employee&);
};

void date::display(employee& model)
{
    cout << model.name << "\n"
        << (*this).day  << "\n";
}

main()
{
    date  today = "October 24, 1990";
    employee model = "William J. Heinze";
    today.display(model);
}
```

———————— **Program's Output** ————————
William J. Heinze
October 24, 1990

In this example, display() is declared a member function of class date. However, it passes as an argument an object of class employee. In class employee, display() is declared a friend of class date – notice the syntax of this declaration.

friend void date::display(employee&);

The name of this function is date::display() because it is a member of class date. If we had only said

friend void display(employee&);

would have gotten a compiler or linker error because this function would not have been defined. The function was defined as a date member function and was called as a date member function.

An often–asked question is when should you use member functions and when should you use friend functions. The best answer that we can give is; *Use member functions unless there is a compelling reason for using friend functions.*

7.2 Operator Overloading

Operator overloading is not a new concept in programming. In C, many operators were overloaded although you may not have been aware of it. For example, the + operator could be used to add two shorts, ints, longs, floats, and doubles. However, + could not be used to add together two complex objects, because complex objects were not defined when the compiler was written. In C++ however, you can overload the + operator to add together two complex numbers.

In C, if we needed to add together two complex numbers, we could have written a member function for class complex called sum() that would add together the complex objects.

```
#include <iostream.h>

class complex {
    double real, imag;
public:
    complex(double r = 0, double i = 0) {real=r; imag=i;}
    void display() {cout << real << " + " << imag  <<"i";}
    complex sum(complex&);
};
```

```
complex complex::sum(complex& x)
{
    complex temp;
    temp.real = this–>real + x.real;
    temp.imag = this–>imag + x.imag;
    return temp;
}

main()
{
    complex first(2.3, 3.3), second(4.4, 5.5), third;
    third = first.sum(second);
    third.display();
}
```

————————————————— Program's Output —————————————————
6.7 + 8.8i

The sum() function is declared and defined. It is a normal member function which must be called through an object of the class. However, when was the last time you wrote a function called sum() that you used to add together two doubles? We would ideally like to use the same interface to work with user–defined data types that we use with built–in data types.

Let us rewrite our class definition, renaming sum() to be the operator+().

```
#include <iostream.h>

class complex {
    double real, imag;
public:
    complex(double r = 0, double i = 0) {real=r; imag=i;}
    void display() {cout << real << " + "
                        << imag <<"i";}
    complex operator+(complex&);
};

complex complex::operator+(complex& x)
{
    complex temp;
    temp.real = real + x.real;
    temp.imag = imag + x.imag;
    return temp;
}
```

```
main()
{
    complex  first(2.3, 3.3), second(4.4, 5.5), third;
    third = first.operator+(second);
    third.display();
}
```

——————— **Program's Output** ———————

6.7 + 8.8i

Although it looks like the only thing that changed was the name of the function used to add together the two complex objects, something else has changed as well. When you use the keyword *operator* with one of C++'s built–in operators (*operator+*) to create a function, you can call this function in two different ways:

1) With the function notation **(third = first.operator+(second);)**

2) With infix notation **(third = first + second;).**

We could have called our function by

```
main()
{
    complex  first(2.3, 3.3), second(4.4, 5.5), third;
    third = first + second;
    third.display();
}
```

In this example, we create a class called complex. Because the + operator is overloaded, we can add two complex objects using the same interface that is used when adding two integers.

You can also do this with member functions but in many cases you would use the same notation used for built–in data types, such as

- **+**   instead of **sum()**

- **–**   instead of **minus()**

- **/**   instead of **divide()**

- *****   instead of **multiply()**

- **++**   instead of **increment()**

- – –   instead of **decrement()**

Rules about Operator Overloading

C++ provides the following operators:

new	**delete**	**sizeof**						
+	–	*	/	%	^	&	|	~
!	=	>	<	+=	–=	*=	/=	%=
^=	&=	|=	<<	>>	>>=	<<=	==	!=
<=	>=	&&	||	++	– –	,	–>	–>*
()	[]	.	.*	::	?:			

All of the operators except the following can be overloaded:

.   .*   ::   ?:   **sizeof**

The preprocessing symbols cannot be overloaded as well

 # and ##

The following rules apply to operands when overloading unary and/or binary operators:

For unary operators such as +, there is only one argument passed to the operator+() function, and that argument is the operand for the operator.

For binary operators such as +, there are two arguments passed to the operator+() function. The first argument is the left operand of the operator and the second argument is the right operand of the operator.

Accounting for the few exceptions listed above, you can overload all of the predefined operators of C++. You cannot create new operators. The overloaded operators have the same arity (unary, binary, or ternary operators), precedence, and associativity of their predefined operators.

- Unary operators can only be overloaded as unary operators.

- Binary operators can only be overloaded as binary operators.

- Ternary operators cannot be overloaded (there is only one).

- Operators that are both unary and binary can be overloaded as either unary or binary operators(e.g., + and –).

- You can overload the pre–increment and post–increment versions of ++. The same can be done for the – – operator. In pre–2.1, you could only overload the operator ++ as pre–increment or post–increment but not both, because you could only write one function for the two operators. The same is true for the decrement operator. For example, the ++ operator can only be defined as one function and that function is called whether you use the operator as a pre– or post–increment operator.

- You cannot change the precedence of any operator from the precedence that it has as a built–in C++ operator. Therefore, you should carefully choose the operators that you use – it would be foolish to use the comma operator as an address operator.

- You cannot change the associativity of an operator by overloading it. The assignment will be right to left associative when it is overloaded, and the addition operator will be left to right associative.

- You cannot change the meaning of an operator for a built–in data type. To prevent this, you must pass at least one class object as an argument to an overloaded operator. This argument will be one of the operands of the operator.

- You provide the meaning of the operator for a user–defined data type; the meaning is in the code that is executed when the operator is used. The overloaded operator does not have to have the original meaning of the operator. You could use the minus operator (–) as the overloaded operator for summing two class data members, but it would not be wise to do so.

- You should be careful of getting carried away with operator overloading. You might create a class called screen and then overload a lot of operators to use with the class, but in the end, it would be difficult for another person to understand your code. Don't make C++ look like APL by incautious operator overloading.

Overloading Operators as Friends and Member Functions

To overload an operator use a special function notation

operator+(...)

There is no difference between this function and any other function. You can use + as an infix operator or you can invoke the function:

object.operator+(...);

An overloaded operator does not have to be a member function but it must take at least one class argument. This prevents the overloading of an operator for built–in data types. An overloaded operator can be declared as either a member function or as a friend function. A member operator always uses one less argument than a friend function because its first argument is the implicit pointer *this*.

```
#include <iostream.h>

class complex {
    double real, imag;
public:
    complex(double r = 0, double i = 0) {real=r; imag=i;}
    void display() {cout << real << " + "
                         << imag <<"i";}
    complex operator+(complex&);
    friend complex   operator–(complex&, complex&);
};

complex complex::operator+(complex&  x)
{
    complex  temp;
    temp.real = real + x.real;
    temp.imag = imag + x.imag;
    return temp;
}

complex operator–(complex&  x, complex& y)
{
    complex  temp;
    temp.real = x.real – y.real;
    temp.imag = x.imag – y.imag;
    return temp;
}

main()
{
    complex  first(2.3, 3.3),  second(4.4, 5.5),  third;
    third = first + second;
    third.display();
    third = second – first;
    third.display();
}
```

———————— **Program's Output** ————————

6.7 + 8.8i
2.1 + 2.2i

In the above example, we overloaded the + operator as a member function and the – operator as a friend function. In this case, it would have been better to overload both as friend functions. If we did, the following main() function would execute as

```
main()
{
    complex  first(2.3, 0.0),  second(4.4, 5.5),  third;
    third = 22.22 + second;                 // operator+(22.22, second);
    third.display();
    third = 44.57 – first;                  // operator–(45.57, first);
    third.display();
}
```

———————— **Program's Output** ————————

26.62 + 5.5i
42.27 + 0.0i

This program executes because the actual functions called (operator+() and operator–()) are not member functions and do not have to be called through a complex object. If they were defined as member functions, the calls would have been

```
complex  first(2.3, 0.0),  second(4.4, 5.5),  third;
third = 22.22 + second;   // 22.22.operator+(second);
third = 44.57 – first;      // 44.57.operator–(first);
```

However, these calls are not possible (44.57 and 22.22 are not objects) and the compiler generates an error.

Overloading Overloaded Operators

An overloaded operator function can itself be overloaded.

```
#include <iostream.h>

class complex {
    double real, imag;
public:
    complex(double r = 0, double i = 0) {real=r; imag=i;}
```

```
        void display() {cout << real << " + "
                              << imag <<"i";}
        complex&   operator+();
        friend complex   operator+(complex&, complex&);
};

complex& complex::operator+()
{
     return *this;
}

complex operator+(complex&  x, complex& y)
{
complex  temp;
     temp.real = x.real + y.real;
     temp.imag = x.imag + y.imag;
     return temp;
}

main()
{
     complex  first(2.3, 3.3),  second(4.4, 5.5),  third;
     third = first + second;
     third.display();
     third = +first;
     third.display();
}
```

——————— **Program's Output** —————
6.7 + 8.8i
2.3 + 3.3i

In this example, the + operator is overloaded as a unary operator and a binary operator. Because operator+() is just another C++ function, it can be overloaded as long as the compiler can tell the two functions apart by looking at their argument lists. These functions are clearly different and therefore can be overloaded.

Overloading a Unary Operator

Unary operators can be overloaded by passing the function only one argument. This single argument will be the operand of that operator.

Overloading a Unary Operator as a Member Function

The following example shows you how to overload a unary prefix operator as a member function:

```
#include <iostream.h>

class Unary  {
    int x;
public:
    Unary() {x = 0;}
    Unary(int a) {x = a;}
    Unary&    operator- -() {- -x;
                        return *this;}
    void display(void) {cout << x << "\n";}
};

main()
{
    Unary  example = 57;
    for(int i = 5; i > 0; i- -) {
        - -example;              // example.operator- -();
        example.display();
    }
}
```

The unary operator- -() function is declared; because it is a member function, the system passes the *this* pointer implicitly. Therefore, the object calling the member function becomes the operand for this operator.

Overloading a Unary Operator as a Friend Function

The following function was defined as a friend function:

```
#include <iostream.h>

class Unary  {
    int x;
public:
    Unary() {x = 0;}
    Unary(int a) {x = a;}
    friend Unary&   operator++(Unary y) {++y.x; return y;}
    void display(void) {cout << x << "\n";}
};
```

```
main()
{
    Unary  example = 57;
    for (int i = 5; i > 0; i– –) {
        ++example;                   // operator++(example);
        example.display();
    }
}
```

The unary operator++() function is defined; because it is a friend function, the system does not pass the *this* pointer implicitly. Therefore, you must explicitly pass the object.

The above code also contains an implicitly inlined friend function. A friend function is implicitly inlined by defining its code body inside a class definition. This is the same technique that we used to implicitly inline member functions.

Overloading a Post–increment and Post–decrement Operator

As you have seen, the pre–increment and pre–decrement unary operators ++ and – – can be overloaded just like any other operators. However, the post–increment and post–decrement unary operators ++ and – – have different specifications: they are specified using binary operator syntax, with the second argument being an int! This syntax was chosen because it is an easy way to force the compiler to distinguish them from the pre–increment and pre–decrement versions. Note: This is a 2.1 compiler capability and is not possible in pre–2.1 versions.

The following example illustrates overloading the post–increment operator ++:

```
#include <iostream.h>


class Camera  {
    int      picture_member;
    void     take_picture() { /* Some code to do it */ }
    void     advance_film() { /* Some code to do it */ }
public:
    Camera() { picture_number = 0;}
    void     operator++(int);
};
```

```
void      Camera::operator++(int )
{
//    object++  means take the picture and then
//    advance the film.  Later we could use pre-increment
//    to advance the film and then take the picture

    take_picture();
    advance_film();
}

main()
{
    Camera Cheryls_minolta;
    Cheryls_minolta ++;          // Picture # 1
    Cheryls_minolta ++;          // Picture # 2
    return 0;
}
```

The following statement

```
++ Cheryls_minolta;
```

would cause a compile error if it were placed in main() because only the post–increment operator is overloaded for class Camera. Prefix ++ is undefined.

In pre–2.1 versions of C++, if either the prefix ++ or – – operator were overloaded, the same function would be called by using the operator as a prefix or postfix operator.

Overloading a Binary Operator

Binary operators can be overloaded by passing the function two arguments. The first argument is the left operand of the overloaded operator and the second argument is the right operand.

Overloading a Binary Operator as a Member Function

The following example shows how to overload a binary operator as a member function:

```
#include <iostream.h>
class Binary  {
    int x;
public:
    Binary() {x = 0;}
```

```
        Binary(int a) {x = a;}
        Binary    operator+(Binary&);
        void display(void) {cout << x << "\n";}
};

Binary Binary::operator+(Binary&  a)
{
        Binary  temp;
        temp.x = x + a.x;
        return temp;
}

main()
{
        Binary  first(2.3),  second(4.4),  third;
        third = first + second;
        third.display();
}
```

——————— **Program's Output** ———————
6.7

The binary operator+() function is declared; because it is a member function, the system passes the *this* pointer implicitly and you pass the Binary object explicitly. Therefore, the object calling the member function becomes the left operand for this operator and the argument you pass becomes the right operand.

Overloading a Binary Operator as a Friend Function

The following function is defined as a friend function:

```
#include <iostream.h>

class Binary  {
        int x;
public:
        Binary() {x = 0;}
        Binary(int a) {x = a;}
        friend  Binary  operator+(Binary&, Binary&);
        void display(void) {cout << x << "\n";}
};
```

```
Binary operator+(Binary&  a, Binary& b)
{
    Binary  temp;
    temp.x = a.x + b.x;
    return temp;
}

main()
{
    Binary  first(2.3),  second(4.4),  third;
    third = first + second;
    third.display();
}
```

————————— Program's Output —————————
6.7

The binary operator+() function is declared; because it is a friend function, the system does not pass the *this* pointer implicitly, and therefore you must pass the Binary object explicitly as both arguments. Therefore, the first argument of the member function becomes the left operand for this operator and the second argument you pass becomes the right operand.

Predefined Operators

C++ provides three predefined operators that can be used with objects of all user–defined classes. The following operators do not have to be overloaded:

- assignment (=)
- address (**&**)
- sizeof

Overloading the Assignment Operator

The pre–defined assignment operator is used with class objects to perform memberwise assignment. Each data member value of one object is assigned to the corresponding data member of the other object, providing the two objects are of the same class. There are occasions when it is a good idea to overload the assignment operator.

Whenever a class has a data member that is a pointer, the pointer is used when dynamically allocating memory on the heap and the class also has a destructor function that does a delete on the pointer, you should provide an overloaded assignment operator.

```
#include <iostream.h>
#include <string.h>

class Assignment {
    int x;
    char* y;
public:
    Assignment() {x = 0;   y = NULL};
    Assignment(int a, char* b) { x = a;
                    y = new char[strlen(b) + 1]; strcpy(y, b); }
    ~Assignment() {delete y;}
    void display(void) {cout << y << x << endl;}
};

main()
{
    Assignment aaa(57, "B"), bbb(33, "b");
    bbb.display();
        bbb = aaa;
    bbb.display();
}
```

The above example looks fine, but there is a potential bug. The system generates the following function to carry out the assignment statement:

```
Assignment& Assignment::operator=(const Assignment& q)
{
    x = q.x;
    y = q.y;
}
```

Therefore the character pointers in objects *aaa* and *bbb* both contain the same address (see Figure 7.1). The first object that goes out of scope has its destructor do a delete on that memory address and the system is free to use the de–allocated memory. When the second object goes out of scope, its destructor does a delete on the same memory address and de–allocates the memory, which can then be owned by some totally different object. This can lead to intermittent bugs (if the objects go out of scope close enough to each other before the de–allocated memory is reallocated to another object, no problem will occur; but do not count on it, these objects do not have a mutual suicide pact). Worse yet, when bugs occur, they do not always have the same behavior (we do not know who gets the de–allocated memory). We can think of nothing worse than having intermittent bugs with different behaviors caused by the same problem.

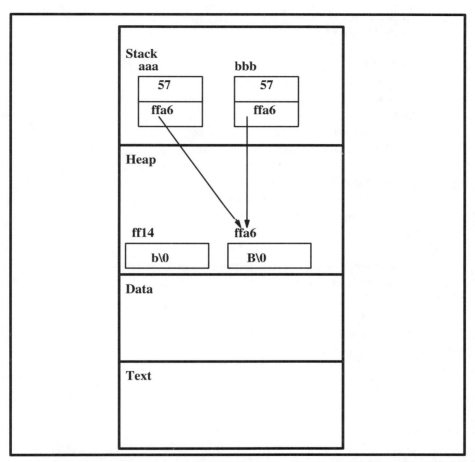

Figure 7.1 Memory layout using the default assignment operator with objects.

These problems can be resolved by providing our own overloaded operator

```
#include <iostream.h>
#include <string.h>

class Assignment {
    int x;
    char* y;
public:
    Assignment() {x = 0;   y = NULL};
    Assignment(int a, char* b) { x = a;
                    y = new char[strlen(b) + 1]; strcpy(y, b); }
    ~Assignment() {delete y;}
    Assignment&  operator=(const Assignment&);
    void display(void) {cout << y << x << endl;}
};

Assignment& Assignment::operator=(const Assignment& q)    {
    if(this != &q) {
        x = q.x;
        delete y;
        y = new char[strlen(q.y) + 1];
        strcpy(y, q.y);
    }
    return *this;
}

main()
{
    Assignment aaa(57, "B"), bbb(33, "b");
    bbb.display();
    bbb = aaa;
    bbb.display();
}
```

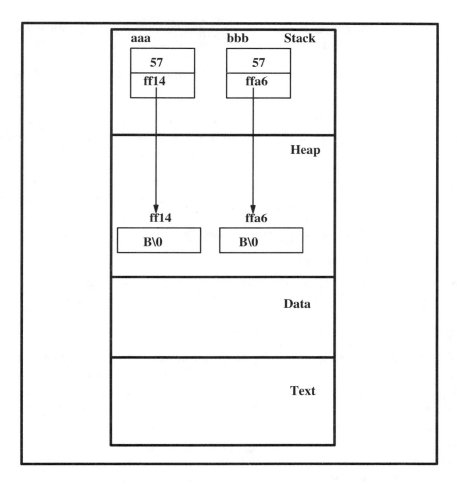

Figure 7.2 User–defined assignment operator memory space.

In our new example, we have overloaded the assignment operator. The syntax of this declaration is important if you want to use your version of the operator, and not the default version provided by the system. You can see the implementation of the member function. The following features should be noted:

- We checked to see if we were assigning an object to itself. If so, we immediately returned the object. If the objects were different, we continued.

- We copied the int from one object to the corresponding data member of the other object.

- We deleted the dynamically allocated memory. This is important because we did not leave garbage on the heap (remember that the object being assigned to already exists and has its pointer pointing to some heap data).

- We dynamically allocated a new block of memory on the heap for the object being assigned to and then copied into that area the data in the object being assigned from (look at Figure 7.2 to see that each object controls its own block of memory on the heap and that these areas contain the same data).

- We returned the object.

With our overloaded assignment operator, we can now assign one object to another without having to worry about two pointers pointing to the same area on the heap.

Operators that Return a Memory Address: []

There will be times when you will want an overloaded operator to return a memory address. You can write to the memory location that is referenced by this address when it is at the left side of an assignment operator and read the contents of the memory location that is referenced by this memory address when it is at the right side of an assignment operator. The address returned can be used as both an lvalue and an rvalue.

To illustrate this point, we will overload the square brackets operator.

```
#include <iostream.h>

class    DoubleArray {
    int      a;
    float *  boat;
public:
    DoubleArray() { a = 0;  boat = NULL;}
    DoubleArray(int  x)
    {
        a = x;
        boat = new float [a];
        for(int i = 0; i < a; i++)
```

```
                        boat[i] = (float) i;
                }
        DoubleArray(const DoubleArray &);
        DoubleArray& operator=(const DoubleArray& );
        float&    operator[](int b)
        { return boat[b]; }


        void  display()
        {
            for(int i = 0; i < x; i++) {
                cout << boat[i]  << '\n';
            }
        }
};              // End of class DoubleArray

DoubleArray::DoubleArray(const DoubleArray& q)
{
        boat = new float[q.x];
        a = q.a;
        for(int i = 0; i < a; i++)
                boat[i] = (q.boat)[i];
}

DoubleArray&   DoubleArray::operator=(const DoubleArray& q)
{
    if(this != &q) {
        delete boat;
        boat = new float[q.x];
        a = q.a;
        for(int i = 0; i < a; i++)
                boat[i] = (q.boat)[i];
    }
    return *this;
}

main()
{
    DoubleArray     quick(5);
    quick.display();
    for (int i = 0; i < 5; i++) {
        quick[i] = quick[i] + 5;
```

```
        cout << quick[i] << '\n';
    }
}
```

In this example, the square brackets operator is overloaded and returns a floating point reference. A reference had to be returned because, when used as an lvalue, we wanted to write to that memory location. Had we returned a float, we could have read the value of the float, but we could not change the value.

float   operator[](int) { return boat[b]; }

would have produced an error because you cannot assign one number the value of another (1 = 6 is not correct).

quick[i] = quick[i] + 5;

We can also see the use of the overloaded square brackets operator; at the right side of the assignment statement, we read the present value, add five to it, and then write the result to the same memory location. Here we are using the return value of the operator[]() function as both an lvalue and an rvalue.

Additionally, **quick[i] = quick[i] + 5;** could have been written as follows:

quick.operator[](i) =quick.operator[](i) + 5;

7.3   **Example : String Concatenation**

In the following example, we will overload the following operators:

- =
- +=
- []
- <<

```
#include <iostream.h>
#include <string.h>

class MyString  {
    int length;
    char* string;
```

```
public:
    MyString() {string =  NULL; length = 0;}
    MyString(const char*);
    MyString(const MyString&);
    ~MyString() {delete string;}
    MyString&  operator=(const MyString&);
    friend ostream&  operator<< (ostream & sout)
            {sout << string << "\n";
              return sout;}
    void operator+=(char*); //A char* variable is passed
    friend void operator+=(char*, MyString&);
    void operator+=(MyString&);
    char& operator[](int x);
};


MyString::MyString(const char* str)
{
    length = strlen(str) + 1;
    string = new char[length];
    strcpy(string, str);
}


MyString::MyString(const MyString& str)
{
    length = str.length;
    string = new char[length];
    strcpy(string, str.string);
}


MyString& MyString::operator=(const char& str)
{
    if (this != &str) {
        length = str.length;
        string = new char[length];
        strcpy(string, str.string);
    }
    return *this;
}
```

```
void MyString::operator+=(char* str)
{
    char* buffer;
    length += (strlen(str) + 1);
    buffer = new char[length];
    strcpy(buffer, string);
    strcat(buffer, str);
    delete string;
    string = buffer;
}

void operator+=(char* str, MyString&  obj)
{
    obj.length = obj.length + strlen(str) + 1;
    char* buffer;
    buffer = new char[obj.length];
    strcpy(buffer, str);
    strcat(buffer, obj.string);
    delete obj.string;
    obj.string = buffer;
}

void MyString::operator+=(MyString& str)
{
    char* buffer;
    length += (strlen(str.string) + 1);
    buffer = new char[length];
    strcpy(buffer, string);
    strcat(buffer, str.string);
    delete string;
    string = buffer;
}

inline char& MyString::operator[](int x)
{
    return string[x];
}
```

```
main()
{
    MyString  object("William "),
                 lesson("Joseph "), grid("Heinze");
    cout << object;
    object += "Heinze";
    cout << object;
    cout << lesson;
    "William " += lesson;
    cout << lesson;
    lesson += grid;
    cout << lesson;
    lesson[0] = 'w';

    cout << lesson;
}
```

—————— Program's Output ——————
William
William Heinze
Joseph
William Joseph
William Joseph Heinze
william Joseph Heinze

The class MyString is defined and it contains the following:

- A default constructor

- A conversion constructor

- A copy constructor

- A destructor

- An overloaded assignment operator

- An overloaded output operator

- Multiply overloaded += operators

- An overloaded [] operator.

8

References

References are very important in C++ because they provide the capability to define interfaces that are not definable in C. References have several uses. They are frequently used when overloading operators. They are also used to pass an argument by reference rather than by value, and this allows the called function to modify the argument's value in the calling function. In C you had to use pointers to do this. A function can also return its argument by reference; this also was not possible in C. Lastly, a reference can be used as a synonym or alias name for a variable or object. This chapter describes references and shows you how to use them.

A reference is a way to construct a new type from an existing object of a type. You already know several other ways to construct new types from other types. Together, they include the following ways of making declarations:

Description	Declarator
functions	()
arrays	[]
pointers	*
references	&
constants	const
classes	class
structures	struct
unions	union
enumerations	enum
pointers to members	class–name::*

The following program illustrates a use of each declarator listed and thus provides a brief review:

```
int f(int);                 // Declares function f which takes an int
                            // and returns an int

class   C;                  // Declares C to be a class; OK but not needed here

class   C {                 // Defines class C, which also declares it
      int a;
};

struct  S {                 // Defines struct S, which also declares it
      int a;
};

union   U {                 // Defines union U, which also declares it
      double d;
      int   i;
};

enum    E {red, white, blue};
                            // Defines enum E, which also declares it

int C::* pma;               // Defines pma to be a pointer
                            // to a class C member that is an int

main()
{
      int a[13];            // Define array a
      int* p;               // Define pointer p
      int& r = a[3];        // Define reference r  (explained below)
      const int K =5;       // Define constant int K
      C c;                  // Define a class  C object
      S s;                  // Define a struct S object
      U u;                  // Define a union  U object
      E e;                  // Define a enum  E object

      return 0;
}

int f(int i) { return i * i; }     // Defines function f
```

In the above example a was declared to be an array of 13 ints. The statement

    int& r = a[3];

declares r to be a reference to an integer and it references the integer defined by a[3]. Thus, r is an synonym, or alias for the integer that corresponds to the expression a[3]. Using r is the same as using a[3] and their use is interchangeable in any expression.

The key differences between a reference and a pointer is that

- A reference is an object

- A pointer is the memory address where an object resides, or the value NULL (0).

The following program illustrates their differences:

```
#include <iostream.h>
void f(char  &x)      { cout <<  x << endl; }
void g(char* x)       { cout << *x << endl; }

main()
{
    char  a = 'A';          // Object a has the character value A
    char* p = &a;           // p is initialized to the address of a

    cout << a << endl;
    cout << *p << endl;

    // Pass an object
    f( a);   f(*p);

    // Pass an address
    g(&a);
    g( p);

    return 0;
}
```

——— **Program's Output** ———
A
A
A
A
A
A

8.1   Declaring a Reference

The symbol & is used to declare a reference and you should not confuse this use of & with the address operator. The symbol & means reference, address operator, or the and operator, depending on its use; the symbol * means pointer, dereference, or multiplication, depending on its use. This means that & now has an additional meaning in C++ that it did not have in C. After using C++ for awhile, reference declarations will look as natural to you as C pointer declarations.

8.2   References Used as Aliases

The following code declares a double, a pointer to the double and a reference to the double:

```
double d = 1.23;
double* pd = &d;        // Pointer to double
double& rd = d;         // Reference to double
```

The name d is a double and it is initialized to 1.23. The name pd is a pointer to a double and it is initialized to the address of d; thus, pd points to d. The name rd is a reference to a double and it is initialized to the double d. Note that it is initialized to object d and not the address of d. Also, whenever a reference is declared, it must be initialized; a reference can only reference one thing and it cannot later be changed to reference something else. In fact, a reference is like a constant pointer that the system automatically dereferences whenever it is used, and compilers implement references as constant pointers.

A pointer is always dereferenced to access what it points to; a reference accesses what it references. The following code illustrates these points:

```
cout <<   d;          // Prints 1.23
cout << *pd;          // Prints 1.23
cout <<  rd;          // Prints 1.23
```

```
double t;
t = rd + 10;            // Using rd as an rvalue
cout <<  t;             // Prints 11.23
rd = 4.56;              // Using rd as an lvalue
cout <<  d;             // Prints 4.56
cout <<  rd;            // Prints 4.56
```

As the example code shows, the use of references is very easy. There are several applications of reference. We have used references as aliases when converting FORTRAN code to C++ code and in simplifying references to complicated expressions. This section shows some applications of references and section 8.7 discusses converting FORTRAN code.

This program illustrates using a reference as an alias for a complicated long expression. This can make a program much more readable when the reference is used in several places.

```cpp
#include <iostream.h>

struct {
    struct {
        // ...
        struct {
            // ...
            double Pi;
        } transcendental;
    } mathematical;
} constants = {3.14159};




main()
{
    // If just used once, this is probably OK

    cout << constants.mathematical.transcendental.Pi << endl;

    // If used many times, this is much better
    // Also note that because the reference has a different
```

```
// scope (main's scope) than the struct that contains
// the constant of interest (Pi), you can use the same name,
// which makes the code very readable and also makes
// it quick and easy to pick a name.

double& Pi = constants.mathematical.transcendental.Pi;

cout    << Pi/2      << " "
        << Pi        << " "
        << 3*Pi/2    << " "
        << 2*Pi      << endl;
return 0;
}
```

——— Program's Output ———
3.14159
1.570795 3.14159 4.712385 6.28318

A math textbook gave the following definition for complex division:

$$\frac{a + bi}{c + di} = \frac{(ac + bd) + (bc - ad)i}{c*c + d*d}$$

In the next program, complex division is implemented by the function operator/, which takes two complex parameters. References are used to give names to the real and imaginary components of the parameters so that they correspond to the variables a, b, c, and d in the above formula. This simplifies writing the division algorithm because the code directly reflects the following formula:

return Complex((a*c + b*d), (b*c − a*d)) / (c*c + d*d);

The program below also implements a simplified complex class with the complex operators +, −, /, and << :

```
#include <iostream.h>

class Complex {
    double re;
    double im;
```

```
public:
    Complex()   { re = 0; im = 0; }
    Complex(double r, double i = 0) { re = r; im = i; }

    friend double& re(Complex x)    { return x.re; }   // Allow write
    friend double& im(Complex x)    { return x.im; }  // Allow write

    friend Complex operator+ (Complex x, Complex y)
                { return Complex(x.re+y.re, x.im+y.im); }

    friend Complex operator– (Complex x, Complex y)
                { return Complex(x.re–y.re, x.im–y.im); }

    friend Complex operator/ (Complex, Complex);

    friend ostream& operator<< (ostream& s, Complex x)
    {
        s    << x.re
             << ((x.im < 0) ? " – " : " + ")
             << x.im
             << 'i';
        return s;
    }
};

Complex operator/ (Complex x, Complex y)
{
    double& a = x.re;
    double& b = x.im;
    double& c = y.re;
    double& d = y.im;

return Complex((a*c + b*d), (b*c – a*d))  /  (c*c + d*d);
}
```

```
// A textbook gave the following complex division example:
//
//        4 + i    5 + 14i
//       ───────  =  ───────
//        2 – 3i     13


main()
{
    Complex n(4,1);
    Complex d(2,–3);
    Complex z;

    z = n / d;

    cout << z<< endl;
    cout << re(z)*13 << endl;    // should be 5
    cout << im(z)*13 << endl;    // should be 14

    return 0;
}


──────── Program's Output ────────
0.384615 + 1.076923i
5
14
```

In the above program, references were used to give names to expressions.

8.3 Declaring Non–trivial References

Like other declarations, reference declarations can be arbitrarily complex. In complex situations, using typedefs significantly simplifies writing declarations and aids in writing them correctly.

The following program illustrates defining references to an array of char (a string), an array of struct, and an array of array of int (a two– dimensional array):

```
#include <iostream.h>

struct S {
    int a;
};

S   u[6]  = { 1, 2, 3, 4, 5, 6};

char a[]      = "Art";
int   b[]     = { 1, 2, 3};
int   c[][3]  = {{1, 2, 3},  {4, 5, 6}};

typedef int T[3];
T   tt[2]  = {{1, 2, 3},   {4, 5, 6}};

main()
{
    // Create alias names for some existing 1–D and 2–D arrays
    // using typedefs simplifies dealing with involved expressions
    char*  (&r)   = a;          // ref to a 1–D array of char
    int*   (&s)   = b;          // ref to a 1–D array of int
    S*     (&v)   = u;          // ref to a 1–D array of struct
    T*     (&w)   = tt;         // ref to a 2–D array of ints

    // Use the references
    cout << r      << endl;
    cout << s[2]   << endl;
    cout << v[3].a  << endl;
    cout << w[1][1] << endl;

    // Use references to give a simple name to some array elements
    char*&    rr  = r;
    int&      s2  = s[2];
    int&      v3a = v[3].a;
    int&      w11 = w[1][1];
```

```
// Use the new references
cout << rr   << endl;
cout << s2  << endl;
cout << v3a << endl;
cout << w11 << endl;

return 0;
}
```

———— Program's Output ————
Art
3
4
5
Art
3
4
5

8.4   Passing a Function Parameter by Reference

In C, when a parameter is passed to a function, it is always passed by value. This means that the called function has a local copy of the parameter passed; modifying the local copy has no effect on the value in the calling function. The following program illustrates passing a parameter by value:

```
#include <iostream.h>

void f(int a) { a = 123; }

main()
{
    int x = 7;
    f(x);                       // x is passed by value
    cout << x << endl;          // prints 7
    return 0;
}
```

In the above example, the function f() has a local variable named a . When the function is called, the local variable is initialized to the value of the passed argument. It is important to note that parameter passing has the semantics of initialization; a parameter is not passed with the semantics of assignment. This becomes significant when passing constant arguments and reference arguments, because they both require initialization. Neither of them can be assigned a value. It is also significant when passing a user–defined type by value. The copy constructor initializes the value, not the overloaded assignment operator operator=.

Some computer languages, including FORTRAN, Pascal, and C++ can pass parameters by reference, and FORTRAN cannot pass parameters any other way! The following program illustrates passing an argument by reference:

```
#include <iostream.h>
void f(int& a) { a = 123; }

main()
{
    int x = 7;
    f(x);                    // x is passed by reference
    cout << x << endl;       // Prints 123
    return 0;
}
```

In the above program, the function f defines its parameter to be passed as a reference to an int. This means that when the function is called, the user passes an int but internally, the compiler actually passes the address of the int. Also, inside the code body of the function f, the formal parameter a is used as if it were an int, even though internally the compiler passes the int's address. When the int a is used, the compiler automatically does the dereferencing. In main, the function f is called with the variable x, which has a value of 7. When the function returns to main, the value of x changes to 123.

When user–defined objects are passed to a function, some of them may be quite large and passing them by value (making a copy of them) is inefficient. Passing them by reference only passes their addresses and this is much more efficient. A pointer could be used. The choice between a reference and a pointer usually is dictated by the user interface that is needed. When a reference is used, the interface looks as if an object were passed (from the call, you cannot tell whether the argument is a reference or object); when a pointer is used, either the address of an object or a pointer to an object is passed (from the call, you can tell when a pointer is used).

When overloading an operator, the choice for large objects is either a reference or a const reference. A constant reference means and guarantees that the called function will not modify the argument. Assume that we have a class named Big_thing whose objects have a size of 1000 bytes and that we want to pass it to operator! but do not want to modify its value. The following shows an appropriate prototype:

> **Big_thing operator! (const Big_thing& x);**

The following few statements show a use of it:

> **Big_thing pi(7); // pi represented with 10,000,000 digits**
> **Big_thing x;**
> **x = !pi;**

8.5   Returning a Function's Result by Reference

In C, a function always returns its result by value, which means that a copy of the returned result is made into the calling function. In C++, you have the choices of return–by–value and return–by–reference. A key feature of a function that returns its result by reference is that the function appears to return an object, and the return value can be used as an rvalue or an lvalue.

The following program illustrates the definition and use of a function that returns its result by reference:

```
#include <iostream.h>

class Int_array {
    int  n;                    // Size of the array
    int* p;                    // The array is kept on the heap
public:
    Int_array(int a = 10)
    {
        n = a;
        p = new int[n];
        for (int i = 0; i < n; i++)
            p[i] = i;
    }
```

```
        int size() { return n; }

                    // This function returns its result by reference.
                    // Thus, it can be used as an lvalue or an rvalue.

        int& operator[] (int index)
        {
            return p[index];
        }

};


main()
{
    Int_array a;
    int      i;

    i = a[4];                        // Use function operator[] as an rvalue
    cout << i   << endl;

    a[4] = 44;                       // Use function operator[] as an lvalue
    cout << a[4] << endl;

    a[5] = a[4] + 11;                // Use as both an lvalue and an rvalue

    for (int j = 0; j < a.size(); j++)
        cout << a[j] << '\t';
    cout << endl;

    return 0;
}
```

──────────── Program's Output ────────────
```
4
44
0   1   2   3   44  55  6   7   8   9
```

The example shows a very useful application of functions that return references. Another area where they are useful is in implementing associative arrays or other data structures. In these cases the same function can be used to either access or update associative information.

You must exercise some caution when using return–by–reference. The following code has a terrible bug:

```
class A {
     int a;
public:
     A()     { a = 1; }
     int& f() { A t; return t.a; }        // Never do this!
};

main()
{
     A   x;
     int y;
     y = x.f();                           // Bug, y refers to a temporary that is gone
     return 0;
}
```

In this program, the function f() in its code body creates a temporary object named t on the stack and returns by reference a part of the temporary object. When x.f() is executed in main, the function is called and it creates a temporary A object named t on the stack. Then it returns a reference to data on the stack and returns to main. At this point in main, the function's stack frame is popped off the stack and that area of the stack is available for reuse: the data that were there are possibly now gone. Thus, as a rule of thumb, never return a reference or a pointer to a function's local data.

8.6   Using References to Define Cascading Functions

The iostream library overloads the operators operator<< and operator>> so that operations on a stream can be cascaded. For example,

```
cout << 1 << 2.3 << 'c' << "A string" << endl;
int   a;
char* b = 0;
cin >> a >> b;
```

A cascading function takes a parameter by reference, possibly modifies the parameter, and then returns the parameter by reference. When it is returned, it can be used in the next cascaded call, and so on. You can look at the header file iostream.h to see how the operator<< and operator>> functions pass and return their parameters.

If an I/O error occurs, this fact is stored in the state of the stream object that was passed by reference and returned by reference. Later, the stream object's state can be checked to see if any I/O errors occurred.

The following program illustrates writing a cascading function that returns its parameter by value (usually return–by–reference is wanted):

```
#include <iostream.h>

class A {
    int state;
public:
    A()     { state = 0; }
    void display()   { cout << state << endl; }

                // The cascading function
    friend A operator<< (A& a, int i)
    {
        a.state += i;
        return a;
    }
};

main()
{
    A a;
    a.display();
    a << 1 << 2 << 3;
    a.display();

    return 0;
}
```

————— **Program's Output** —————

0

1

The main function creates object a and the constructor initializes its state variable to 0. The a.display() outputs a 0, verifying the initial value. The next statement

a << 1 << 2 << 3;

uses the operator << which has left–associativity and is equivalent to the fully parenthesized statement

(((a << 1) << 2) << 3);

When this expression is evaluated, the following occurs:

1. (a << 1) is evaluated, which modifies the state of a that was passed in by reference to 1 and returns a temporary copy of the a object, which we will call temp1.

2. (temp1 << 2) is evaluated which modifies the object temp1 to have a value of 3 and returns a new temporary copy of temp1, which we will call temp2.

3. (temp2 << 3) is evaluated which modifies the object temp2 to have the value 6 and returns a new temporary copy of temp2, which we call temp3.

4   temp3 is returned as the final value of the expression, which is not used.

5. The temporaries temp1, temp2, and temp 3 are frequently destroyed by the com–piler before the next statement is evaluated; however, at which time they are actu–ally destroyed is compiler–dependent.

The next statement in the program a.display() displays the value of object a, which is 1, as indicated by the program's output. While you might have expected and wanted a to have the final value of 6, this did not occur because the operator returned its result by value. The next program remedies this problem.

The following program illustrates writing a cascading function that returns its results by ref-erence:

```
#include <iostream.h>
class A {
    int state;
public:
    A()      { state = 0; }
    void display()   { cout << state << endl; }

    // The cascading function
    friend A& operator<< (A& a, int i)
    {
        a.state += i;
        return a;
    }
};

main()
{
    A a;
    a.display();
    a << 1 << 2 << 3;
    a.display();

    return 0;
}
```

——— Program's Output ———

0

6

When the expression

$$(((a << 1) << 2) << 3);$$

is evaluated, the following occurs:

1. The expression (a << 1) is evaluated and it modifies the a object that was passed in by reference to a value of 1. It then returns the object a as the result.

2. The expression (a << 2) is evaluated. Object a's value is modified to 3 and it is returned by reference as the result.

3. The expression (a << 3) is evaluated. Object a's value is modified to 6 and it is returned by reference as the final result.

Notice that no temporaries were used in evaluating the expression. All modifications were done to the original object a. The next statement a.display() displays the value of a, which is 6 as shown by the program's output. This is the behavior that we wanted and that we need to implement cascaded functions correctly.

8.7 Using References to Convert FORTRAN Code to C++

References significantly contribute to the conversion of FORTRAN source code to C++ code. FORTRAN passes all of its parameters by reference and the same semantics are kept by passing all corresponding parameters by reference. Another area of conversion is mapping FORTRAN common, named common blocks, and equivalence statements to corresponding C++ code. Common blocks are converted to structs, and unions are used with some dummy variable padding. References are used to map struct member names to the corresponding FORTRAN names; this means that the converted code looks the same as the original code, except for the translation of all upper–case characters to lower–case.

The strategy that we have used to convert one–dimensional, two–dimensional and three–dimensional arrays to C++ is to keep 1–origin indexing in the converted code rather than convert all expressions to use C's and C++'s 0–origin indexing. By doing this, FORTRAN–to–C++ converted code that uses array indexing does not get converted. When an array is allocated, its 0–row, 0–column, and 0–plane are allocated but not used. The allocated arrays are 1 larger in each dimension and their 0–th index is not used. While converting 1–origin indexing code to 0–origin indexing code is feasible, the authors have had very good success with sticking to 1–origin indexing: less code to modify and thus fix during debugging.

The following program illustrates how to use references to handle FORTRAN equivalence statements and common statements:

```
// Implement the following FORTRAN equivalence statement
// that includes a FORTRAN array of 2 elements which
// is implemented as a 3–element array with the index 0
// not being used as discussed above:
//
//     Equivalence    (p1, p(1), p12),
//                    (p2, p(2))

// A FORTRAN equivalence mapped into C++ unions and structures
union {
```

```
    struct {
        int  dummy1;
        int  p1;
        int  p2;
    } st0;

    int p[3];

        struct {
        int  dummy2;
        long p12;
    } st1;
} un0;


#include <iostream.h>


main()
{
    // Local names for the common block elements
    // Often, elements in a common block are given
    // different names in different routines.
    //
    int&        p1  = un0.st0.p1;
    int&        p2  = un0.st0.p2;
    int*        p   = un0.p;
    long&       p12 = un0.st1.p12;

    // The converted FORTRAN code
    p1 = 12;
    p2 = 34;

    cout << p1 << " " << p2   << "   " << p12 << endl;
    cout << p[1] << " " << p[2] << endl;

    return 0;
}
```

——— **Program's Output** ———
12 34   2228236
12 34

8.8   Interesting Issues About References

There is an interesting situation that can occur when using references and it depends on the properties of pointers. As we previously described, compilers typically implement a reference as a pointer and whenever you use a reference, the compiler automatically dereferences the pointer to access the reference's value. You also should know that a pointer with a zero value (null value) is guaranteed to not point to any variable or object in memory. Likewise, it is meaningless to dereference a null pointer. Given this information, what would happen if somehow the address of a reference gets set to zero? Can you test for this situation? What happens if you output such a reference? The following program illustrates the peculiar behavior of references that get initialized to what is equivalent to *NULL.

```
#include <iostream.h>


int*  p;                   //Uninitialized data is set to 0
int   our_swiss_bank_account_number;

main()
{
                           // The missing code was supposed to set p to point
                           // to the important number above, but because of
                           // an oversight by some anonymous programmer,
                           // it never happened.

    int& i = *p;
    cout << i << endl;
            // You can test for this situation and appropriately handle it.

    if (&i == NULL)
        cout << "*NULL" << endl;
    else
        cout << i     << endl;
```

```
        return 0;
}
```

──────── **Program's Output** ────────
0
NULL

In the above program, the pointer p is initialized to zero, or a NULL pointer value, by the mere act of defining it as an uninitialized global variable. The variable i is defined to reference the integer that p points to, which means, in this case, that a compiler's implementation of the reference i, a pointer, is set to the value of pointer p (NULL) without ever evaluating *p. Now, whenever i is used, the null pointer is dereferenced and an error occurs. Many systems will detect the dereference of a null pointer and cause some action like a bus error and core dump. Some systems produce an appropriate behavior. Other systems, such as a Personal Computer (PC) with the DOS operating system, do not detect the error and actually return the value at location 0. The above example was executed on a PC and the actual results that you get are system dependent. As the above program shows, you can test for such a situation and avoid dereferencing a "bad" reference.

8.9   How References in Classes Affect Constructors

When a class contains a data member that is a reference, the reference must be initialized in the constructor initialization list of every constructor in the class. This is because a reference must be initialized when it is created, and, a reference is created whenever an object of its class is constructed. If the reference is not initialized, a compile error will occur. The following program illustrates the constructor initialization of a reference data member:

```
int y;

class A {
    int& a;
  public:
    A()     : a(y) {}
    A(int i): a(i) {}
};
```

```
main()
{
    A x;
    A y;
    return 0;
}
```

9

Inheritance and Virtual Functions

Until now, we have explored many of the data abstraction features of C++. Although these features are very powerful and allow you to create better programs, they do not constitute object–oriented programming. C++ provides two capabilities that allow you to write object–oriented programs:

- Derivation (Inheritance)

- Virtual functions (dynamic binding)

Object–oriented programming extends the use of ADTs to permit a new type to be derived through the mechanism of inheritance and to delay until run–time whether a base class version of a redefined function or the derived class version is called through the mechanism of dynamic binding.

C++ implements inheritance through the mechanism of derivation. A *derived class* is derived from a *base class*. A derived class inherits the template of all the data members and the ability to call all of the non–private member functions of the base class. It is important to note that what is inherited is the template of the memory layout of data from the base class definition and not any data from a base class object; *you do not inherit from objects*. Member functions can be called through objects of either class without having to reimplement the functions. Therefore, the same function definition can be used for different objects of the original (*base*) class and different objects of a *derived* class. This code sharing is a very efficient way of programming.

Another important advantage of inheritance is class extensibility. If you have a class that does not have all the functionality that you require, you can derive a new class from it and then implement the new code in the derived class and use the other code from the base class.

C++ implements dynamic binding through the mechanism of virtual functions. A *virtual function* is a special member function that is invoked through a public base class pointer. The selection of the code to be executed when a virtual function is called through a pointer is delayed until run–time. The code that is executed is determined by the class type of the actual object addressed by the pointer or reference. The resolution of a virtual function is transparent to the user.

If we did not have virtual functions but had overloaded derived functions, we would be responsible for determining just what function would be called for a specific class type of an object. We would have to determine an object's class type by inspecting it and then, based on that information, call the appropriate function. Usually, this would be done with a switch statement. If we derived a new class with its overloaded function, we would have to modify all our switch statements to take into account the new class function. This means that we would have to have the source code for all places where the switch statements were found. By using virtual functions, the compiler automatically does what is necessary (manage and use virtual tables) to use dynamic binding.

9.1   Class Derivation and Single Inheritance

Here is an example of a base class that will be used by a derived class:

```
#include <iostream.h>
#include <string.h>

class employee {
protected:
    char *name, *address;
    int age, depend, job_class;
public:
    employee(char*, char*, int, int, int);
    ~employee() {delete name; delete address;}
    void display() {cout << name << '\n'
                        << address << "\n\n";}
    int get_age() {return age;}
    int get_depend() {return depend;}
    int get_job_class() {return job_class;}
};

employee::employee(char* nm, char* ad, int ag, int dp, int jc)
{
    name = new char[strlen(nm) +1];
    strcpy(name, nm);
    address = new char[strlen(ad) +1];
    strcpy(address, ad);
```

```
        age = ag;
        depend = dp;
        job_class = jc;
}
```

The base class is set up like any other class. However, because we intended that this class have a class derived from it, we put the data members in the protected access region because we wanted the derived class member functions to have direct access to these data. The class has one constructor that requires arguments and it also has a destructor which is used to de–allocate the memory on the heap which is pointed to by name and address. The class has an output function, display(), and three access functions, get_age(), get_depend(), and get_job_class().

Occasionally very little is done with a base class. We may not declare any objects of a base class, because a base class object is not required to declare a derived class object. Base classes can be created to provide data members and member functions that will be shared by a variety of different derived class definitions.

The derived class is

```
class workdata : public employee {
    char* occupation;
public:
    workdata(char*, char*, char*, int, int, int);
    ~workdata() {delete occupation;}
    const char* get_occupation() {return occupation;}
    void display() {cout << name << '\n' << address
                    << '\n' << occupation << "\n\n";}
    int get_age() {return age;}
};

workdata::workdata(char* nm, char* ad, char* oc, int ag,  int dp, int jc)
            : employee(nm, ad, ag, dp, jc)
{
    occupation = new char[strlen(oc) +1];
    strcpy(occupation, oc);
}
```

Class workdata is a derived class which inherits from the public base class employee. We include the derived class tag name, followed by a colon, followed by the name of the base class. The base class for this derived class can be either *private, protected,* or *public* (more will be said of this later, but for now, *do not forget to include the keyword public* because the default is a private base class. A base class must be defined before another class can be derived from it.

A derived class will inherit all the data members and member functions of its base class and can declare some of its own. The member functions of the derived class can see the public and protected data members of the base class, but not the private data members. (The base class member functions cannot see the data members of any of its derived classes. How could it? The base class has no idea what classes may be derived from it.) The derived class can only indirectly access the private data members of the base class by using the protected or public member functions of the base class (there is no relaxing of access restriction in inheritance).

This example class has a constructor with six arguments, although the class has only declared one data member of its own, which is

> **char* occupation**

One argument is used to give occupation a value, the remaining five arguments are used to initialize the memory inherited from the base class. We will say more about this when we discuss base class initialization. The destructor is used to de–allocate the memory allocated for occupation.

The constructor for workdata is responsible for initializing the base class portion of a derived class object and also its own data member. See the subsection on base class initialization for a further discussion of this constructor.

The derived class inherits the ability to use the following functions of the base class:

> **display()**
> **get_age()**
> **get_dependent()**
> **get_job_class()**

In addition, the derived class has added a new function called

> **get_occupation()**

and redefines the functions

> **display()**
> **get_age()**

for this class. It is important to realize that these redefined functions are not examples of function name overloading because both the base class and derived class functions have identical prototypes. The derived class can use two display() functions and two get_age() functions: those defined in employee and the others defined in workdata.

If a derived class object invokes a display() or get_age() function, it gets the local version by using the following calls:

> **workdata   obj("Bill", "EB2", "Trainer", 49, 1, 57);**
> **obj.display();**
> **int x = obj.get_age();**

The derived class can access the member functions of the base class by using the form

> **int x = obj.get_dependent()**

It can also use the scope resolution operator with the following call:

> **obj.employee::display()**

The scope resolution operator is required when functions in base and derived classes have the same name (overridden) or when two different base class parents have the same function or data name (see Section 9.2).

A derived class can act as a base class for classes derived from it, allowing you to create a hierarchy of derived classes.

Base Class Initialization

C++ has an unique concept, children (derived classes) must take care of their parents (base classes). If a base class constructor requires a value, the derived class constructor must provide it. The mechanism for doing this is as follows:

In the general form, a derived class constructor argument list is followed by a constructor initialization list. This is specified by a colon and a comma–separated list of initializers before the opening brace of the function body. In the above example, the code

> **workdata::workdata(char* nm, char* ad, char* oc,**
> **   int ag, int dp, int jc) : employee(nm, ad, ag, dp, jc)**

contains the constructor initialization list

> **: employee(nm, ad, ag, dp, jc)**

argument

This constructor ~~initialization~~ list has only one item which is used to initialize the part of the derived class workdata template that was inherited from the base class employee. The order of the arguments in the argument list for workdata(...) is unimportant, but the order of the arguments in employee(...) is important; this will be the order expected by the base class constructor. The third argument is the age variable and the fourth argument is the number of dependents. If we were to pass these arguments in the wrong order, the base class constructor would set the age to 1 and the number of dependents to 49 (this would be very interesting biologically).

A derived class is only responsible for sending values to its base class constructor. It does not have to worry about whether the base class is a derived class from its own base class. Another way of saying this is that a derived class has to look up only one level. It takes care of its base class and nothing else.

The driver function that is used to test our inheritance hierarchy is

```
main()
{
        employee bill("Bill", "EB2" 47, 1, 57);
        workdata bev("Bev", "Bonny Doon", "writer", 45, 0, 0);

        bill.display();
        bev.display();

        const char* occupation;
        occupation = bev.get_occupation();
        cout << occupation << "\n\n";

        int age;
        age = bill. get_age();
        cout << age << "\n\n";
        age = bev.get_age();
        cout << age << "\n\n";
        age = bev.employee::get_age();
        cout << age << "\n\n";
}
```

————————— Program's Output —————————

Bill
EB2

Bev
Bonny Doon
writer

writer

47

45

45

In the above code, an object bill of type employee is declared and its constructor is passed values to initialize the bill object.

A separate object bev of type workdata is declared, its constructor is passed data and its constructor is invoked. The bev object constructor executes and immediately invokes the employee constructor passing it the values in the constructor initialization list. When the employee constructor is finished executing, the body of the derived class constructor executes.

At this time it may be informative to see what is in the object's data space. Figure 9.1 shows the memory layout of the example program.

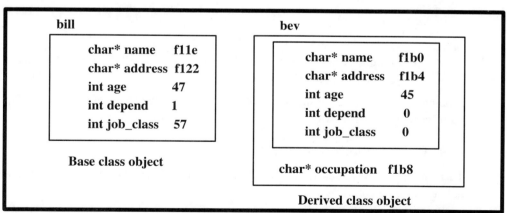

Figure 9.1. Memory layout for a base class object and a derived class object.

The first thing to notice is that the two objects are separate – they have different addresses. Notice next that the bev object inherits the template from the employee class but does not inherit anything from the bill object. The bill object contains only the employee class template, while the bev object (the derived object) contains both the employee class template and the workdata template. When the bill object was created, its constructor initialized the data members of the object with values. When the bev object was created, its constructor passed values to the employee class constructor to initialize the data members of the employee class template and then assigned values to the workdata data member.

You should also notice that that when display() was called through a bill object, the values of the bill object were displayed, but when display() was called through a bev object, the values of the bev object were displayed. This resulted because the compiler knew that the bill object was of class employee; it then called the employee version of display(). It worked on the bill object because the implicit first argument was the *this* pointer (the address of the bill object). The compiler called the workdata::display() (the local version of display()) for the bev object because the compiler knew that bev was a workdata object; it printed the values from the bev object because the *this* pointer *(the address of the bev object)* was passed as the first argument to the display() function.

You should also be aware of the three ways that the function get_age() was called.

- **bill.get_age()** called the function on the bill object using the employee version of get_age()

- **bev.get_age()** called the function on the bev object using the workdata version of get_age()

- **bev.employee::get_age()** called the function using the employee version of get_age(), but on the bev object

A pointer to occupation was also created and it assigned the value that was returned by the bev object executing the workdata:: get_occupation() call.

Base Class Initialization Issues

There are several different situations that occur when initializing the base class portion of a derived class object.

- If a base class does not have a constructor, the derived class constructor (if it has one) does not have to worry about the base class portion of the derived class object.

- If a base class only has constructors that require arguments, the derived class constructor must explicitly initialize the base class by providing the values that the base class requires in the derived class constructor's initialization list. The previous example illustrated this case.

- If a base class has a default constructor (one that requires no arguments), the derived class does not have to specify any values to send to the base class portion of the derived class object. However, the compiler generates code during the constructor initialization phase of the derived class constructor to call the default base class constructor (remember, if a class has a constructor, a constructor must be called when the object of that class is created; otherwise, a compile error results).

- If a base class has a default constructor and the derived class does not have a constructor, the compiler will automatically generate a default constructor for the derived class. Thus, when an object of the derived class is created, the system–generated constructor for the derived class will execute and initialize the base class.

- If a base class has a constructor that requires arguments, does not have a default constructor, and the derived class does not specify a constructor, the compiler will generate an error. A derived class constructor must be written and it must explicitly initialize the base class in its constructor initialization list because the compiler has no idea which values should be used with which to initialize the base class portion of the derived class object.

Things That Are and Are Not Inherited

A derived class inherits data members and member functions from its base classes. Inherited members can be used with derived class objects, even though they were originally usable only with base class objects. If an inherited member is redefined in a derived class, the redefined name masks or hides the inherited name in the scope of the derived object. To reference a masked inherited member it is necessary to qualify its name with its class name and the :: operator.

A derived class inherits all data members except, static data members, from each of its base classes. Thus, a derived class contains all of the data members that it inherits, and also the data members that it defines itself. The size of a derived class is never smaller than its base class or base classes; its size is increased by the amount of extra memory space that its locally–defined data members require.

A derived class inherits member functions from its base classes. This means that it inherits the ability to call base class member functions on derived class objects.

The following are not inherited:

- Constructors

- Destructors

- Friend functions

- Static class functions

- Static class data

- Overloaded assignment operator (operator=).

The following example illustrates inherited members:

```
class A {                    // The base class
protected:
    int dm1;
    int dm2;
    static int si;
public:
    void f1() {}
    void f2() {}
    static void sf() {}
    A() {}
    ~A() {}
    friend void ff() {}
};

class B : public A {         // The derived class
    int dm1;
    void f1();
};
```

```
void B::f1()
{
    dm1= 10;            // Sets B's dm1
    A:dm1= 11;          // Sets B's A::dm1
    dm2 = 12;           // Sets B's A:: dm2
    A::si = 13;         // Sets class A's si
}

int A::si;             // Must define a static to allocate its memory space

main()
{
    B b;
    b.f1();            // Uses B's f1()
    b:A::f1();         // Uses B's inherited A::f1()
    b::f2();           // Uses B's inherited A::f2()
    return 0;
}
```

Class B has its locally–defined function f1(), the inherited functions A::f1() and A::f2(), and the following compiler–generated functions: the default copy constructor and overloaded assignment operation (the function operator =). Class B does not inherit class A's constructor A(), compiler–generated copy constructor A(const&A), destructor ~A(), friend function ff(), compiler–generated overloaded assignment, static function sf(), or static data si.

In the above function main, the object b of type class B, contains three data members; two are inherited from class A (dm1 and dm2) and one (dm1) is defined locally in class B. When f1() is called through the b object, the most locally–defined f1() is called, which is B::f1(). To call B's f1() that was inherited from class A, it was necessary to fully qualify its name and use A::f1() .

The function definition B::f1() sets its data member to a value and also sets the value of class A's static data si. Even though si was not inherited, it is accessible as protected data from class B, and thus is directly accessible to class B's member functions.

Copy Constructors and Overloaded = Issues

If a derived class's base class has defined its own copy constructor, you must make sure the base class's copy constructor is invoked when the derived class's copy constructor is invoked. This situation commonly occurs when a class has a pointer data member (e.g., a char*) and a constructor initializes it to point to some allocated memory on the heap, Also, recall that if a correctly coded class has defined its own copy constructor, it generally overloads the assignment operator (operator =) as well. This means that you must also make sure that when a derived class is overloaded assignment operator is invoked, it invokes the base class's assignment operator as well. When a derived class has multiple base classes (multiple inheritance), all properties of copy constructors and overloaded assignment operators apply to each of the base classes.

There are a few cases to consider. If a derived class does not define a copy constructor, there is nothing extra to do because the compiler will automatically generate a default copy constructor for the derived class that invokes the base class copy constructor(s) as required. Also, if a derived class does not overload the assignment operator, the compiler will automatically generate a derived class overloaded assignment operator that properly invokes the base class(s) assignment operation(s). This case is simple and it always works correctly.

If both a derived class and its base class define copy constructors, the derived class's copy constructor must invoke the base class's copy constructor in the derived class copy constructor's initialization list. Also, if a derived class has more than one base class with a defined copy constructor, the derived class copy constructor must invoke each base class's defined copy constructor.

If both a derived class and its base class overload the assignment operator, the derived class's overloaded assignment operator must invoke the base class's assignment operator in the code body of the derived class's operator = function definition. Also, if a derived class has more than one base class with a defined operator =, the derived class operator = must invoke each base class's defined operator =.

The following example illustrates invoking a base class's defined copy constructor and overloaded assignment operator from a derived class's defined copy constructor and overloaded assignment operator:

```
#include <iostream.h>
#include <string.h>              // For strlen and strcpy

class A {
    char* p;
public:
    A() { p = 0; }               // Initialization constructor
    ~A() { delete p; }           // Destructor
    A(const A&);                 // Copy constructor
```

```
        A& operator= (const A&);        // Overloaded assignment operator
};


A::A(const A& a)                        // Copy constructor
    { cout << "A::A(const A&) called. \n";
    p = new char[strlen(a.p) + 1];
    strcpy(p, a.p);
}


A& A::operator= (const A& a)           // Overloaded assignment operator
    cout << "A::operator= (const A&) called. \n";
    if (this != &a) {                  // If not assigning an object to itself
        delete p;
        p = new char[strlen(a.p) + 1];
        strcpy(p, a.p);
    }
    return *this;
}


class B : public A {
    char* q;
public:
    B() { q = 0; }                     // Initialization constructor
    ~B() { delete q; }                 // Destructor
    B(const B&);                       // Copy constructor
    B& operator= (const B&);           // Overloaded assignment operator
};


B::B(const B& b)                       // Copy constructor
 : A(b)                                // Invoking A's copy constructor
{
    cout << "B::B(const B&) called. \n";
    q = new char[strlen(b.q) + 1];
    strcpy(q, b.q);
}
```

```
B& B::operator= (const B& b)          // Overloaded assignment operator
{
    cout << "B::operator= (const B&) called. \n";
    if (this != &b) {                 // If not assigning an object to itself
        A(*this) = A(b);              // Invoking A's assignment operator
        delete q;
        q = new char[strlen(b.q) + 1];
        strcpy(q, b.q);
    }
    return *this;
}

main()
{
    B x;
    cout << "\nExecuting the statement \"B y(x);\"\n";
    B y(x);                     // Use B's copy constructor

    cout << "\nExecuting the statement \"x = y;\"\n";
    x = y;                      // Use B's assignment operator
    return 0;
}
```

_____ Program's Output _____

Executing the statement "B y(x);"
A::A(const A&) called.
B::B(const B&) called.

Executing the statement "x = y;"
B::operator= (const B&) called.
A::A(const A&) called.
A::A(const A&) called.
A::operator= (const A&) called.

In the above program, class A defines a copy constructor and an overloaded assignment operator. Class B also defines a copy constructor and an overloaded assignment operator. Class B's copy constructor invokes A's copy constructor in its constructor initialization list

        : A(b)

and the b argument is implicitly converted to a type A argument as required by A's copy constructor A(const A&). (Whenever a derived class object is used where a base class object is required, the system implicitly converts the derived class object to a base class object.) Class B's assignment operator (function B::operator=) invokes A's assignment operator on the A part of the B class using the statement

     A(*this) = A(b);   **// invoking A's assignment operator**

In this statement *this is the left–hand argument of the B's assignment operator and b is its right–hand argument. A(*this) is the A part of *this and A(b) is the A part of b; both of the parts are of type A. Because both of the operands of = are of type A, A's overloaded assignment operator is called. Thus, B's overloaded assignment operator invokes A's overloaded assignment operator on its arguments.

Main's code and the corresponding program output shows that when the y object of class B is initialized to the x object of class A, B's copy constructor is called, which also calls A's copy constructor. The output prints A's copy constructor output first because B's initialization list is executed before B's code body is executed.

The program output also shows that when the B object y is assigned the B object x, B's assignment operator is called and it calls the A assignment operator to assign y's A part to x's A part. The two copy constructors, A::A(const A&)are called to do the type conversion of y and x to their corresponding A parts before the A::operator= is called.

Constructor Initialization List Use

A constructor's initialization list occurs between the closing parenthesis of its argument list and the opening brace of the code body. The list begins with a colon and its elements are separated by commas. A constructor's initialization list is used to initialize its class's inherited base classes and class data members.

The following code fragment illustrates these uses:

```
#include <stdlib.h>                    // For the function "int rand();"

class A {
     int          i;
     const int    j;
public:
     A(int a) : i(1), j(a+2) {};
};
```

```
class B : public A {
    int     x;
    A       y;
    A       z;
public:
    B(int b) : A(b), x(b+1), y(b*2), z( rand() ) {}
};
```

Class A's constructor has the constructor initialization list

: i(1), j(a+2)

and an empty code body. The initialization list *initializes* the class A data members i to the value 1 and j to the value a+2. Instead of being initialized, i could have been *assigned* a value in the A's code body (it is a matter of programmer preference); however, the data member j had to be initialized because it is a constant.

Class B's constructor initializes both its inherited base class part and its data members; its code body is also empty. The initialization list

: A(b), x(b+1), y(b*2), z(rand())

initializes its base class A by invoking A's constructor A(int) with the argument b and initializes x to b+1. The initialization list also initializes the data members y and z, which are objects of user–defined type A. The member y is initialized by the constructor A(int) which is passed the argument b+1; z is initialized similarly with an argument that has the value returned by the function rand().

We believe that it is generally a better coding style to initialize members in a constructor initialization list rather than assign them values in a constructor's code body. This is because the purpose of a constructor is to initialize (not assign), and using the constructor initialization list preserves the semantics of initialization.

9.2 Class Derivation and Multiple Inheritance

There are times when you want to derive a class from more than one base class and this is called *multiple inheritance*. Multiple inheritance is a key feature in object–oriented programming and in release 2.0 and later versions, C++ supports multiple inheritance. Not all object–oriented languages support multiple inheritance. In multiple inheritance, each base class has data and functions that you will want to access from a derived class object. Therefore, when creating a derived class, base classes are specified in the *base class list*.

Problems Better Solved by Multiple Inheritance

Multiple inheritance allows inherited information to be placed locally where it is needed; without multiple inheritance, inherited information is often placed more globally than desired.

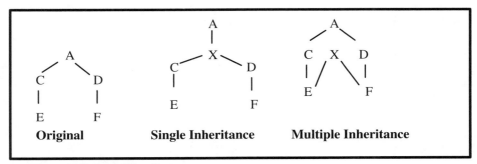

Figure 9.2. Locality of scope.

In Figure 9.2, if we needed data from X in both classes E and F, in single inheritance, we would have to designate X as the base class of C and D. Unfortunately, data from X would also be found in both C and D where they are not needed or wanted. However, in multiple inheritance, both E and F can have X as one of their base classes, and the data from X will only be found in E and F, but not in C or D.

Class Hierarchy Diagrams

When classes are related by single inheritance, the relationship of the classes can be represented by a directed tree diagram.

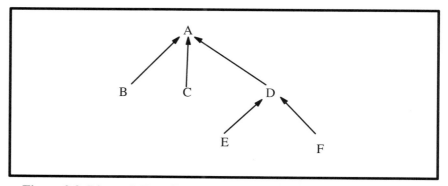

Figure 9.3. Directed Tree Structure of Single Inheritance.

A node in Figure 9.3 represents a class and an arrow extends from a derived class to its base class. These diagrams are useful to explain complex class hierarchies.

When classes are related by multiple inheritance, the relationship of the classes can be represented by a *directed acyclic graph*, which is also called a *class lattice*. Directed means that the classes are connected from a derived class to a base class in a single direction, which is represented by an arrow. Acyclic means that you cannot go from a class such as E, through a cycle, and end up back at E. Directed Acyclic Graphs (DAGs)are more general than trees and they can solve more general problems.

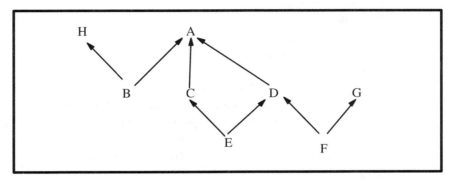

Figure 9.4. Directed Acyclic Graph (DAG) of Multiple Inheritance.

In Figure 9.4, we have B inheriting from both H and A; F is inheriting from D and G,;and E is inheriting from A, C, and D. A, C, D, and E form a DAG which is allowed in multiple inheritance.

Multiple Inheritance Example

An example of using multiple inheritance is

```
#include <string.h>
#include <iostream.h>

class employee {
    char* name;
protected:
    int  identification;
public:
    employee( char*,  int );
    ~employee() {delete name;}
    void display() {cout << name << identification  << "\n\n";}
    const char* get_name() {return name;}
    int get_identification() {return identification;}
};
```

```
class family_data {
protected:
    char *spouse;
    char *address;
public:
    family_data(char*, char*);
    ~family_data() {delete  spouse; delete address}
    void display() {cout << spouse << address  << '\n';}
    const char*  get_spouse() {return spouse;}
    const char*  get_address() {return address;}
};

employee::employee(char* nm, int id)
{
    identification = id;
    name = new char[strlen(nm) +1];
    strcpy(name, nm);
}

family_data::family_data(char* sp, char* ad)
{
    spouse = new char[strlen(sp) +1];
    strcpy(spouse, sp);
    address = new char[strlen(ad) +1];
    strcpy(address, ad);
}
```

The above code shows the definition of two base classes along with their data members, constructors, and other member functions. The following shows the definition of a derived class that has both of the above classes as base classes;

```
class record : public employee, public family_data {
    char* occupation;
public:
    record(char*, char*,char*, char*, int);
    ~record() {delete occupation;}
    void display() {cout << get_name() << '\n' << identification
                    << '\n' << occupation << '\n'
                    << spouse << '\n'
```

```
                              << address << endl;}
};

record::record(char* nm, char *spouse, char* address,  char* oc, int id)
                    : employee(nm, id), family_data(spouse, address)
{
        occupation = new char[strlen(oc) +1];
        strcpy(occupation, oc);
}
```

Base classes of a derived class record are declared as a comma–separated list after the colon that follows the derived class tag name. The order in which they are declared determines the order in which their data go into the object space of any derived class and also determines the order in which the destructors are called. Notice that the keyword *public* precedes each base class name. If you leave out the second public keyword in the list, class employee will be a public base class and class family_data will be a private base class; we do not think that you will want to do this.

Notice the constructor for the derived class. The order of the parameters in the constructor argument list is not important; however, it is your responsibility to see that the right parameters get sent to the appropriate base class constructors. In the example, nm and id go to class employee; whereas, spouse and address go to class family_data base class constructor. The order of the base classes in the constructor initialization list is not important, because the constructors will always be called in the order that the base classes were declared when the derived class was defined.

The template for a derived class object would look like Figure 9.5.

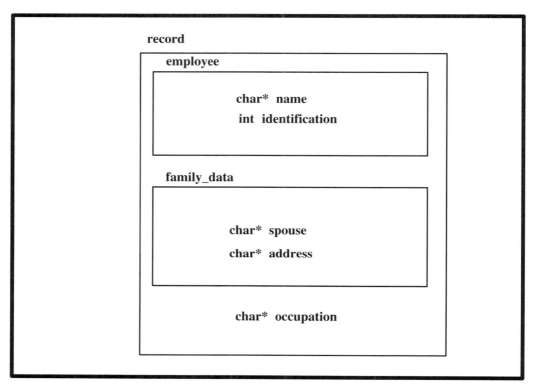

Figure 9.5. Memory layout for class record.

Notice that the template for employee goes in first, followed by the template for family_data, and ends with the record part of the template. When a record constructor is called by the system for a record object being created, it passes values to the employee constructor, then to the family_data constructor, and finally executes the body of the record constructor.

The driver code to test our multiple inheritance example looks like the following:

```
main() {
    int identification;
    const char* name;
    const char* spouse;
    const char* address;
    const char* occupation;
    employee  bill( "William Heinze", 9966);
    family_data  bev("Beverly Heinze", "Bonny Doon");
    record mudlark("Bill", "Bev", "Santa Cruz","Educator", 48);

    bill.display();
    bev.display();
    mudlark.display();
    identification =bill.get_identification();
    cout << identification << "\n\n";
    identification = mudlark.get_identification();
    cout << identification << "\n\n";

    name = bill.get_name();
    cout << name << "\n\n";
    name = mudlark.get_name();
    cout <<  name << "\n\n";

    spouse = bev.get_spouse();
    cout << spouse << "\n\n";
    spouse = mudlark.get_spouse();
    cout << spouse << "\n\n";

    address = bev.get_address();
    cout << address << "\n\n";
    address = mudlark.get_address();
    cout << address << "\n\n";

    occupation = mudlark.get_occupation();
    cout << occupation << "\n\n";
}
```

───────── **Program's Output** ─────────
William Heinze9966

Beverly Heinze Bonny Doon
Bill
48
Educator
Bev
Santa Cruz
9966

48

William Heinze

Bill

Beverly Heinze

Bev

Bonny Doon

Santa Cruz

Educator

The Execution Order of Constructor Initialization List Items

A constructor initialization list is a comma–separated list of initializers. You can specify the initializers in any order that you choose. A typical coding style is to initialize inherited base classes, then embedded data members of user–defined types, and finally, other data members of built–in data types. When a constructor is compiled, the compiler decides the order in which the initializers will execute. The actual order is compiler–dependent. The order is generally determined by an object's memory layout, and a part of an object that is lower in memory is initialized before a part that is higher in memory.

The Dominance Rule

An expression that refers to a class member is ambiguous if the expression refers to more than one function, object, type, or enumerator. In an inheritance hierarchy, the *dominance rule* is used to resolve ambiguities. If a base class and derived class have a member with the same name and declaration, the one in the derived class is the dominant one.

Figure 9.6 shows a base class and derived class with member functions that have the same prototype:

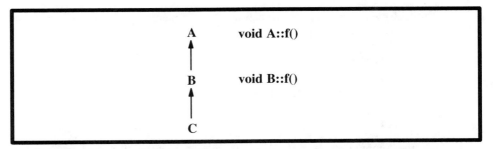

Figure 9.6. Class hierarchy diagram and associated member functions.

In the context of a either a B–type object or a C–type object are appropriate, f() refers to B::f() because B::f() dominates A::f().

In the following example of multiple inheritance, it is possible for two copies of A to get into an object of D. To prevent this, the mechanism of virtual base class is used (virtual base classes will be described in detail later). The following definitions create the virtual base class seen in Figure 9.7:

```
class A {// ...};
class B : virtual public A {// ...};
class C : virtual public A {// ...};
class D : public B, public C {// ...};
```

Figure 9.7 illustrates the use of the dominance rule when a class has a virtual base class .

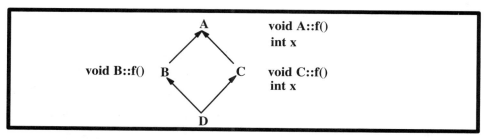

Figure 9.7. A diamond shaped class hierarchy diagram with annotations.

Both classes A and C have a function f() and a member x. Let class D have the following member function that references f and x:

```
void D::d()
{
    f();    // B::f() or A::f()?
    x;      // B::x or A::x ?
}
```

By the dominance rule, B::f() dominates over A::f(); also, B::x dominates over A::x. Therefore, in the function D::d(), f() and x refer to B::f() and B::x.

Figure 9.8 illustrates a more subtle application of the dominance rule.

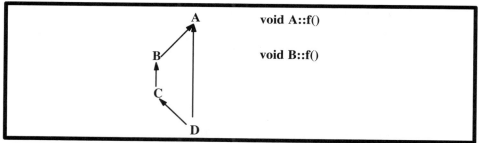

Figure 9.8. A four–sided class hierarchy diagram with annotations.

Both classes A and B have a member function f() and class D has the following member function that references f():

```
void D::d()  { f(); }
```

Which function f() is referenced in D::d()? The function A::f() looks closer than the function B::f(); it is one hop from D to A, but two hops from D to B (D –> C –> B). Even though A::f()

looks closer than B::f(), by the dominance rule, B::f() dominates B::f(). Therefore, when D::d() calls f(), B::f() is the called function.

Figure 9.9 shows a class hierarchy diagram that has the shape of a hexagon and it also summarizes the associated member functions.

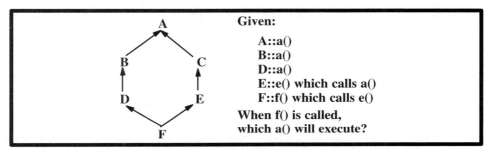

Figure 9.9. A six–sided class hierarchy diagram with annotations.

Classes A, B, and C each have a member function a(). Class C has no member functions. Class E has a member function that calls function a(). Class F has a member function f() that calls member function e(). When the following function is executed:

```
main()
{
      F obj;
      obj.f()        // f() calls e() which calls a()

      return 0;
}
```

which function a() is executed: A::a(), B::a(), or D::a()? The answer is A::a().

The following discussion explains why A::a() is called. When the statements

```
      F obj;
      obj.f();
```

are executed, the member function F::f() is called with its *this* pointer of type F* pointing to obj. When f() calls the function e()

```
      e();            // this–>E::e()
```

it calls e() through its *this* pointer, but the E::e() expects to be called with an E* pointer. Wherever a base class pointer is expected, but a derived class pointer is provided, the derived class pointer is implicitly converted to a base class pointer. This means that the e() function is really called using code similar to the following:

(E(this))–> E::e();

and when e() executes, it executes on the E part of the F object obj. The E part contains F's members that were inherited from classes A, C, and E. When the e() function calls the function a(), it calls the a() function that is within scope of an E type of object. Because A::a() is the only function within this scope, the statement

a();

in function E::e() calls the function A::a(). The dominance rule was not used in this example; however, if A::a() had been a virtual function, the dominance rule would have been used. The section on virtual functions contains this example with A::a() declared as a virtual function.

9.3   Inheriting a Class Multiple Times

Although a base class may appear only once in a derivation list, it can appear multiple times in a derivation hierarchy; as Figure 9.10 illustrates.

class employee { ... };

class dependents : public employee {...};

class workData : public employee {...};

class deductions : public dependents, public workData
        {// ...};

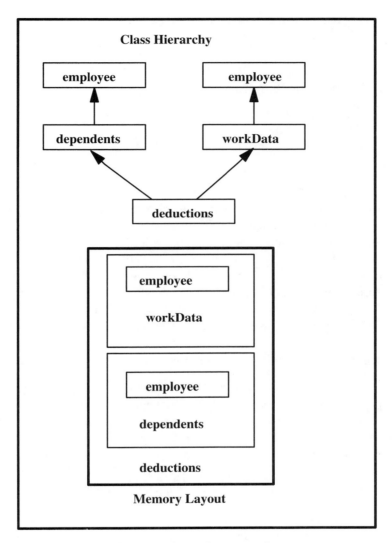

Figure 9.10. Class hierarchy and memory layout.

Figure 9.10 shows a class hierarchy diagram and memory layout of a class deductions object. Notice that in the deductions object, the memory template for class employee was included twice: once through class dependents and the other through class workData. This may not be what you want. In the next subsections, we will show you how to get only one copy of employee in the deductions object.

A More General Meaning of ::

Class *deductions* contains two sets of *employee* data members:

- One inherited from *dependents*

- One inherited from *workData.*

If we wish to access a data member of employee called *name*, do we get it through the *dependents* chain or through the *workData* chain? Using *employee::name* does not help. If we wish to call a function called *display( )*, do we call it through the *dependents* chain or through the *workData* chain? Using *employee::display( )* does not help. If we call display as dependents::display() we call through the dependents chain on the employee data that are in the dependent template of the deductions object. If we use workData::display(), we call it through the workData chain on the employee data that are in the workData template of the deductions object. This naming convention of :: applies to both data members and functions.

Explicit Cascaded Conversions

As we know, a derived class object, pointer, or reference can be converted to a base object, pointer, or reference, respectively. For example, a deductions object will implicitly be converted to either a dependents object or a workData object, if one of them is needed, and we have a deductions object, pointer, or reference. If we have a deductions object and we want the employee object from dependents, how can we get it? There is no way to obtain it through an implicit conversion, because that would be ambiguous (do we go through dependents or workData?). We cannot explicitly cast it as

```
dependents      alpha;
(employee)  alpha;
```

because this is ambiguous for the same reason as the implicit conversion. By using the following cascading conversion, we can obtain an unambiguous conversion:

        (employee)(dependents) alpha;

or

        (employee)(workData) alpha;

Some Limitations On Accessing Members

When using multiple inheritance there are some cases when there is no syntax in C++ to construct an identifier to use an inherited data member or member function. This problem does not occur when using single inheritance.

Assume that in the single inheritance Figure 9.11,

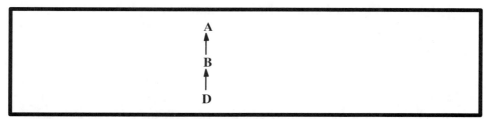

Figure 9.11. A class hierarchy diagram of three classes.

classes A and B each have a data member m and a member function f(). In class D, using m and f() corresponds to using B::m and B::f(), respectively, and they mask or hide the inherited members in the class with the same names. In class D there is no problem accessing the masked members m and f() that were indirectly inherited from class A because their fully–qualified names A::m and A::f() refer to them.

There are multiple inheritance situations where a fully–qualified member name is insufficient to access an inherited member. This can occur when a class gets inherited a multiple number of times. For example, let class D have the class hierarchy shown in Figure 9.12:

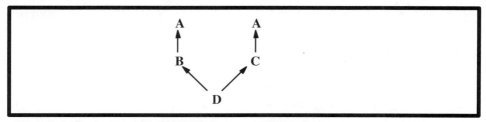

Figure 9.12. A class hierarchy diagram of five classes.

and let each of the classes A, B, and C have a data member m and a member function f() in their protected access regions. In class D, B::m and C::m refer to the m data member in classes B and C, respectively. Also, B::f() and C::f() refer to the classes B and C f(), respectively. In class D, to which members m and f() do A::m and A::f() refer? The answer is both the m and f() in the A inherited by B and the m and f() in the A inherited by C; this is an ambiguity and using either A::m or A::f() in class D will cause a compile error. How can this problem be resolved?

One way to resolve the problem is to eliminate name conflicts by renaming conflicting members. In the example above, renaming A's members m and f() to am and af() fixes the problem. Now in class D, B::am and B::af() refer to the A members that were inherited from B. Likewise, C::am and C::af() refer to the A members that were inherited from C. (This more general use of :: was discussed previously.) If you cannot change class A(possibly it belongs to someone else), classes B and C could be altered.

If clashing names either are not changed or cannot be changed, there is a still a partial solution to the problem. In class D it is possible to access the value of m in both the A inherited by B and the A inherited by C, but there is no good way to change either of their values. This solution uses multiple castings (chained casts). The following member function reads and prints the value of m in each of the inherited As and also calls the f() in each of the As:

```
void D::display()
{
        cout << ( (A)(B) *this ).m;        // The m in B's A part
        cout << ((A)(C) *this ).m;         // The m in C's A part
        ((A)(B) *this ).f()                // The f() in B's A part
        ((A)(C) *this ).f()                // The f() in B's A part
}
```

In the above code, the *this returns the object that the member is called on, the (B) converts the D type of object to a temporary B type of object (the B part of D); the (A) converts the temporary B object to a temporary A type of object (the A part of B); and, the . operator selects the desired member.

If the following code statement:

```
((A)(B) *this ).m = 123;              // Assume m is type int
```

were added to the D::display() function, it would not change the value of the m in the B's A part because the casting operations create a temporary copy of the A part of B and the assignment changes the value of the m member in the temporary copy.

Virtual Base Classes

Virtual base classes provide a method of overriding the default inheritance mechanism, allowing you to specify a class that is a shared base class.

```
class employee {/* ... */ };
class dependents : virtual public employee {/* ... */};
class workData : virtual public employee {/* ... */};
class deductions : public dependents, public workData
          {/* ... */};
```

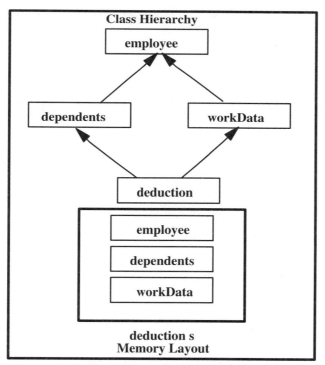

**Figure 9.13. Virtual base class hierarchy and
memory layout.**

In the example code, to declare a base class virtual, the keyword virtual is used in the base class declaration list in the derived class definition.

> **class dependents : virtual public employee {...};**
> **class workData : virtual public employee {...};**

If some derived class inherits it multiple times, only a single copy of the virtual base class template gets into the derived class object – the object is shared.

Figure 9.13 shows the class hierarchy of the deductions class and the memory layout of the deductions class object. By looking at the diagram, you can see that employee is a virtual base class because both dependents and workData point to it. Note that only one copy of the employee template gets into the deductions object – it is shared.

Initialization of Virtual Base Classes

In version 2.1 of C++, if a base class has any constructors, it must define one that requires no arguments (takes no argument in 2.0) or one that has defaults for each argument. Otherwise, there are no other changes to the class.

In initializing its base classes, a derived class normally only initializes its immediate base classes. For virtual base classes, the derived class that shares the base class from two paths of derivation must supply the base class with its values. The following program illustrates this point:

```cpp
#include <iostream.h>

class A {
    int x;
public:
    A(int a): x(a) {cout << "A::A(int)"  << '\t' << x << endl;}
};

class B : virtual public A {
    int m;
public:
    B(int a) : A(a * 2), m(a) {cout << "B::B(int)" << endl;}
};

class C : virtual public A {
    int p;
public:
    C(int a) : A(a * 3), p(a){cout << "C::C(int)" << endl;}
};
```

```
class D : public B, public C {
     int t;
public:
     D(int a) : A(a*4), B(a), C(a) {cout << "D::D(int)" << endl;}
};


main()
{
     cout << "\nD object" << endl;
     D delta(1);

     cout << "\nB object" << endl;
     B beta(1);

     cout << "\nC object" << endl;
     C gamma(1);

     cout << "\nA object" << endl;
     A alpha(1);

     return 0;
}
```

——————— Program's Output ———————

```
D object
A::A(int)     4
B::B(int)
C::C(int)
D::D(int)

B object
A::A(int)     2
B::B(int)

C object
A::A(int)     3
C::C(int)

A object
A::A(int)     1
```

When an object of class D is declared, it is responsible for initializing the data member of class A. From the output of the delta object, we see that the value of A's data member is set to 4. This is the value passed by the D constructor; even though the B and C constructors are also called, their initialization of A is ignored and only the D constructor is used for initializing the A part of delta. When an object of B or C is declared, however, its constructors initialize the A part of its objects.

The order of initialization of a class object is controlled by its DAG. The order is depth first, left to right, and all virtual base classes before non–virtual base classes.

The most derived class (the lowest class in the hierarchy that shares the virtual base class) constructor must initialize all the virtual base classes. It must have in its constructor initialization list all the base class data. This means that the derived class must know not only what its immediate base classes require, but also, what is required by all its virtual base classes.

9.4 Public, Private, and Protected Base Classes

A derived class may inherit a base class as either a public base class, a protected base class, or a private base class. By default, a derived struct inherits its base as public base and a derived class inherits its base as private base. Normally you will want to use public base classes. A common error of beginning C++ programmers is to forget to specify the keyword public when inheriting a base class; this results in unexpected access violation compilation errors. The following code fragment illustrates how base classes are inherited and the use of the public, protected, and private keywords:

```
class    A {/ ...};
struct   B   :            A {/ ...};        // Default is public
struct   C   : public     A {/ ...};
struct   D   : protected  A {};
struct   E   : private     A {};
class    F   :            A {};             // Default is private
class    G   : public     A {}:
class    H   : protected  A {};
class    I   : private     A {};
```

In the following code fragment:

```
class A {};
class B {};
class C {};
class D : public A, B, C {};
```

class D inherits A as a public base class, B as a private base class and C as a private base class. In this case, because the keyword public was not specified for each base class, B and C are private by default. If class D's definition were changed to

class D : public A, public B, public C {};

classes A, B, and C would be inherited as public base classes. As mentioned above this is normally how base classes are inherited and most likely how you will want them inherited.

Public Base Classes

Typically you will want to inherit a base class as a public base class. The inherited members of a public base class maintain their access level in the derived class and any classes derived from the derived class, etc. The following rules also apply:

- Private members remain private

- Protected members remain protected

- Public members remain public.

Inheritance is often used to create a new user–defined type that is a specialization of a more general user–defined type. A derived class has the same or more state (data members) and behavior (member functions) than its base class (or base classes) because it has all of the inherited characteristics plus the members that it (the derived class) defines. If you are creating a derived class that is a specialization of a base class (e.g., creating class eagle from class bird), make the base class a public base class. If multiple classes are inherited, make each of them public base classes.

Protected Base Classes

You will not use protected base classes very often. When a class is inherited as a protected base class, the inherited members have the following access level in the derived class:

- Private members remain private

- Protected members remain protected

- Public members change to protected members.

The following example class B has a protected base class:

```
class A {
        public:        int a;
        protected:     int b;
        private:       int c;
};

class B : protected A {              // Protected base class A
        public:        int d;
        protected:     int e;
        private:       int f;
};

class C : public B {
        public:        int g;
        protected:     int h;
        private:       int i;
};

main()
{
    A x;
    B y;
    C z;

    x.a = 1;                    // Legal, a is public
    y.a = 2;                    // Illegal, compile error
    z.a = 3;                    // Illegal, compile error
}
```

In the above example, it is illegal to access the data member a from the object y because the data member a has an access level of protected when referenced from a B class object. It is also illegal to access the data member a from the C class object z. The A class data member a was inherited by class B as a protected data member. Wherever class B appears in a class hierarchy, from that point down in the hierarchy, data member a has an access level of protected. It is possible for a class that inherits either directly or indirectly from class B to increase the data member a's access level to private.

It is not possible to lower a members' access level. A private member cannot become protected or public; a protected member cannot become public.

Private Base Classes

When a class is inherited as a private base class, all of its inherited members have a private access level in the derived class and

- Private members remain private

- Protected members change to private

- Public members change to private.

A private base class is used when a derived class is not a specialization of the base class. Objects of a derived class do not have any of the external behavior or characteristics of the base class; all of the inherited data members and member functions are private (not externalized). For example, if the handle of an old broken shovel with a missing blade were used as a makeshift baseball bat to play baseball, the new derived class object (the makeshift baseball bat) does not have the characteristics of a shovel. The makeshift baseball bat is not a special kind of shovel; the bat is something entirely different. (In computer science terminology, a derived class is not a subtype of the base class.)

The following example class B has a private base class:

```
class A {
    public:        int a;
    protected:     int b;
    private:       int c;
};

class B : private A {                        // Private base class A
    public:        int d;
    protected:     int e;
    private:       int f;
    public:        void  bf() { a; b;}
};
```

```
class C : public B {
      public:           int g;
      protected:        int h;
      private:          int i;
      public:           void cf() { d; e; }
                        void cg() {a; b;}     // Error, a and b are private
};

main()
{
      A x;
      B y;
      C z;

      x.a = 1;                               // Legal, a is public
      y.a = 2;                               // Illegal, compile error
      z.a = 3;                               // Illegal, compile error
}
```

In the example class B inherits class A as a private base class. Notice that this has no effect on the member function bf() of the derived class because it can still access the public and protected data members of its private base class. However, no class derived from B, such as C, can access the data and members from the private class A. In the statement

public: void bf() { a; b;)

the function bf() accesses the public member a and the protected member b; member c cannot be accessed because class A defines it as private. How a base class is inherited (public, protected, or private) does not affect derived class member function access to inherited members. A derived class member function can always access the public and protected members of an inherited base class.

In the above program example, the statements

y.a = 2;   // Illegal, compile error
z.a = 3;   // Illegal, compile error

cause compile errors because the data member a is private for class B and class C objects.

Normally, wherever a base class object is required and a derived class object is provided, the derived class object is implicitly converted to a base class object. However, this implicit conversion does not occur if the derived class object's class inherits the base class object's class as a private base class. The following program illustrates these points:

```
class A {};
class B : public  A {};
class C : private A {};
class D : public  C {};

void f(A a) { a = a; }

main ()
{
     A a;
     B b;
     C c;
     D d;

     f(a);               // OK
     f(b);               // OK
     f(c);               // Compile error
     f(d);               // Compile error

     return 0;
}
```

In the example program the function f() requires an argument of type A. When f(b) is called, the b object is implicitly converted to an A type object and passed to the function f(). When f(c) is compiled, a compile error occurs because the c object is not implicitly converted to an A type object. The implicit conversion does not occur because c's class C inherits class A as a private base class. When f(d) is compiled, a compile error also occurs because d is not implicitly converted to an A type object. Class D inherits from class C and class C inherits class A as a private base class. Therefore, class D inherits its class A part as a private base class and a D class object cannot be implicitly converted to an A class object.

In the following example:

```
class A {};
class B {};
class C : public A, private B {};
```

```
void f(A a) { a = a; }
void g(B b) { b = b; }

main()
{
    C c;
    f(c);                    // OK
    g(c);                    // Compile error

    return 0;
}
```

class C inherits public base class A and private base class B. In the function main(), when f(c) is called ,the c object is implicitly converted to an A type object and passed as the function's argument. When g(c) is called, a compile error occurs because the class C object c is not implicitly converted to a class B object. The conversion does not occur because class C inherits class B as a private base class.

Retaining the Access Level of Specific Members

You can restore the access level of data members and member functions for private and protected base classes by specifying the base class name, followed by ::, followed by the member's identifier in the derived class.

```
#include <string.h>
#include <iostream.h>

class employee {
    char* name;
protected:
    int identification;
public:
    employee( char * int );
    void display() {cout << name << identification  << "\n\n";}
    const char* get_name() {return name;}
    int get_identification() {return identification;}
};
```

```
class family_data {
protected:
    char *spouse;
    char *address;
public:
    family_data(char*, char*);
    ~family_data() {delete  spouse; delete address}
    void display() {cout << spouse << address  << '\n';}
    const char*  get_spouse() {return spouse;}
    const char*  get_address() {return address;}
};

class record : private employee, private family_data {
    char* occupation;
protected:
    family_data::spouse;
    family_data:: address;
public:
    record(char*, char*,char*, char*, int);
    ~record() {delete occupation;}
    void display() {cout << get_name() << '\n' << identification
                         << '\n' << occupation << '\n'
                         << spouse << '\n'
                         << address << endl;}
    employee::get_name;
    family_data::get_spouse;
};
```

In the example, the data members of class family_data that were protected in that class are protected in class record. Also, the member functions, get_name() from class employee and get_spouse() from class family_data, are public in class record. It is important to point out that you could not have made the data members spouse and address public by escaping them in the public part of record. They keep in the derived class the same level of access they had in the base class.

```
class record : private employee, private family_data {
    char* occupation;
public:
    record(char*, char*,char*, char*, int);
    ~record() {delete occupation;}
    void display() {cout << get_name() << '\n' << identification
                         << '\n' << occupation << '\n'
                         << spouse << '\n'
                         << address << endl;}
    employee::get_name;
    family_data::get_spouse;
    family_data::spouse;
    family_data:: address;
};
```

The reason for keeping the same level of access should be obvious. If it were possible to change the level of access, you could use derivation to make all the private and protected members of a class public, and this would defeat the purpose of having access restrictions.

9.5   Virtual Functions

A virtual function is a special member function that is invoked through a public base class, reference, or pointer. A virtual function is declared in a base class by preceding the function declaration with the keyword *virtual*.

The following example does not use any virtual functions for its member functions that are redefined in the derived class:

```
#include <iostream.h>
#include <string.h>

class employee {
protected:
    char *name;
    int age;
public:
    employee(char*, int);
    ~employee() {delete name;}
```

```
        void display() {cout << name << '\n'; }
        int get_age() {return age;}
};

class dependents : public employee {
    char* occupation;
public:
    dependents(char*, char*, int);
    ~dependents() {delete occupation;}
    char* get_occupation() {return occupation;}
    void display() {cout << name << '\n'<< occupation << '\n';}
};
```

The following example uses virtual functions for get_age() and display():

```
#include <iostream.h>
#include <string.h>

class employee {
protected:
    char *name;
    int age;
public:
    employee(char*, int);
    ~employee() {delete name;}
    const char* get_occupation() {return "TRAINER";}
    virtual int get_age() {return age;}
    virtual void display(void) {cout << name << '\n'};
};

class dependents : public employee {
    char* occupation;
public:
    dependents(char*, char*);
    ~dependents() {delete occupation;}
    const char* get_occupation() {return occupation;}
     virtual int get_age() {return (age – 10);}
    void display(void) {cout << name << '\n'<< occupation << '\n';}
};
```

In the class employee, display() is declared to be a virtual function. display() is redefined in class dependents and it is also a virtual function (you may use the keyword virtual if you wish, but its virtualness is inherited). If dependents itself is a base class for its own derived class, which also has a display() with the same prototype, display() would be virtual in that class also. The redefinition of a virtual function must have the exact declaration as the virtual function:

In employee,

> **virtual void display(void);**

In dependents,

> **virtual void display(void);**

The following are the implementations of the constructors:

```
employee::employee(char* nm)
{
    name = new char[strlen(nm) + 1];
    strcpy(name, nm);
    age = 57;
}

dependents::dependents(char* nm, char* oc)
        : employee(nm)
{
    occupation = new char[strlen(oc) + 1];
    strcpy(occupation, oc);
}
```

The following main() function tests the virtual functions:

```
main()
{
    employee  *ptr = new employee("Bill");
    const char* cp = ptr->get_occupation();
    cout << cp << '\n' << endl;
    ptr->display(); // employee::display();
    delete ptr;
```

```
        ptr = new dependents("Bev", "Writer");
        cp = ptr->get_occupation();
        cout << cp << endl;
        ptr->display(); // dependents::display();
        delete ptr;
}
```

─────────── Program's Output ───────────

TRAINER
Bill

TRAINER
Bev
Writer

The get_occupation() function is not a virtual function and therefore the base class version is called twice and TRAINER is displayed both times. The display() function is a virtual function and the appropriate code is called when the pointer has the address of first a base class object, and then a derived class object.

Although virtual functions are resolved at run–time they must still obey the access rules of C++. The following is an example of virtual functions as they might be used in a real example:

```
#include <iostream.h>
#include <string.h>

class general_drawing {
protected:
    char* graphic;
public:
    general_drawing(char*);
    virtual ~general_drawing();
    virtual void draw_me();
};

general_drawing::general_drawing(char* shape)
{
    graphic = new char[strlen(shape) + 1];
```

```
        strcpy(graphic, shape);
}

general_drawing::~general_drawing() {delete graphic;}

void general_drawing::draw_me()
{
        cout << "general_drawing" << '\n';
}


class sphere : public general_drawing {
        double radius;
public:
        sphere(char*, double);
        void draw_me();
};

sphere::sphere(char* object, double dimension)
            : general_drawing(object)
{
        radius = dimension;
}

void sphere::draw_me()
{
        cout << "sphere" << '\n';
        cout << graphic << '\t' << radius << '\n';
}


class oval : public general_drawing {
        double major_radius, minor_radius;
public:
        oval(char*, double, double);
        void draw_me();
};
```

```
oval::oval(char* object, double dim1, double dim2)
        : general_drawing(object)
{
    major_radius = dim1;
    minor_radius = dim2;
}
void oval::draw_me()
{
    cout << "oval" << '\n';
    cout << graphic << '\t' << major_radius << '\t'
            << minor_radius << '\n';
}

class square : public general_drawing {
    double side;
public:
    square(char*, double);
    void draw_me();
};
square::square(char* object, double dimension)
        : general_drawing(object)
{
    side = dimension;
}

void square::draw_me()
{
    cout << "square" << '\n';
    cout << graphic << '\t' << side << '\n';
}

class rectangle : public general_drawing {
    double major_side, minor_side;
public:
    rectangle(char*, double, double);
    void draw_me();
};
```

```
rectangle::rectangle(char* object, double dim1, double dim2)
        : general_drawing(object)
{
    major_side = dim1;
    minor_side = dim2;
}

void rectangle::draw_me()
{
    cout << "rectangle" << '\n';
    cout << graphic << '\t' << major_side << '\t'
            << minor_side << '\n';
}

sphere              earth("Earth", 23.34),
                    moon("Moon", 12.1),
                    sun("Sun", 39.48);
oval                earth_orbit("Earth orbit", 12.3, 12.5),
                    moon_orbit("Moon orbit", 9.3, 9.99);
square              room("Bedroom", 33);
                    den("Den", 44);
rectangle           hall("Hall", 12, 44);

main()
{
    static general_drawing *obj_arr[] = {
        &earth, &earth_orbit,
        &moon, &moon_orbit,
        &sun,
        &room, &den,
        &hall};


    for(int i = 0; i <  8; i++) {
        obj_arr[i]->draw_me();
        cout << '\n';
}
```

―――――――― **Program's Output** ――――――

sphere
Earth   23.34

oval
Earth orbit 12.3   12.5

sphere
Moon   12.1

oval
Moon orbit 9.3 9.99

sphere
Sun   39.48

square
Bedroom   33

square
Den   44

rectangle
Hall   12   44

As a general rule, if a class has a virtual function and also a destructor, you must make the destructor a virtual function also or there will be times when a wrong destructor is called.

The Virtual Function Mechanism

A major feature of virtual functions is that the same function is called for an object independently of the type of expression used to access the object. The C++ virtual function mechanism implements this feature.

The virtual function mechanism of C++ is extremely efficient and this distinguishes it from other object–oriented languages (Lisp, SmallTalk, etc.), which have very high run–time overhead mechanisms to implement dynamic binding. C++'s efficiency in this area is one of the major reasons why we believe that C++ will dominate the object–oriented arena.

This section describes a conceptual C++ virtual function mechanism at a high level; actual implementations of the mechanism are compiler– and linker–dependent. While it is not necessary to understand the virtual function mechanism to be a proficient and expert C++ programmer, it will give you a better understanding of how virtual functions work and eliminate the belief that it is all done with mirrors.

When a non–virtual member function is called, the compiler decides at compile time which particular function to call. In contrast, every time a virtual function is called, the executable code decides at runtime, during the call, which version of the virtual function to call. This run–time determination is referred to as *dynamic binding*.

If a class has a virtual function, the compiler generates a *virtual table* for the class and adds a pointer to the class's definition. When an object of the class is created, the pointer is automatically initialized to point to the class's virtual table. The virtual table contains an entry for every virtual function in the class. This includes all of the virtual functions defined in the class and all of the virtual functions that the class inherits. An entry in the table contains the address of a particular virtual function in the text segment and some offset information to locate inherited parts within the class template (memory layout). Within an entire class hierarchy, all of the variants of a virtual function with the same prototype will have the same index into the virtual tables. This makes it easy and extremely efficient for the executable code to call a particular variant of a virtual function that corresponds to a particular object. The following program uses virtual functions:

```
#include <iostream.h>

class A {
    public:
        virtual void f() { cout << "A::f() was called \n"; }
};

class B : public A{
    public:
        virtual void f() { cout << "B::f() was called \n"; }
};

main()
{
    A   *a[2] = { new A, new B },
    A   *p;
```

```
        for (int i = 0; i < 2; i++) }
            p = a[i];
            p->f();              // a virtual function call
        }


        return 0;
}
```

──────── **Program's Output** ────────
A::f() was called
B::f() was called

In the program, a[0] points to a class A object that contains a pointer to the class A virtual table and a[1] points to a class B object that contains a pointer to the class B virtual table. When the statement

p->f();

executes with p pointing to the class A object, the version of the virtual function f() that executes is A::f(), and when the statement executes with p pointing to the class B object, the virtual function B::f() executes. This shows that the program dynamically selects at run–time which version of a virtual function to call.

The executable code uses the virtual function mechanism to determine which variant of the virtual function to call. When a program is compiled, the compiler generates a class A virtual table and a class B virtual table (see figure 9–14). The first entry of the class A virtual table contains &A::f() and the first entry of the class B virtual table contains &B::f(). When a virtual function is called, it is called using a pointer (or a reference) to an object. The execut–ing code uses the pointer to access the virtual table pointer in the object and then uses the virtual table pointer to dereference f()'s entry in the table, which calls the appropriate ver–sion of f(). Thus the compiler translates the statement p–>f() into an equivalent statement similar to the following code:

(*(p–>pvt) [0]) ( );

The following list explains the components of the above statement when p points to an object of class B:

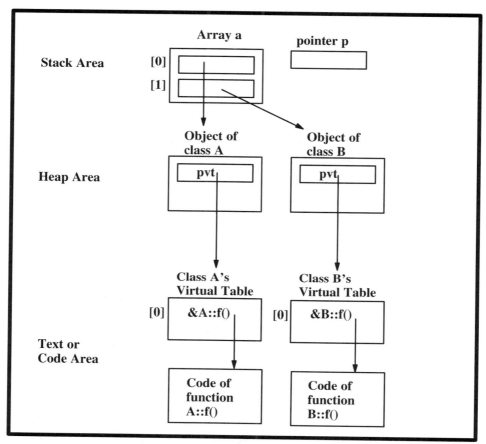

Figure 9.14. Memory layout of the above program with virtual functions.

- p points to an object of class B

- Assuming pvt is a pointer in the object that points to a virtual table, it points to class B's virtual table.

- (p–>pvt) is the address of class B's virtual table.

- (p–>pvt)[0] is the first entry in class B's virtual table, which contains the address of the virtual function B::f().

● (*(p–>pvt)[0]) ( ) calls the function B::f and passes the empty argument list ( ).

In the above explanation it only takes three dereferences to select the appropriate variant of a virtual function and call it. In general there is a bit more to the virtual function mechanism than is described here and it involves using a couple of offsets that are also contained in each virtual table entry; however, it is unnecessary to understand these lower–level details to grasp the basic concept of the C++ virtual function mechanism. This direct lookup mechanism of C++ is very efficient compared to most other languages which have to search for and find the appropriate variant before it can be called. Searching is very slow compared to a direct lookup.

Virtual Functions in a Multiple–inheritance Class Hierarchy

Virtual functions are a general feature of the C++ language, which are used with classes that have single inheritance and multiple inheritance. In both situations virtual functions have the same behavior. The same virtual function is called for an object independently of the type of expression used to access the object.

Figure 9.15 shows a multiple–inheritance class hierarchy diagram that has the shape of a hexagon:

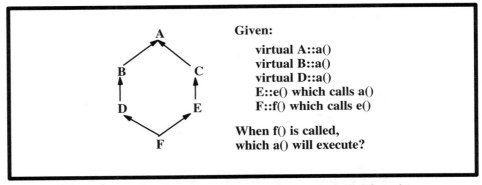

Figure 9.15. A hexagon class diagram with associated virtual functions.

Classes A, B, and D each have their own version of the virtual function a(). Class F has the member function f() that calls the member function e(). Class E has the member function e() that calls the virtual function a(). When an F class object is used to call F::f(), which version of the virtual function a() is called? Taking a quick glance at the diagram, one might wrongly expect that when E::e() calls a(), it would call A::f(), which is the f() that is found by following the arrows from class E. This is the wrong answer. The correct answer, which is explained below, is D::a().

Let the header file *hexagon.h* contain the following class definitions:

```
// hexagon.h

class A {
    public:
        virtual void a() { cout << "A::a() called. \n; }
};

class B : virtual public A {
    public:
        virtual void a() { cout << "B::a() called. \n; }
};

class C : virtual public A {
    public:
        virtual void a() { cout << "C::a() called. \n; }
};

class D : public B {
    public:
        virtual void a() { cout << "D::a() called. \n; }
};

class E : public C {
    public:
        void e() { a(); }   // which version of a() is called?
};

class F : public D, public E {
    public:
        void f() { e(); }   // which version of a() is called?
};
```

The following program determines the correct answer to the question asked:

```
#include <iostream.h>
#include "hexagon.h"
```

```
main ()
{
    F obj;
    obj.f();

    return 0;
}
```

This program prints the following output, which is the correct answer to the question:

D::a() called.

This output is correct because the virtual function a() is called for an F class object. Class F inherits function D::a() from class D because of the dominance rule. Whenever a() is called for an F object, D::a() is called independently of the type of expression used to access the object. In this case a() is called with E::e()'s *this* pointer, which points to the E part of an F type of object. Independent of the pointer pointing to a subpart of the F type of object, the object's virtual function D::a() is used.

The next two programs use pointers and references to emphasize that the same virtual function is called for an object independently of the type of expression used to access the object.

This example uses pointers to call a virtual function

```
#include <iostream.h>
#include "hexagon.h"

main ()
{
    F* pf = new F;          // create an F type of object

    A* pa = pf;             // some pointer expressions
    B* pb = pf;
    C* pc = pf;
    D* pd = pf;
    E* pe = pf;

    pa->a();                // call a() using pointers
    pb->a();
    pc->a();
    pd->a();
```

```
        pe->a();
        pf->a();

        return 0;
}
```

——————— **Program's Output** ———————
D::a() called.
D::a() called.
D::a() called.
D::a() called.
D::a() called.
D::a() called.

The program's output shows that the same virtual function of an object is called, irrespective of which subpart of the object was used to access the virtual function. (Each class that a derived class inherits contributes a subpart to the derived class.)

The following example is similar to the above program, but uses references to call a virtual function:

```
// Use references to call a virtual function
#include <iostream.h>
#include "hexagon.h"

main ()
{
        F& rf = *new F;                 // Create an F type of object

        A& ra = rf;                     // Some references
        B& rb = rf;
        C& rc = rf;
        D& rd = rf;
        E& rd = rf;

        ra.a()                          // Call a()  using references
        rb.a();
        rc.a();
        rd.a();
```

```
              re.a();
              rf.a();

              return 0;
        }
```

────────── **Program's Output** ──────────

D::a() called.
D::a() called.
D::a() called.
D::a() called.
D::a() called.
D::a() called.

The output again shows that the same virtual function of an object is called, irrespective of which subpart of the object was used to access the virtual function.

In the previous three programs, derived class pointers and references were (implicitly) cast to base class pointers and references, respectively. The conversions did not create a new object; they just pointed to or referenced subparts of the original object.

The conversion or casting of a derived class object to a base class object creates a new object, distinct from the original object. The following example shows that casting a derived class object to a base class object can affect which virtual function is called:

```
#include <iostream.h>
#include "hexagon.h"

main ()
{
        F obj;

        A(obj).a();
        B(obj).a();
        C(obj).a();
        D(obj).a();
        E(obj).a();
        F(obj).a();
```

```
        return 0;
}
```

——————— **Program's Output** ———————

A::a() called.
B::a() called.
A::a() called.
D::a() called.
A::a() called.
D::a() called.

The statement

      A(obj).a();

creates a new A type of object, initializes it with the A part of the object obj, and then calls the virtual function a() using the newly created object. Calling a() an A type of object invokes A's version of a(), which is A::a(). This is exactly what the first line of output above shows. The B class has its own version of a() and uses it: B::a(). Class C is derived from class A. It inherits the function a() from class A: A::a(). Class D has its own version of a() and class D objects use D::a(). Class E is derived from class C and class C is derived from class A. E inherits a() from class C, which uses A::a(); therefore, class E uses A::a(). Class F has base classes D and E. By the dominance rule, D::a() is dominant over A::a(); therefore; class F inherits D::a().

Virtual Function Usage Summary

The following points about virtual functions should be noted:

- Virtual functions only have meaning in the context of an inheritance hierarchy.

- Virtual functions are called through a reference, or pointer which generally a pointer to the top–most base class.

- All virtual functions must have the same prototype, including the type of the return value.

- You can override the virtualness of a function by using the class name::function name; however, avoid doing this unless it is absolutely necessary. It can lead to problems.

- In a multiple inheritance class hierarchy, a particular virtual function should only occur on a single path of the hierarchy. This practice avoids ambiguities.

9.6   Pure Virtual Functions and Abstract Base Classes

Many times virtual functions are declared in a base class and are not intended to be used in the base class but are only for derived classes. You can indicate this by modifying a declaration as follows:

virtual void display(void) = 0;

Initializing a virtual function to zero means that it cannot be used in that base class but will be a standard virtual function in all classes derived from the base class. These are called *pure virtual functions*. It is illegal to create objects of classes that have pure virtual functions or use abstract classes as argument types or function return types. It is legal to declare pointers and references to an abstract class.

A class that is derived from a class that has a pure virtual function can either inherit the pure virtual function or define the function. (In earlier versions of C++, a derived class could not inherit a pure virtual function; however, it could declare it to be a pure virtual function.)

10

Conversions

All of the implicit conversions that are possible in C are also possible in C++. For a complete description of the C conversions provided by C++, consult the *C Reference Manual* by Harbinson and Steele. In addition to the standard C conversions, there are additional conversions to be considered for C++.

10.1 Conversions to void*

The pointer void* is extensively used in C++. Any pointer type can be converted to void*. But in C++, the converse is not true: void* pointers cannot be converted to anything else but other void* pointers (this is not true in ANSI C). If you have a pointer implicitly cast to void* by the compiler and then you want to use the pointer later, you must explicitly cast it back to the appropriate pointer type.

```
#include <iostream.h>
enum pointer_type {string, integer, real, character};
void     f(void*,  pointer_type);

main()
{
     int     x = 57;
     char    b = 'B'
     float   x = 33.33;
     char*   sp = "Bill";

     int*    ip = &x;
     char*   cp = &b;
     float*  fp = &x;

     f(ip, integer);
     f(cp, character);
```

```
            f(fp, real);
            f(sp, string);
    }

    void    f(void* vp, pointer_type  pointer)
    {
        switch(pointer)  {
           case character:
                cout << *((char *)vp) << endl;
                break;
           case integer:
                cout << *((int *)vp) << endl;
                break;
           case real:
                cout << *((float *)vp) << endl;
                break;
           case string:
                cout << ((char *)vp) << endl;
                break;
        }
    }
```

10.2 Conversions from Built–in Data Types to User–defined Data Types

There will be situations where you will require an object of a user–defined data type but instead have a built–in data type. Conversion constructors can be used to convert built–in data types to user–defined data types. Remember that a conversion constructor is one that takes a single argument and converts the type of that argument into an object of the const-ructor's class. Conversion constructors often work together with overloaded operators.

```
        #include <iostream.h>

        class A {
            int y;
          public:
            A()     { y = 0; }
            A(int a) { y = a; }
```

```
        friend  A operator+(A& a, A& b)
        {
            A temp;
            temp.y = a.y + b.y;
            return temp;
        }
        void display() { cout << y << endl; }
};


main()
{
    A alpha(15), beta(16), gamma;   gamma = alpha + beta;
    gamma.display();

    gamma = alpha + 66;          // Conversion constructor called
    gamma.display();

    gamma = 77 + beta;           // Conversion constructor called
    gamma.display();

    return 0;
}
```

——————— **Program's Output** ———————
31
81
93

By providing a conversion constructor, it is possible to add A objects and ints together. The ints are converted to temporary A objects and the operator+() function is called.

10.3   Conversions from User–defined Data Types to Built–in Data Types

In C++ you can create standard conversions from user–defined types to built–in data types by using a new member function called: the operator data type.

```
class A  {
     int x;
public:
     A() {x = 57;}
     operator int() {return x;}
};
```

You can create a conversion operator that take a user–defined argument and converts it into a built–in type of argument; you can also create a conversion operator that take a user–defined argument and converts it into a user–defined type of argument. You can define several conversion operators. In our example,

```
operator int() {return x;}
```

converts a user–defined integer type into a built–in int type. This function has a very special syntax. Like constructors and destructors, you cannot declare any return type, not even void, even though the function is returning a value. You cannot provide any arguments to the function. The code in the function body must return a variable of the type specified in the function identifier, or something which can be safely converted to the appropriate data type.

The following is a driver function for our class:

```
main()
{
     A alpha, beta;
     int xx;
     xx = alpha + 32;
     cout << xx << '\n';
     xx = alpha + 33.33;              // Converted to 33
     cout << xx << '\n';
     double yy;
     yy = beta + 55;
     cout << yy << '\n';
     yy = beta + 111.111;
     cout << yy << endl;
}
```

——————— **Program's Output** ———————

89	**int xx = alpha + 32**
90	**int xx = alpha + 33.33**
112	**double yy = beta + 55**
168.111	**double yy = beta + 111.111**

In the example, there is an operator int conversion defined, but there is no conversion from an int to an A as was in the previous example. Therefore, all the objects of type A are converted to ints. If a conversion constructor that converted an int to an A object were provided, ambiguity compile errors could occur.

10.4   Conversions with Inheritance

There are five predefined standard conversions between a derived class and its public base class:

- A derived class object is implicitly converted into a public base class objects.

- A derived class reference is implicitly converted into a public base class reference.

- A derived class pointer is implicitly converted into a public base class pointer.

- A pointer to a class member of a base class is implicitly converted into a pointer to a class member of a publicly derived class.

- A pointer to any class object is implicitly converted into a pointer of type void*.

10.5   Conversions Used When Passing Arguments to Functions

Functions can be overloaded to provide functions that handle class objects. For example,

extern complex& sqrt(complex&);

When passed an argument, the function checks the argument using the following algorithm:

- Look for an exact match. If the function requires a double and you pass it a double, there is an exact match and the function call is made.

- If there is no exact match, look for an implicit standard conversion. If the function expects a double and you pass it a float, the float will be converted to a double. If the function expects a void* and you pass a complex*, the complex* is converted to a void*. If the function expects a reference to a base class and you pass a reference to a derived class, the derived class reference is converted to a base class reference.

- If no standard conversion is possible, look for a user–defined conversion. If the function expects a double and you passed an object of type complex, does the complex class contain an operator double() function? If the function expects an object of type complex and you passed a double, does the class contain a conversion constructor (complex(double))?

- If none of the three above conditions hold, the function call fails and a compile error is generated.

When providing user–defined conversions, be careful not to introduce ambiguity. Look at the following example:

```
#include <iostream.h>

class A {
    int     y;
public:
    A() { y = 0;}                          // Default constructor
    A(int a) { y = a;}                     // Conversion constructor
    operator int() {return y;}             // Operator data type
    friend A operator+(const A& a, const A& b)
        { return a.y + b.y; }
    void display() { cout << y << endl;}
};

main()
{
    A       alpha(16),  beta(33), gamma;
    int     y,  x = 57;
```

```
        y        =    x        + 100;       // Exact match;
        gamma    =    alpha    + beta;      // Exact match;
        y        =    x        + alpha;     // Ambiguous
        gamma    =    alpha    + x;         // Ambiguous
    }
```

The above code fails when we try to add an int and an A object. The system does not check to see what the assignment is (it does not look on the left side of the assignment operator). The system does not know whether to convert the A object to an int or the int to an A object, so a compile error ensues. Explicit casts are required to resolve the ambiguity.

```
    #include <iostream.h>

    class A {
        int      y;
    public:
        A() { y = 0;}                        // Default constructor
        A(int a) { y = a;}                   // Conversion constructor
        operator int() {return y;}           // Operator data type
        friend A operator+(const A& a, const A& b)
            { return alpha.y + beta.y; }
        void display() { cout << y << endl;}
    };

    main()
    {
        A        alpha(16),  beta(33), gamma;
        int      y,  x = 57;
        y         = x       + 100;           // Exact match;
        gamma     = alpha + beta;            // Exact match;
        y         = x       + (int) alpha;   // alpha cast to int
        gamma     = alpha + (A)x;            // int cast to A object
    }
```

10.6   Examples

Look at the following examples and try to determine which functions, if any, will execute:

Example 1:

```
#include <iostream.h>

class foo {
public:
    int x;
    foo(int a) {x = a;}
};

class bar {
public:
    float y;
    bar(float c) {y = c;}
};

void obtain(foo& a) { cout << a.x << endl;}
void obtain(bar& a) { cout << a.y << endl;}

main()
{
    foo argus = 57;
    bar  none = 33.33;
    obtain(argus);
    obtain(none);
}
```

The first example ran because there were exact matches in the arguments to obtain().

Example 2:

```
#include <iostream.h>

class foo {
public:
    int x;
    foo() {x = 0;}
    foo(int a) {x = a;}
};
```

```
class bar : public foo {
public:
    float y;
    bar(float c) {y = c;}
};

void obtain(foo& a) { cout << a.x << endl;}

main()  {
    foo argus = 57;
    bar  none = 33.33;
    obtain(none);
}
```

The second example worked because a derived class object, reference, or pointer was implicitly converted into a corresponding base class object, pointer, or reference. Therefore, tit was like calling:

```
obtain(foo&).
```

Example 3:

```
#include <iostream.h>

class foo {
public:
    int x;
    foo() {x = 0;}
    foo(int a) {x = a;}
};

class bar : public foo {
public:
    float y;
    bar(float c) {y = c;}
};

void obtain(bar& a) { cout << a.x << endl;}
```

```
main()
{
    foo argus = 57;
    obtain(argus);
}
```

The third example fails because there is no standard conversion from a base class object to a derived class object; therefore, passing a base class object fails if there is a function that only takes a derived class argument.

Example 4:

```
#include <iostream.h>

class foo {
public:
    int x;
    foo() {x = 0;}
    foo(int a) {x = a;}
};

class Alpha {
public:
    int z;
    Alpha() { z = 66;}
};

class bar : public foo, public Alpha {
public:
    float y;
    bar(float c) {y = c;}
};

void obtain(foo& a) { cout << a.x << endl;}
void obtain(alpha & a) { cout << a.z << endl;}

main()  {
    bar none = 33.33;
    obtain(none);
}
```

This call is ambiguous because the compiler does not know whether to convert the derived class object to the base class foo or base class alpha. This call could be made if an explicit cast was made; such as

obtain(alpha(none));

Now the system would convert the derived class object to an alpha base class object.

Example 5:

```
#include <iostream.h>
class foo {
public:
     int x;
     foo() {x = 0;}
     foo(int a) {x = a;}
};

class Alpha {
public:
     int z;
     Alpha() { z = 66;}
     Alpha(int a) {z = a;}
};

class bar : public foo, public Alpha {
public:
     float y;
     bar(float c) {y = c;}
};

void obtain(foo& a) { cout << a.x << endl;}
void obtain(void*) {cout << "Hello" << endl;}

main()  {
     Alpha  *bet = new Alpha(26);
     obtain(bet);
}
```

The fifth example works because a pointer of any class is implicitly converted into a pointer of type void*.

Example 6:

```
#include <iostream.h>

class foo {
public:
    float x;
    char y;
    foo(float a) {x = a;  y = 'B';}
    operator char() {return y;}
};

class bar  {
public:
    char* y;
    bar(char* a)  {y = a;}
};

void obtain(foo&) { }
void obtain(bar&) { }

main()
{
    float  alpha = 3.0;
    obtain(alpha);
}
```

The sixth example works because the user–defined conversion constructor

```
foo(float a)  { x = a;}
```

converts obtain's alpha argument to a foo object and calls the function obtain(foo&).

11

Input and Output – iostream Library

This chapter describes the C++ iostream library and how to use it. The iostream library is organized into major components. This chapter gives an overview of I/O concepts, the over-all structure of the iostream library and then describes how to use the library's interface components: iostream.h, fstream.h, strstream.h, iomanip.h, and stdiostream.h.

Like C, the C++ input/output facilities are not part of the C++ language but are provided by a library. The (defacto) standard C++ I/O library is called iostream, and its specification is defined by AT&T. C++ programs can also use all of the standard C libraries, including C's input/output library stdio; however, unless there is a compelling reason, as a general rule, only the iostream library should be used.

C++'s iostream library provides two powerful software–engineering features: type–safe I/O and a straightforward, single, unified I/O approach for all types, including user–defined types (classes). From type–safe I/O, we gain all the same benefits for I/O that were gained from type–safe expressions and statements. From unified I/O we gain a single way to handle all of our I/O. Thus, when a new class is defined, it can define I/O for its objects so they have the same look and feel as built–in types. Combined, these capabilities make it easier to develop new and reliable software and to use and/or reuse existing C++ developed software.

11.1 A Simplified Model

What is an I/O stream? A stream is a linear sequence of eight–bit bytes (octets). The bytes may represent binary data and have some particular meaning, such as IEEE standard binary floating–point numbers or colored pixel values of a window image. Likewise, the bytes may represent text characters, such as ASCII characters, which are very common in many environments. If data are transferred as they are and unmodified between a program and a file, the I/O operation is called unformatted or binary I/O. If data, which are in internal machine representation (i.e., a double), are transferred with modification between a program and a file, and which are in text character representation (i.e., ASCII), the I/O operation is called formatted I/O. The iostream library supports both unformatted and formatted I/O operations and expects the user to control specific formatting operations with manipulators.

There is a common I/O model that many systems use. A program uses a system–provided interface (library routines) to read and/or write a sequence of bytes in a file. A file may represent a collection of persistent data on a disk storage device or it may represent an input or output interface to a keyboard or color monitor device. Typically a user accesses a file in a device–independent way and the system (libraries and operating system) handles the device–dependent details. Some devices are called character devices and they support single character data transfers to and from the device. Some devices are called block devices and they support the transfer of data to and from them in multiples of a fixed block size (e.g.,1024 bytes). Often, a single device is treated as either a character device or a block device, depending on which operating system device driver is used.

For performance reasons, disks are typically used as block devices and a file that resides on a disk has blocks of the file data read into a memory buffer (synonym: file buffer) or written from a memory buffer by the operating system in response to a user's I/O request. Programmers rarely transfer data chunks of a particular fixed size (1024 bytes) to a file; they usually transfer some variable number of characters per line of I/O. Because the programmers transfer data in variable size chunks, systems provide a user interface (library routines) to handle the transfer of user data between a file buffer and the user. The interface routines automatically flush a write buffer when it fills up (makes room for more data in the buffer by writing blocks of data to the file) and automatically refills a read buffer that a user empties by reading more blocks of data from a file. Figure 11.1 shows a buffered file I/O model writing data:

11.2   iostream Library Example

Frequently, a disk file or standard file (like C's stdin, stdout, or stderr) is associated with a particular stream and the user uses a standard stream interface (library–provided routines) to read from and/or write to a file. In C++, the iostream library provides the predefined stream objects cin, cout, cerr, and clog to use with iostream (member) functions to perform I/O with the corresponding C files stdin, stdout, stderr (unbuffered), and stderr (buffered). Thus in C++, I/O can be performed on standard files without having to explicitly associate any files with streams. These predefined streams are sufficient to write the majority of programs

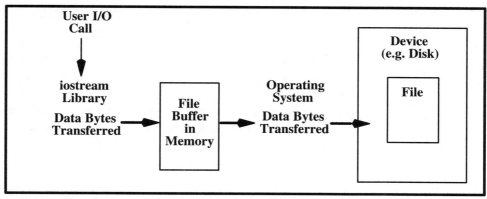

Figure 11.1. A buffered I/O model writing data.

(called filters) and command line redirection is used to redirect a program's I/O to other files. If the following program were compiled and linked into an executable file named hello:

```
#include <iostream.h>

main()
{
    cout << "Hello world, from C++!" << endl;
    return 0;
}
———— Program's Output ————
Hello world, from C++!
```

the following command on a DOS or UNIX system would write the program's output to a file named keep_me:

hello > keep_me

11.3 iostream Library Structure

The iostream library is very powerful (over 250 functions and approximately 20 classes). It supports a single unified style of I/O for both built–in data types (i.e., doubles, ints, etc.) and user–defined types, like class Complex below. Additionally, it does this with strong type checking: safe I/O!

Because of its size, the interface to the iostream library is partitioned into five distinct header files:

- iostream.h   If you do any iostream I/O, you need to use this file. It is the primary interface and contains much of the stream library's capabilities. It contains the base classes of the other derived classes in the library. It contains the objects cin, cout, cerr, and clog. It handles formatted and unformatted I/O operations and also contains common manipulators like endl.

- fstream.h   If you need to open, position, and close files, you will use the features defined in this interface.

- strstream.h   If you need to do in–core formatting (formatting into a string or character array), you must include this file.

- iomanip.h   If you are doing formatting or creating your own manipulators to tailor I/O formatting (e.g., adding a tab manipulator), you will include this file.

- stdiostream.h This file is rarely if ever used when writing new programs in C++. It is only used when you must use C's FILE descriptors mixed with C++ iostream operations. This can occur if you are enhancing an existing C program with code written in C++.

Because the above five header files specify the interfaces of the iostream library, we recommend that you print a hard copy of them and refer to the appropriate sections of your code while reading this chapter. As mentioned above, the iostream library contains about 20 classes (user–defined types). Figure 11.2 in the next section shows the iostream library's class hierarchy and it also shows in which header file a class resides.

The example that follows illustrates type–safe I/O, the output of some built–in types and how I/O for a user–defined type looks just like the I/O for built–in types. This chapter will discuss how to extend stream I/O for user–defined types, as is done here with class Complex.

```
#include <iostream.h>

class Complex {
     double real_part;
     double imaginary_part;
public:
```

```
            Complex(double x = 0, double y = 0)  // constructor
            {
               real_part     = x;
               imaginary_part = y;
            }

            friend ostream& operator<<(ostream& s, Complex z)
            {
               s << z.real_part    << " + "
                  << z.imaginary_part << "i";
               return s;
            }
      main()
      {
            char    a = 'A';
            double  b = 1.2;
            Complex c = Complex(3.4, 5.6);

            cout << a << "   " << b << "   " << c << endl;
            return 0;
      }
```

——————— Program's Output ——————
A   1.2   3.4 + 5.6i

Note that the compiler has type checked each of the operands of the overloaded operator <<
and called the appropriate overloaded operator<< functions. I/O for the built–in types char
and double is defined in iostream.h and I/O for Complex is defined in the Complex class.
The endl is not an object to be printed. It is called a *manipulator* and its particular purpose is
to send a newline character to the stream and then to flush the stream. Manipulators are used
to control streams and, as we will see later in this chapter, they are used to specify I/O formatting too.

11.4   iostream Class Hierarchy

The iostream contains three base classes and over fifteen derived classes. The base classes
are

- class streambuf;
- class ios;
- class iostream_init;

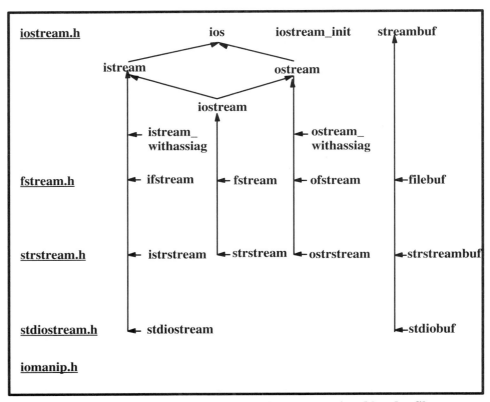

Figure 11.2. Iostream library class hierarchy and associated header files.

Figure 11.2 shows the iostream library class hierarchy and the header files that contain the interfaces to the various classes. The diagram is used to identify which file contains a particular class and to determine the inheritance hierarchy of data and functions. For example, class ostream is defined in iostream.h and it inherits from class ios. This means that its functionality (behavior and state) is documented in the classes ios and ostream.

The class ios is the root of the class hierarchy and it contains the state variables and functions that are common to the various derived stream classes. The class streambuf is the base class for buffers and supports insertion and extraction of characters. Class iostream_init is present for technical reasons related to initialization and is used to initialize the predefined streams for standard input, output, and errors.

Whenever stream I/O is used, the iostream.h header file is included. It contains the root base class ios and the following derived classes:

- class istream   :   virtual public ios;
- class ostream   :   virtual public ios;
- class iostream   :   public istream, public ostream;

The class istream supports formatted and unformatted character conversion from character sequences fetched from streambufs. The class ostream supports formatted and unformatted conversion to sequences of characters stored in streambufs. The class iostream combines istream and ostream and it is intended for situations in which bidirectional operations are desired.

Whenever file I/O is used, the fstream.h header file is included. It contains the following classes:

- class filebuf   :   public streambuf;
- class fstream   :   public iostream;
- class ifstream   :   public istream;
- class ofstream   :   public ostream;

Class filebuf supports I/O through the use of file descriptors. Its member functions support opening, closing, and seeking in files. Class fstream associates a file to a program for both input and output operations. The class ifstream associates a file to a program for input. The class ofstream ties a file into a program for output.

Whenever in–memory (in–core) I/O is used ,the strstream.h header file is included. It is also used to associate a file with a user–defined buffer. It contains the following classes:

- class strstreambuf: public streambuf;
- class istrstream   :   public istream;
- class ostrstream   :   public ostream;

Class strstreambuf inserts and extracts characters from arrays of bytes in memory (i.e., strings). Class istrstream fetches characters from an array. Class ostrstream stores characters into an array.

To support existing C programs with standard I/O and add new C++ code with compatible stream I/O capability, the header file stdiostream.h is included. It is not used for writing new C++ programs. This header file contains the following classes:

- class stdiobuf   :   public streambuf;
- class stdiostream :   public ios;

The class stdiobuf supports I/O through stdio FILE structs. It is intended for use when mixing C and C++ code. Class stdiostream specializes in iostream for stdio FILEs.

11.5   Stream Fundamentals

To make it easy to do stream I/O, the following streams are predefined:

- cin
- cout
- cerr
- clog

cin is an object of istream and is associated with standard input (file descriptor 0). cout is an object of ostream and is associated with standard output (file descriptor 1). cerr is an object of ostream and is associated with standard error (file descriptor 2). Output through this stream is unbuffered and characters are flushed after each insertion operation. clog is an object of ostream and is associated with standard error (file descriptor 2). Output through this stream is buffered and characters are not flushed after each insertion operation.

Streams have two operators that are overloaded for all C++ built–in data types. They are

- <<
- >>

For streams, the operator << is called the insertion operator and it is used for output operations. The operator >> is the extraction operator and it is used for input operations. Data are said to be extracted from an input stream and diverted to some memory location. By default, the input stream comes from the keyboard and the output streams go to a screen/window.

11.6   Standard Output

To perform standard output you must use the header file iostream.h. Next you use the object cout which is predefined for you. With cout, you use the insertion operator. If you want the output buffer to be flushed after each operation, you can use manipulators which will be discussed in Chapter 13.

#include <iostream.h>

```
main ()
{
     cout << "Hello world, from C++ \n";
     cout << flush;
     return 0;
}
```

————— **Program's Output** —————
Hello world, from C++

Two manipulators can be used to flush the buffer after an insertion operator. They are

- flush   This empties the buffer.

- endl   This appends a new line character to the output and then flushes the buffer.

Rules for using the insertion operator:

- The function operator<<() returns an ostream&, so the extraction operator can be cascaded.

- The insertion operator has been multiply overloaded so it can be used with all the built–in data types.

- You must explicitly overload the insertion operator to be used with user–defined data types.

It is not important to specify the type of the data being inserted. Because << is overloaded, the compiler will check to see what the type is and call the appropriate operator<<() function.

Any complex expression can be specified as long as it can evaluate to a data type accepted by the insertion operation.

```
#include <iostream.h>
#include <string.h>

char* string = "William J. Heinze";

main()
{
    cout << string;
    cout << '\n';
    cout << "The length of Heinze is: ";
    cout << strlen("Heinze");
    cout << '\n';
    cout << flush;
}
```

The insertion operator knows how to handle char* variables. Therefore, it prints out the associated string. The expression strlen("Heinze") evaluates to the integer 6 which is printed by cout. The string literal which evaluates to a char* and character constants are recognized by << and are printed by cout. Because the operator<<() returns an ostream object, you can concatenate the insertion operator into a single statement.

```
#include <iostream.h>
#include <string.h>

char* string = "William J. Heinze";

main()
{
    cout    << string << '\n'
            << "The length of Heinze is: "
            << strlen("Heinze") << endl;
}
```

This code is equivalent to making five calls to the operator<<() function, each call returning a cout object, which is used with the next call.

The operator<<() can also be used to print out memory addresses

```
#include <iostream.h>

main()
{
    float f = 33.33, *fp;
    fp = &f;
    cout    << "f:\t" << f << '\t'
        << "&f:\t" << &f << '\n';
    cout    << "*fp:\t" << *fp << '\t'
            << "fp:\t" << fp << "\n\t\t"
            << "&fp:\t" << &fp << endl;
}
```

————— **Program's Output** —————

f:	33.33	&f:	0xefffe38
*fp:	33.33	fp:	0xefffe38
		&fp:	0xefffe34

The output is in hexadecimal. If you want it in decimal, you must cast it to a long

```
#include <iostream.h>

main()
{
    float f = 33.33, *fp;
    fp = &f;
    cout    << "f:\t" << f << '\t'
            << "&f:\t" << (long)&f << '\n';
    cout    << *fp:\t << *fp << '\t'
            << "fp:\t" << long(fp) << "\n\t\t"
            << "&fp:\t" << long(&fp) << endl;
}
```

——————— Program's Output ———————

f:	33.33	&f:	251657784
*fp:	33.33	fp:	251657784
		&fp:	251657780

The following program wants to print out the address contained in name

```
#include <iostream.h>

main()
{
        char *name = "Bill";
        cout    << "The address of name is:\t"
                        << name << endl;
}
```

——————— Program's Output ———————
The address of name is: Bill

The problem here is that cout knows how to process char* variables as strings. We need to override this default behavior to get the address of name. We can accomplish this by casting the char* variable to a void* variable

```
#include <iostream.h>

main()
{
        char *name = "Bill";
        cout << "The address of name is:\t"
                        << (void *)name << endl;
}
```

——————— Program's Output ———————
The address of name is: 0x200c8

There are two more output functions found in ostream. They are

- put()

- write()

put(char) is used to insert a character into the stream

cout.put('B');

write(const char*, int) is used to insert a sequence of bytes into the stream:

cout.write("William J. Heinze", 17);

The put() function can be used with either unsigned or signed characters and it returns an **ostream** object. The put() function can also be concatenated

cout.put('B').put('i').put('l').put('l').put('\n');

The write() function can be used with either unsigned or signed characters and it returns an ostream object. The int value is for the length of the byte sequence to be written. The write function is for binary output. The write() function can also be concatenated

cout.put('\t').write("Bill", 3).put('k').put('\n');

─────────── **Program's Output** ───────────
Bilk

There are six manipulators that are defined in iostream.h. They are

- ostream&   endl(ostream&);

- ostream&   ends(ostream&);

- ostream&   flush(ostream&);

- ios&   dec(ios&);

- ios&   hex(ios&);

- ios&   oct(ios&);

The following list gives a brief description of each of the manipulators:

- **endl**   Ends a line by inserting a newline character and flushing.

- **ends**   Ends a string by inserting a null(0) character and is typically used with strstream.

- **flush**   Flushes the output buffer.

- **dec**   Sets the stream object's base 10 flag.

- **hex**   Sets the stream object's base 16 flag.

- **oct**   Sets the stream object's base 8 flag.

Once you change the conversion base, it remains at the new setting until it is changed to some other base or the process terminates.

The following program uses the dec, hex, and oct manipulators:

```
#include <iostream.h>

main()
{
    int  i = 1024;
    cout << "Default:\t" << i << '\n';
    cout << "Octal:\t\t"n << oct << i << '\n';
    cout << "Hex:\t\t"n << hex << i << '\n';
    cout << "Decimal:\t"n << dec << i << endl;
}
```

─────────── **Program's Output** ───────────

Default:	**1024**
Octal:	**2000**
Hex:	**400**
Decimal:	**1024**

There are no predefined insertion operators for user–defined data types. If you want to use stream I/O on your classes, you must use the overload operator<<() to work on your class.

```
#include <iostream.h>

class smallint
{
    int  x;
    friend ostream& operator<<(ostream&, smallint&);
public:
    smallint(int i = 0) {x = i;}
};
```

```
        ostream& operator<<(ostream &os, smallint& si)
        {
                os << ”<” << si.x << ”>” << endl;
                return os;
        }

        main()
        {
                int aaa = 333;
                smallint zzz = 444;
                cout << zzz << aaa << endl;
        }
```

We previously discussed why you must use a friend function to overload the **<<** operator.

11.7   Standard Input

To perform standard input you must use the header file iostream.h. Next you use the object cin which is predefined for you. With cin, you use the extraction operator.

```
        #include <iostream.h>

        main()
        {
                int  i;
                float m;
                cout << ”Enter an integer and a real number: ”;
                cin >> i >> m;
                cout << ”i:\t” << i << ”\nm:\t” << m << endl;
        }
```

The extraction operator is **>>**. You do not have to specify the address of a variable. It would be an error to specify

```
        cin >> &a;
```

The operator>> function reads the current input stream skipping over leading whitespace until it encounters a non–whitespace character. It finishes its operation when it once again encounters a whitespace character. The following would read three ints into their respective memory locations:

```
int a, b, c;
cin >> a >> b >> c;
cout << a << ' ' << b << ' ' << c << endl;
```

The following input data are provided:

\n\t\t   233\t\t\n\n57\t\n \n\t\n 33\t\n

If you are interactively entering these data to a program, for the \n newline character you would press the *enter* or *return* key and for the \t tab character you would press the *tab* key. After reading the input, the program produces the following output:

223 57 33

Leading whitespace (spaces, newlines, and tabs) are skipped by the operators >> that are defined in the iostream library.

You must be sure to pass the right type of data to the extraction operator. If an integer and a character were passed to the following program, the results would be unpredictable:

```
#include <iostream.h>

main()
{
    int  i;
    float m;
    cout << "Enter an integer and a real number: ";
    cin >> i >> m;
    cout << "i:\t" << i << "\nm:\t" << m << endl;
}
```

data passed: 33a57.57

_____ **Program's Output** _____

```
i:      33
m:  5.51375e–30
```

The extraction operator parses the stream until it comes upon whitespace or data that are inconsistent with the type that should go into the memory location. It reads 3, then 3, and then a, which is not part of the integer. An unpredictable value is then printed because the stream was corrupted and no longer works for input. Whatever value is at the m memory location is printed.

Many of the rules for output are the same for input

- The function operator>>() returns an istream&, so the extraction operator can be cascaded.

- The extraction operator has been overloaded so it can be used with all the built–in data types.

- You must explicitly overload the extraction operator to be used with user–defined data types.

A general method of using cin on character data is to place it within a while loop

```
#include <iostream.h>

main()
{
    char  i;
    cout << "Enter a sequence of characters. ";
    cout << "Enter Ctl–d when finished.\n";
    while(cin >> i)
        cout << i;
}
```

The while loop will continue to loop until an end–of–file is reached, which results in the expression

```
cin >> i
```

returning the value of 0. Why this occurs is explained later in this chapter.

 When you are entering input from a keyboard on PC DOS a Control–Z is used to signal an end–of–file, and on UNIX a Control–D is used to signal an end–of–file . A program will never input the character that is entered to signal an end–of–file; only the end–of–file status is provided.

Another important characteristic of this program is that it will not read whitespace characters.

This is the C++ idiom that is equivalent to the C idiom:

```
while((c = getchar()) != EOF)
    putchar(c);
```

You can use cin with char* variables

```
#include <iostream.h>
#include <string.h>

main()
{
    char  i[57];
    cout << "Enter a sequence of characters. ";
    cout << "Enter Ctl–d when finished.\n";
    while(cin >> i) {
        char* ptr = new char[strlen(i) + 1];
        strcpy(ptr, i);
        cout << ptr << '\n';
        delete ptr;
    }
}
```

This program reads in one string (input between successive whitespace) and then puts it into i. The following input would be treated as seven separate strings:

"The time has come the Walrus said"

This program will not read white space characters. If you want to read whitespace characters there are other member functions of istream that can be used, such as

- **get()**

- **getline()**

- **read()**

If a string is larger than the size of the buffer, inBuff would overflow and the program might fail. To prevent overflow you can use the manipulator setw()

```
#include <iostream.h>
#include <iomanip.h>

const int buffLength = 5;

main()
{
```

```
        char  inBuff[buffLength];
        cout << "Enter a string. ";
        cout << "Enter Ctl–d when finished.\n";
        while(cin >> setw(buffLength) >> inBuff)
            cout << inBuff << endl;
    }
```

The input abcdefghijklmnop would be output as follows:

```
        abcd
        efgh
        ijkl
        mnop
```

To use the setw() manipulator, you must include iomanip.h. The string is broken up into substrings of buffLength –1 length. The manipulator places a null character at the end of each substring.

iostream has two member functions that can be used to extract characters from a stream:

- istream&   get(char&);

- int   get();

The following programs illustrate using these functions:

```
        #include <iostream.h>

        main()
        {
            char  c;
            cout << "Enter characters – then Ctl–d";
            while(cin.get(c))
                cout.put(c);
        }
```

or

```
        #include <iostream.h>

        main()
        {
```

```
int    i;
cout << "Enter characters – then Ctl–d";
while((i =cin.get()) != EOF)
    cout.put(i);
}
```

get() extracts and returns a single value from the input stream including EOF. EOF is implemented as an int on many machines, i must be declared as an integer instead of a char. The int returned by get() must be tested against EOF.

get(char& c) extracts a single character from the input stream and places it in **c**. This is the inverse function of put(char c). It returns the istream object that invoked it (here, cin). If EOF is detected, 0 is returned and the result of the while expression becomes false.

get(char* ptr, int length, char delimiter = '\n') is a member function that returns an istream&. This function extracts characters from the stream (including all leading whitespace characters) and stores them into the byte array, starting at ptr. Extraction ends when one of the following conditions occurs:

- Length – 1 characters have been extracted

- A delimiter character was encountered

- The stream has no more characters.

This function always stores a terminating \0 character into the ptr array, even if no characters are extracted. If a delimiter stops the extraction, the delimiter is left in the stream; it is not extracted. If get() encounters an EOF before any characters are extracted, the stream's ios::fail bit is set to indicate this situation.

getline(char* ptr, int length, char delimiter = '\n') is a member function that returns an istream&. This function behaves similarly to the get just described but it *does* extract the delimiter character from the stream and then throws it away; it is not put into the ptr array. If length –1 characters have been extracted and the next character is a delimiter, the ptr is terminated as usual with a null character ('\0') and the delimiter is not extracted. In this case the full array, and not the delimiter, terminates the getline() function.

If the next two lines of input data (each terminated by a newline)

Sammy
A guide dog

are read by the following code:

```
char    word[30], line[200];
cin >> word;
cin.getline(line, 200);
```

the result is probably not what you would expect. The first input statement

```
cin >> word;
```

inputs the characters Sammy into the array word and then encounters a whitespace character (newline), which terminates character extraction but leaves newline in the stream (it is not extracted) and the input data in the array word are terminated with a '\0' character. The next statement

```
cin.getline(line, 200);
```

extracts the newline character from the stream which terminates the extraction. Because the first character getline() extracts is the newline, line[0] is set to '\0'. The getline() does not input the string

A guide dog

into the line array as we expect. If the first statement were changed to

```
cin >> word >> ws;
```

this code would work correctly and getline() would do what we wanted (ws is a manipulator that consumes whitespace).

It is important to make sure that a stream is good each time before you use it. This is particularly true when looping and reading input until an EOF is detected. The following code fragment will always terminate when an EOF is read because it guarantees that the stream is good:

```
while (cin.good() && cin.getline(buf, buf_size))
    cout << buf;
```

However, the following code fragment, under some circumstances, will not terminate when an EOF is read; rather it will loop forever:

```
while (cin.getline(buf, buf_size))
    cout << buf;
```

Whenever this code fragment sees a line of one or more characters that is terminated with an EOF (control–D on UNIX) the function getline() sets the io_state of cin to 1 (set the eofbit) and the code loops forever. The expression

> **cin.getline(buf, buf_size)**

in the while loop returns a cin object but the while loop requires an int as an argument. The overloaded operator void* implicitly converts the cin object to void* and a built–in conversion implicitly converts the void* to an integer. It returns true if cin's io_state bits failbit, badbit, and hardfail are all 0 and returns false otherwise. Notice that the eofbit does not affect the value returned by the conversion operator void*. Therefore, the infinite loop occurs because after getline() reads the data it also sets the eofbit in the cin object. The data are printed inside the while's code block and then the while expression is again executed. getline() does nothing because the stream is not good, the implicit conversion operator void* returns true (eofbit is ignored), and the code body of the while loop is entered. The loop never terminates.

The code fragment above with the while loop will terminate correctly when the function getline() reads a line that has no data and an EOF. In this case, getline() sets the io_state of cin to 3 (sets both the failbit and eofbit). The conversion operator void* returns false because the failbit is set and the while loop terminates as desired.

The following program uses getline() to read lines of text that may contain blanks and it is useful to interactively explore the behavior of getline(). It prints the lines and some additional information: the number of characters read, the io_state of the input stream cin, and the status returned by the getline() function.

```
#include <iostream.h>
#include <string.h>

main()
{
    const int    buf_size = 20;
    char         buf[buf_size];
    void*        status;

    cout << " \n"
        << "Enter some lines of text.\n"
        << "Each line is terminated with the enter or return key. \n"
        << "The last line may be terminated with an end–of–file. \n"
        << "On UNIX, use Control–D to terminate input. \n"
```

```
                 << "On DOS,  use Control–Z to terminate input.  \n";

        while (      cin.good()
            && cout << "\n          Enter your input data: "
            && (status = cin.getline(buf, buf_size))
            )
        {
           cout << '\n'
               << "          You entered the  data: "
               << buf
               << endl;

           cout << "     Number of characters read: "
               << strlen(buf)
               << endl;

           cout << "cin.getline() returned the value: "
               << (int)status
               << endl;

           cout << "cin.rdstate() returned the value: "
               << cin.rdstate()
               << endl;
        }

        cout << "\n————————————————————————————————" << endl;
        cout << "cin.getline() returned the value  " << (int)status << endl;
        cout << "cin.rdstate() returned the value: "
            << cin.rdstate()
        cout << "That's all folks!" << endl;

        return 0;
    }
```

The following text is a sample interactive session with the above program:

Enter some lines of text.
Each line is terminated with the enter or return key.

The last line may be terminated with an end–of–file.
On UNIX, use Control–D to terminate input.
On DOS, use Control–Z to terminate input.

Enter your input data: A line of words.
You entered the data: A line of words.
Number of characters read: 16
cin.getline() returned the value: 1518
cin.rdstate() returned the value: 0

Enter your input data: Leading spaces
You entered the data: Leading spaces
Number of characters read: 17
cin.getline() returned the value: 1518
cin.rdstate() returned the value: 0

Enter your input data: abcdefghijklmnopqrstuvwxyz
You entered the data: abcdefghijklmnopqrs
Number of characters read: 19
cin.getline() returned the value: 1518
cin.rdstate() returned the value: 0

Enter your input data:
You entered the data: tuvwxyz
Number of characters read: 7
cin.getline() returned the value: 1518
cin.rdstate() returned the value: 0

Enter your input data: The end.^Z
You entered the data: The end.
Number of characters read: 8
cin.getline() returned the value: 1518
cin.rdstate() returned the value: 1

---

cin.getline() returned the value 1518
cin.rdstate() returned the value: 1
That's all folks!

The above session inputs the following lines of text:

> **A line of words.**
>   **Leading spaces**
> **abcdefghijklmnopqrstuvwxyz**
> **The end.^Z**

and shows that the function getline() reads all of the data, including whitespace characters. The line of 26 letters of the English alphabet that were entered exceeded the size of the input buffer buf, which is 20 characters. The program read the first 19 characters (a through s) and placed a \0 character in the 20th character in the array to null–terminate the string. The next cycle through the while loop read the remaining seven characters (t through z) of the line. In the last line of input, the characters ^Z indicated where a DOS Ctrl–Z EOF was entered. The function getline() read the character data in the last line and also set the io_state of cin to 1 (set eofbit). Then, the body of the while loop printed its output and the while loop terminated because the function good() returned false if the io_status bits were set: eofbit was set.

If the above program, the input was changed to

> **A line of words.**
>   **Leading spaces**
> **abcdefghijklmnopqrstuvwxyz**
> **The end.**
> **^Z**

The program terminated differently than described above. After reading and printing "**The end.**", the while expression

```
while (   cin.good()
          && cout << "\n        Enter your input data: "
          && (status = cin.getline(buf, buf_size))
      )
```

executed. The stream was good, so the prompt for input was printed and the function getline() executed. It read the EOF by itself, set the io_state of cin to 3 (it set both failbit and eofbit), and assigned status the value 0, which terminated the loop.

gcount() is an iostream member function that returns as an int the number of characters returned by the last unformatted input function (get(), getline(), read(), etc.).

The following program uses the function gcount():

```
#include <iostream.h>
#include <string.h>
```

```
const int stringLength = 81;

main()
{
    int  charRead;
    char  string[stringLength];
    cout << "Enter a string – then Ctl–d";
    while(cin.good() && cin.getline(string, stringLength)) {
        charRead = cin.gcount();
        cout.write(string, charRead).put('\n');
    }
}
```

This program loops reading lines of input into a character array string. The function gcount() is used to determine the number of characters in each input line and its value is assigned to the variable charRead. Each input in string is written to the stream cout using the member function write, which has the character count argument charRead.

There are no predefined extraction operators for user–defined data types. If you want to use stream I/O on your classes, you must overload operator>>() to work on your class.

```
#include <iostream.h>

class smallint {
    int  x;
    friend istream& operator>>(istream&, smallint&);
    friend ostream& operator<<(ostream&, smallint&);
public:
    smallint(int i = 0) {x = i;}
};

istream& operator>>(istream &is, smallint &si)
{
    is >> si.x ;
    return is;
}
```

We previously discussed before why you must use a friend function to overload the **>>** operator.

12

File and In–core I/O

12.1 Introduction to File I/O

In many cases standard I/O is sufficient, but there are times when you must read from or write to a file. C++ provides three new classes to work with file I/O. They are

- ofstream

- ifstream

- fstream.

To use the new classes, you must include the header files iostream.h and fstream.h.

12.2 Creating ofstream Objects

ofstream is used to connect a file to a program for output. You must create an ofstream object and pass it the following two values for its constructor:

- The name of the file to be connected

- The output mode which, is explained later.

For example,

ofstream internalFileName(diskFileName, ios::out);

12.3 Creating ifstream Objects

ifstream is used to connect a file to a program for input. You must create an ifstream object and pass it the following two values for its constructor:

- The name of the file to be connected

- The input mode, which is explained later.

For example,

ifstream internalFileName(diskFileName, ios::in);

12.4 Creating fstream Objects

fstream is used to connect a file to a program for input or output. You must create an fstream object and pass it the following two values for its constructor:

- The name of the file to be connected

- The mode, which is explained later.

For example,

fstream internalFileName(diskFileName, ios::in | ios::app);

12.5 ios Enumerated Types

The class ios works with file I/O and contains three important enumerated types. They are

- enum io_state{goodbit=0, eofbit, failbit, badbit, hardfail};

- enum open_mode{in, out, ate, app, trunc, nocreate,noreplace};

- enum seek_dir{beg, cur, end};

io_state will be discussed in Section 12.8.

open_mode items are:

- **ios::in:**   File opened for input.
- **ios::out:**   File opened for output.
- **ios::ate:**   A seek to the end of a file is performed during the **open()**. **ios::ate** does not imply **ios::out.**
- **ios::app:**   A seek to the end of a file is performed.
- **ios::trunc:**   If a file exists, its contents will be truncated.
- **ios::nocreate:**   If a file does not exist, the **open()** will fail.
- **ios::noreplace:**   If a file exists, the **open()** will fail.

seek_dir items are

- **ios::beg:**   The beginning of the stream.
- **ios::cur:**   The current position in the stream.
- **ios::end:**   The end of the stream (end of file).

12.6   Examples of File I/O

The following program shows how to associate a file with a program. The file will be open for output

```
#include <iostream.h>
#include <fstream.h>
#include <stdlib.h>                        // For exit()

main()
{
    ofstream internalFileOut("diskFile", ios::out);

    if(!internalFileOut) {
        cerr << "File not opened" << endl;
        exit(-1);
    }
```

```
        char c;
        while(cin.get(c))
            internalFileOut.put(c);
}
```

This file could also have been opened for appending.

If we overload a user–defined data type to do output, we can use the insertion operator with file I/O. For example,

```
        smallInt example;
        internalFileOut << example;
```

The following program shows how to associate a file with a program. The file will be open for input

```
        #include <iostream.h>
        #include <fstream.h>
        #include <stdlib.h>

        main()
        {
            ifstream internalFileIn("diskFile", ios::in);

            if(!internalFileIn)  {
                cerr << "File not opened" << endl;
                exit(-1);
            }

            char c;
            while(internalFileIn.get(c))
                cout.put(c);
        }
```

If we overload a user–defined data type to do input, we can use the extraction operator with file I/O. For example,

```
        smallInt example;
        internalFileIn >> example;
```

The following program shows how to associate a file with a program. The file will be open for input, closed, open for output, and closed

```
#include <iostream.h>
#include <fstream.h>

main()
{
    fstream internalFile;

    internalFile.open("diskFile", ios::in);
    // Do some reading
    internalFile.close();

    internalFile.open("diskFile", ios::app);
    // Do some writing
    internalFile.close();
}
```

We used the default constructor when we declared the fstream object. Then, we explicitly opened it with the open() function and set the disk file name and the ios mode. Finally, we explicitly closed the file with the close() function.

We can use an fstream object to open a file for both input and output at the same time

```
#include <iostream.h>
#include <fstream.h>

main()
{
    fstream internalFile("diskFile", ios::in | ios::app);
    // Do some mixed reading and writing
    internalFile.close();
}
```

The bitwise **or** operator | can be used to specify more than one mode.

12.7   Some ios Member Functions

There are two iostream member functions that are used to position the file pointer. They are

- **seekg()**   for ifstream

- **seekp()**   for ofstream

There are two versions of seekg(). They are

- **seekg(streampos)**

- **seekg(streamoff, seek_dir)**

There are two versions of seekp(). They are

- **seekp(streampos)**

- **seekp(streamoff, seek_dir)**

Both streampos and streamoff result from the following:

> **typedef long streamoff, streampos;**

seek_dir is an enumerated type with the following elements:

- **ios::beg**   The beginning of the file.

- **ios::cur**   The current position in the file.

- **ios::end**   The end of the file.

The following code is used to move the file pointer around inside a file. You can use either seekg() or seekp() to navigate through a file – the choice is up to you.

```
#include <iostream.h>
#include <fstream.h>

main()
{
    fstream  internalFile("diskFile", ios::in | ios::app);

    internalFile.seekg(1, ios::beg);
    internalFile.seekg(70, ios::beg);
    internalFile.seekg(-50, ios::cur);
    internalFile.seekg(0, ios::end);
    internalFile.close();
}
```

internalFile.seekg(1,ios::beg) moves the file pointer one byte from the beginning of the file.

internalFile.seekg(70, ios::beg) moves the file pointer 70 bytes from the beginning of the file.

internalFile.seekg(–50, ios::cur) moves the file pointer 50 bytes toward the beginning of the file.

internalFile.seekg(0, ios::end) moves the file pointer to the end of the file.

12.8   ios Internal State Flags

The iostream library also maintains a set of condition flags which are used to monitor the state of the stream. They are listed in the following table:

Flag Name	Value	Meaning
ios::goodbit	0x00	No bit set: everything is OK.
ios::eofbit	0x01	At end of file.
ios::failbit	0x02	Last I/O operation failed.
ios::badbit	0x04	Invalid operation attempted.
ios::hardfail	0x80	Unrecoverable error.

There are several member functions that are used to determine the state of the stream. They are

int   eof() returns non–zero if the stream encounters an EOF.

int   bad() returns non–zero if an error occurs.

int   fail() returns non–zero if an operation fails.

int   good() returns non–zero if no state bits are set.

int   rdstate() returns the stream's current state.

void clear(int = 0) sets the stream state. If there is no argument, or if the argument is zero, all bits are cleared.

13

Manipulators

The iostream interface supports formatted I/O with the member functions width(), precision(), fill(), setf(), etc. When these functions are used, they are directly applied to an object, such as

> **cout.width(10);**
> **cout << "abc";**

which outputs the string "abc" right–justified (default justification) in a field that is ten characters wide. A better interface would support the formatting of the same statement where the I/O is done using << and >>.

13.1   Built–in Manipulators

Manipulators provide the capability to have functions as operands of the insertion << and extraction >> operators. The following manipulators and others are defined iostream.h:

- **dec**

- **oct**

- **hex**

These manipulators set the corresponding flags that control the conversion base of a value.

If dec is set, the conversion base is 10 (decimal); if hex is set, the conversion base is 16 (hexadecimal); and, if oct is set, the conversion base is 8 (octal). If none of the above are set, the default is dec; however, extractions are interpreted according to the C++ lexical conventions for integral constants. The static member ios::basefield identifies these fields.

The following manipulators are also defined in iostream.h:

- ws   This manipulator corresponds to the ios member function skipws, which skips whitespace during extractions.

- endl   This insertion manipulator inserts a newline character and flushes the output stream.

- ends   This insertion manipulator ends a string by inserting a null '\0' character into the output stream, which is typically used for incore conversions with strstream.

- flush   This insertion manipulator inserts a newline '\n' character and flushes the output stream's buffer.

The above manipulators are functions that have no arguments. To use them, you just specify their function name alone (pointer to function) with the insertion << and extraction >> operators. The code fragment

> **int a = 15;**
>
> **cout << dec << a << oct << a << hex << a << dec << endl;**

prints a in base decimal, then in base octal, and then in base hex. The manipulator dec restores cout's base to decimal, the manipulator endl outputs a newline character, and then it flushes cout's buffer.

The header file iomanip.h defines the following additional manipulators:

- **resetiosflags(long)**   This insertion/extraction manipulator corresponds to the ios member function unsetf(long) and it clears the stream's format bits specified by the argument.

- **setfill(int)**   This insertion/extraction manipulator corresponds to the ios member function fill(int) and it sets the stream's fill character.

- **setiosflags(long)**   This insertion/extraction manipulator corresponds to the ios member setf(long) and it sets the stream's formats that are specified in the argument.

- **setprecision(int)**   This insertion/extraction manipulator corresponds to the ios member function precision(int) and it sets the stream's precision state variable to the argument's value.

- **setw(int)** This insertion/extraction manipulator corresponds to the ios member function width(int) and it sets the stream's format width to the argument for the next insertion or extraction operation; then, the stream's width state variable is set to 0.

The header file iomanip.h also contains macros for defining user–defined manipulators, which are discussed in the next section. Manipulators that take one or more arguments are called *parameterized manipulators*. The following program illustrates using parameterized manipulators:

```
#include <iostream.h>
#include <iomanip.h>

main()
{
    double a = 123.4567;
    cout    << setw(10) << setprecision(2) << a
            << setprecision(0) << endl;
    return 0;
}
```

Notice that parameterized manipulators have actual arguments when they are used. Also, the example program outputs the number 123.45 right–justified in a field that is ten characters wide.

13.2 User–defined Manipulators

Manipulators are very handy for specifying formatting in stream insertion and extraction statements. You can define your own manipulators, which is convenient as well.

Manipulators that have no arguments are very easy to define. An insertion manipulator is implemented as a function that takes an ostream& argument and returns an ostream& value. An extraction manipulator is implemented as a function that takes an istream& argument and returns an istream& value.

The following program defines the insertion manipulator tab:

```
#include <iostream.h>

//    tab is a simple manipulator: it has no parameters when used.
ostream& tab(ostream& s)
{
    return s << '\t';
}

main()
{
    cout << "cat" << tab << "Sadie \n";
    cout << "dog" << tab << "Tod  \n";        return 0;
}
```

——— Program's Output ———
cat   Sadie
dog   Tod

On a technical note, remember that the name of a function is a pointer to the function. When tab is used above, it is a pointer to a function that returns an ostream& and takes an ostream& argument. Manipulators with this particular form of prototype get called because operator<< and operator>> are overloaded to take a right operand of a pointer to a function that has a stream (ostream& or istream&) argument and returns a corresponding stream (ostream& or istream&).

Look in iostream.h for a function with a definition like

```
ostream& operator<<(ostream& s, ostream&(*f)(ostream&))
{
    return (*f)(s);            // Call the function f that was passed
}                              // as an argument
```

to see how your system implemented these *dispatcher functions*.

When the statement

```
cout << tab;
```

is executed, it calls the dispatcher function

```
operator<<(cout, tab)
```

which uses the function pointer tab and the stream object cout and calls the function tab() with the argument cout. The tab() function executes, inserts a tab character into the output stream, and returns to the dispatcher. The dispatcher returns the cout value and we are done executing the statement.

A manipulator that takes a single parameter of an int or long is also simple to write, but it requires the use of macros defined in the iomanip.h header file. The following program defines a user–defined manipulator that takes a single int argument:

```
#include <iostream.h>
#include <iomanip.h>


//      nl(int n)
//
//      This manipulator outputs n newline characters.
//
//      Usage:
//          cout << "Line 1" << nl(3) << "Line 4 \n";

ostream& nl(ostream& s, int n)
{
    while (n– – > 0 && s << '\n');
    return s;
}


OMANIP(int) nl(int n)
{
    return OMANIP(int)(nl, n);
}


main()
{
    cout << "Line 1" << nl(3) << "Line 4 \n";        // Note, one nl is
                                                     // for line 1

    return 0;
}
```

——— **Program's Output** ———
Line 1

Line 4

In the above program, the function nl was defined an it injects a specified number of newlines into the stream. Another function is defined using the OMANIP macro that is defined in iomanip.h. OMANIP's definition uses macros in the generic.h header file. The function defined with OMANIP is a dispatching function that gets called when a manipulator is used and it in turn calls the nl function to do the work. It is not necessary to understand the details of these macros to use them; that is why sample code is provided – to show you how to write manipulators.

To define an extraction manipulator, the macro IMANIP is used rather then OMANIP, which is used in defining insertion manipulators.

To create a user–defined manipulator with a single user–defined type argument takes a little more effort. The following code defines such a manipulator:

```
#include <iostream.h>
#include <iomanip.h>

enum Bell_mode { low, medium, high};

IOMANIPdeclare(Bell_mode);

ostream& ring_bell_helper(ostream& s, Bell_mode m)
{
    switch (m) {
    case low:    s    << '\a';        ;     break;
    case medium: s  << "\a\a";       ;     break;
    case high:   s    << "\a\a\a\a\a\a";   break;
    }
    return s;
}

// The ring_bell(Bell_mode) manipulator calls (applies)
//  the ring_bell_helper function to get the work done.

OAPP(Bell_mode) ring_bell = ring_bell_helper;
```

```
void delay() { for (long i = 0; i < 200000; i++); }

main()
{
    cout    << "The low bell"    << ring_bell(low)        << endl;
    delay();
    cout    << "The medium bell"    << ring_bell(medium) << endl;
    delay();
    cout    << "The high bell"    << ring_bell(high)        << endl;
    delay();
    return 0;
}
```

In the above program, the enum Bell_mode defines a new type. The statement

IOMANIPdeclare(Bell_mode);

uses the IOMANIPdeclare macro to declare Bell_mode as a user–defined type that will be the argument of a manipulator.

The function ring_bell_helper is the function that does the actual work of the manipulator. The macro OAPP is used to introduce the name of the manipulator ring_bell and to assign it the value of the manipulator helper function. The ring_bell manipulator is used in the cout << statements.

It is also possible to define user–defined manipulators that take multiple arguments. The technique for using multiple arguments is to package all the arguments in a struct so they can be treated as if they were a single argument. The following program defines a user–defined manipulator that takes two arguments:

```
//      setwp(w, p)
//
//      This manipulator sets the width and precision.
//
//      Usage:
//          cout << setwp(6,2) << 123.4567 << endl;

#include <iostream.h>
#include <iomanip.h>
```

```
struct Setwp_args {
    int w;
    int p;
};

IOMANIPdeclare(Setwp_args);

ostream& setwp_helper(ostream& s, Setwp_args arg)
{
    return s << setw(arg.w) << setprecision(arg.p);
}

OMANIP(Setwp_args) setwp(int width, int precision)
{
    Setwp_args t;
    t.w = width;
    t.p = precision;
    return OMANIP(Setwp_args)(setwp_helper, t);
}

main()
{
    cout    << setwp( 8,2)    << 123.4567
            << setwp( 5,0)    << 123
            << setwp(10,0)        << 123.4567        << endl;
    return 0;
}
```

—— Program's Output ——
123.46 123 123.4567

The above program defines the insertion manipulator setwp(w, p) that sets the width and precision of an output stream. The struct Setwp_args contains data members to hold the values of the width and precision variables. The macro IOMANIPdeclare declares Setwp_args for usage by the other manipulator macros. The setwp_helper function is defined to return an ostream& and to take arguments of ostream& and the single parameter Setwp_args arg, which gets the two manipulator parameters passed as a single argument. The OMANIP macro defines the setwp manipulator function, which takes two arguments as input, packages them into a struct of type Setwp_args, and then does a return using the OMANIP macro to dispatch the helper function with its packaged arguments.

The cout << statements show the usage of the manipulator with its two arguments. Note that a frequent operation, which sets the width and precision, and is usually done with separate built–in manipulators, is simplified by defining a new manipulator.

The above programs define several different manipulators and illustrate how to use the macros defined in iomanip.h. To create your own manipulators, use the above examples as models for writing your code. Remember that the macros that begin with O are for writing (output) insertion manipulators and the macros beginning with I are for writing (input) extraction manipulators.

13.3   The Parameterized Manipulator Mechanism

While the implementation of the parameterized manipulators in iomanip.h is quite involved (take a look at it), the concept of how they work is much easier to understand. The following sequence of transforms illustrates how they work:

1)   The following statement has a manipulator that takes three parameters:

cout << m(a, b, c);

2)   When the statement is evaluated, the function m(a,b,c) executes. This function packages its arguments into a struct, which effectively makes them into a single (aggregate) argument. It then creates an object of a class that we define with two private data members: a pointer that points to the helper function that we want to execute and a struct that will be the helper function's single argument. This object is returned by the function.

3)   Now the statement is transformed into the following statement:

cout << object;

4)   We have an overloaded << operator to take an ostream& and an object of the type that we have. The above statement calls the operator<<() function.

5)   When our operator<<() function executes, it has the ostream cout and the object that we passed. It extracts the function's pointer and the three arguments inside the struct and calls (dispatches) the function through the pointer and passes the three arguments.

6)   Our helper function executes and gets the three parameters a, b, and c. This function uses its arguments and does whatever it needs to – it manipulates.

7)   When done, the helper function returns its stream argument.

8) The dispatcher function (step 5) continues execution and returns the stream that the helper function returned to it.

9) We are done executing the original statement.

14

Formatted Stream I/O

When you do iostream I/O on built–in types, each of them has a default format. The following program illustrates the iostream default formats associated with built–in data types:

```
#include <iostream.h>
main()
{
    char   a = 'A';
    int    b = 1234;
    double c = 123.456;
    double d = 1.2E23;
    char*  e = "abcdefg";
    int*   f = &b;

    cout    << a << endl
            << b << endl
            << c << endl
            << d << endl
            << e << endl
            << f << endl;
    return 0;
}
————— Program's Output —————
A
1234
123.456
1.2e+23
abcdefg
0x1e96fff2
```

The above output reflects the default output formats for some built–in types. A character is output as a single character with a field width of 1. An integer is output with a field width just wide enough to hold the integer. Positive numbers are output without a + sign. Negative numbers are output with a leading – sign. Floats and doubles are output with a field width just large enough to contain the number. They are output as digits and a decimal point if the exponent of the number is not too large; otherwise, they are output in scientific notation. A string (char*) is output in a field width just large enough to hold the character string. A pointer is output in hexadecimal notation with a leading 0x to indicate a hex number and the field width is just large enough to hold it. In general, data are output without any leading or trailing blanks (pad characters).

Input operations, by default, skip leading whitespace (space, tab, newline, and others as defined by isspace() in string.h) and input a data value as determined by a variable's type. Numbers can have an optional leading sign (+ or –) but no whitespace between it and the digits is allowed. Floating–point numbers in scientific notation have the letter e or E followed by an optional sign for the exponent and the exponent's value (e.g., –1.23e+12). Numeric input is terminated by a non–digit character (excludes the exponent part of floating–point numbers). String input is terminated by whitespace.

14.1   Controlling I/O Formatting

Each object of a class derived from class ios, which includes all but the buffer classes, contains private data members that control I/O formatting. Whenever input or output is done on a particular object, the member functions <<, >>, get, put, etc. look at the values of the format control data member variables inside the object to determine how to format the input/ output data. You can read and change the format control member variables (also called format state variables) by using either member functions or manipulators. Manipulators typically use member functions to get their work done. Manipulators are also a notational convenience that simplify formatting and let you cascade format control operations with the data being formatted. A system provides several manipulators, such as endl, and you can also define your own manipulators as well.

The non–public data members below are the format state variables that retain the formatting state within each I/O stream object. They are only accessed using member functions or manipulators; however, they are shown here to help you understand how data are organized:

State Variable	Meaning
long flags	Formatting flag bits
int precision	Floating–point precision on output
int width	Field width on output
int fill	Padding character on output

14.2   The Flags State Variable

Every ios derived stream object (cin, cout, etc.) contains a flags state variable. The flags state variable is a collection of flags (bits) that control formatting. Each flag has a corresponding named constant (actually a bit mask) that is used when accessing and changing the flag within a particular flags variable.

Flag Name	Value	Meaning
ios::skipws	0x0001	Skip whitespace on input (default). If not set, skipping leading whitespace on input is not done.
		Padding Location (ios::adjustfield)
ios::left	0x0002	Left–adjustify output
ios::right	0x0004	Right–adjustify output (default)
ios::internal	0x0008	Padding after sign or base indicator conversion base (ios::basefield)
ios::dec	0x0010	Decimal conversion (default)
ios::oct	0x0020	Octal conversion
ios::hex	0x0040	Hexadecimal conversion. If none of the bits are set, output is in decimal but input is done using C++ lexical conventions for integral constants.
		Modifiers
ios::showbase	0x0080	Use base indicator on output
ios::showpoint	0x0100	Force decimal point (floating output)

ios::uppercase	0x0200	Upper–case all hex and exponent E
ios::showpos	0x0400	Add '+' to positive integers
		Floating–Point Notation (ios::floatfield)
ios::scientific	0x0800	Use 1.2345e2 floating notation
ios::fixed	0x1000	Use 123.45 floating notation. If neither is set, the systems chooses how to format it. If the exponent is less than –4 ,or greater than precision, scientific notation is used. If ios::showpoint is not set, trailing zeros after the decimal point are removed; also, the decimal point shows only if it is followed by a digit
		Flushing Control
ios::unitbuf	0x2000	Flush all streams after insertion
ios::stdio	0x4000	Flush stdout, stderr after insertion

The following member functions are used to read, set, and clear format flags:

```
long    flags();
long    flags(long);
long    setf(long);
long    setf(long,long);
long    unsetf(long);
```

flags() is a member function that returns the current value of the flags state variable

long save_flags = some_stream.flags();

When a function changes flags to do some local formatting, frequently the value of the flags state variable is saved when the function is entered and then later restored just before leaving the function.

flags(long) is a member function that sets the flags state variable to the long parameter's value and returns the previous value of the flags state variable. This function is used the give the flags variable a completely new value.

long old = stream_object.flags(ios::hex | ios::internal);

setf(long) is a member function that sets the flags state variable to its current value that is bitwise ored with the parameters value and returns the result. This function is used to set additional flags in the current flags variable.

setf(ios::showpoint | ios::showpos);

Note that the following statement is equivalent to the above statement:

flags(flags() | ios::showpoint | ios::showpos);

setf(long, long) is a member function that clears the flag bits in the flags state variable specified by the second parameter and then the resulting value is 'bitwise ored' with the first parameter. This final result is stored in the flags state variable and the function returns the previous value of the flags state variable, that is, the value it had just before the setf function was called. The second parameter may be one of the following values:

Value	Flags Represented by the Field
ios::adjustfield	left, right, and internal
ios::basefield	dec, oct, and hex
ios::floatfield	scientific and fixed

setf(long,long) is used with groups of flags (flag fields), where it is only meaningful to have one of the flags within the group (field) set and the others must have a value of 0. For example, a floating–point number can be formatted using either scientific notation or fixed notation; it cannot be formatted with both notations. Using this setf function guarantees that at most one bit is set within a field and that it conforms to proper usage. For the ios::floatfield, an all–zero value has a distinct meaning from having a bit set. The following statement uses setf to change formatting of numbers to hex:

```
setf(ios::hex, ios::basefield);              // Sets hex output mode
setf(0, ios::floatfield);                    // Clears scientific and fixed bits
setf(ios::hex | ios::showbase, ios::basefield);
```

The first statement zeros the basefield and then sets the hex flag within that field. The next statement leaves the floatfield zeroed. The last statement zeros the basefield, then sets the hex flag within that field, and finally sets the showbase flag, which is not within that field but elsewhere within the flags state variable.

Some of the above flag–manipulating member functions also have corresponding manipulator implementations. The manipulator resetioflags, which is described in the manipulator section, also changes the flags like the member function setf. The manipulators dec, oct, and hex are used to set the corresponding flags.

unsetf(long) is a member function that unsets (sets to zero) in the flags state variable the flag bits specified in its argument and returns the previous value of the state variable.

```
long previous = my_stream.unsetf(ios::showpos);
my_stream.unsetf(ios::uppercase | ios::showbase);
```

ios::floatfield within the flags state variable controls the formatting of floating–point output. The following program illustrates using ios::floatfield values of ios::scientific, ios::fixed and 0:

```
#include <iostream.h>

main()
{
        double a = 10;                  // The integer part
        double b = 0.1;                 // The fraction part
        double c = a + b;               // The combined number

        for(int i = 0; i < 5; i++) {

                cout.width(20);                 // Width is explained in next section
                cout.setf(ios::scientific, ios::floatfield);
                cout << c;

                cout.width(20);
                cout.setf(ios::fixed, ios::floatfield);
                cout << c;

                cout.width(20);
                cout.setf(0, ios::floatfield);
                cout << c;

                cout << endl;
                a *= a;
                b *= b;
                c  = a + b;
        }
        return 0;
}
```

──────────── **Program's Output** ────────────

1.01e+01	10.1	10.1
1.0001e+02	100.01	100.01
1e+04	10000.0001	10000.0001
1e+08	100000000	1e+08
1e+16	1000000000000000	1e+16

The columns in the previous example use the formats ios::scientific, ios::fixed, and neither scientific nor fixed (ios::floatfield is zero), respectively. In the last column, the system decides what format to use based on the value of the number. While the numbers printed down each column are formatted representations of the computed numbers

> **10.1**
> **100.01**
> **10000.0001**
> **100000000.00000001**
> **1000000000000000.0000000000000001**

the 1 in the fractional part gets lost when the size of the number exceeds the number of digits that a double can represent when using fixed precision floating–point binary internal representation in our computer hardware.

ios::unitbuf controls when outputs are flushed. Unbuffered output streams are basically flushed when the buffer is full and needs to be emptied for additional insertions. This method is the most efficient. Buffered output streams flush the buffer every character and this method is the least efficient. An ios::unitbuf stream flushes output streams after each insertion and thus forms a compromise between efficiency and buffer flushing.

ios::stdio, when set on an output stream, causes stdio and stderr to be flushed after each insertion of the output stream.

14.3   Width Format Control

The following member functions are used to read and set the field width state variable:

> **int width()**
> **int width(int)**

The width state variable's value is used to affect the field width of the next input >> (extraction) or output << (insertion) operation. After the operation, the width state variable is set to zero. A field width of zero on input only inputs as many characters as necessary to represent the value being input. A field width of zero on output just uses a width wide enough to output the data.

When a field width is non–zero, outputs will output at least that many characters and any unneeded space is filled with the padding character defined by the padding state variable. If a field width is shorter than needed for numeric data, the output uses as much space as it needs. Numbers are never truncated. In this sense, width is interpreted as a minimum field width. On input, a non–zero width limits the number of characters input. The width member function has a corresponding manipulator named setw(int).

width() is a member function and it returns the value of the width state variable.

> **int current_width = some_stream.width();**

width(int w) is a member function that sets the width state variable to its argument and returns the previous value. The width function makes it very easy to output data in columns. The following program uses the width function:

```
#include <iostream.h>

long a[] = { 1, 22, 333, 4444, 55555, 666666};

main()
{
    for (int i = 0; i < sizeof(a) / sizeof(a[0]); i++) {
        cout.width(4);
        cout << a[i];
    }
    return 0;
}
```

————— **Program's Output** —————
1 22 333444455555666666

This output uses the default justification, which is right–justified in the field. All the numbers are printed with a field width of 4. The numbers 1, 22, and 333 are output right– justified with padding on the left; the default padding character is a space. The number 4444 just fits in the field. The numbers 55555 and 666666, which are wider than four characters, are output in a field just large enough to contain them. Numbers are never truncated to fit within a smaller field width.

14.4   Precision Format Control

The following member functions are used to read and set the number of floating–point digits printed after the decimal point:

> **int precision()**
> **int precision(int)**

precision() is a member function that returns the value of the precision state variable that controls the output precision of floating–point numbers.

precision(int) is a member function that sets the precision state variable to the value of its argument and returns the previous value of the state variable. The statement

> **some_stream.precision(5);**

sets the precision state variable of the object some_stream to output five digits of precision for floating–point numbers.

The following program illustrates the precision function:

```
#include <iostream.h>

main()
{
    double n = 9.12345678;

    cout << cout.precision()
        << " is the default value of the precision state variable"
        << "\n\n";

    for (int i = 0; i < 11; i++) {
        cout.precision(i);
        cout << n << "\t\t with precision = " << i << endl;
    }
    return 0;
}
```

———— **Program's Output** ————

0 is the default value of the precision state variable

9.123457	**with precision = 0**
9.1	**with precision = 1**
9.12	**with precision = 2**
9.123	**with precision = 3**
9.1235	**with precision = 4**
9.12346	**with precision = 5**
9.123457	**with precision = 6**
9.1234568	**with precision = 7**
9.12345678	**with precision = 8**
9.12345678	**with precision = 9**
9.12345678	**with precision = 10**

This output shows several interesting results from outputting the number 9.12345678 with a precision ranging from 0 through 10. The default value of the precision state variable is 0; this means, output floating–point numbers with a default of six decimal digits. When output is set with a precision of 0, the number prints as 9.123457. Six decimal digits are printed and the last digit is rounded up. When the precision is set to 3, three digits are printed after the decimal point; when precision is set to, eight decimal digits are printed and that is enough to print the entire original number. When precision is more than eight, as in this example, additional trailing digits of 0 are not printed and trailing zeros are suppressed. Also note that the tabbed fields line up. The variable width of the preceding field (the number) caused this. This could be corrected by printing the number with a fixed field width; the statement "cout.width(12);" just after the for statement would do the job.

setprecision(int) is a manipulator in iomanip.h that provides the same effect as using the member function precision(int).

14.5   Fill Character Format Control

The following member functions are used to read and set the padding character state variable:

char fill()
char fill(char)

The value of the fill state variable is used to pad out or fill in the extra space in a field. A right–justified field is padded on the left; a left–justified field is padded on the right. An ios:internal field is padded between the 0x and the number for a hex number and between the e and the exponent's value for a floating–point number.

fill() is a member function that returns the value of the fill state variable

char pad = cout.fill();   // Get the value of cout's fill character

fill(char) is a member function that sets the fill state variable to the argument's value and returns the previous value.

The following program uses fill() and fill(char):

```
#include <iostream.h>

main()
{

        cout    << "The default fill character is"
                <<" "" << cout.fill() << "". \n";

        cout.width(10);                         // Default fill is a space
        cout << "ABCD" << endl;

        cout.fill('$');                         // Fill with the $ character
        cout.setf(ios::left, ios::adjustfield);
        cout.width(10);
        cout << "ABCD" << endl;

        cout.fill('#');                         // Fill with the # character
        cout.setf(ios::right, ios::adjustfield);
        cout.width(10);
        cout << "ABCD" << endl;

        cout.fill('*');                         // Fill with the * character
        cout.setf(ios::internal, ios::adjustfield);
        cout.setf(ios::showbase);
        cout.setf(ios::uppercase);
        cout.setf(ios::hex, ios::basefield);
```

```
cout.width(10);
cout << 0XABCD << endl;

cout.setf(ios::showpos);
cout.width(10);
cout << 1.2e34 << endl;

return 0;
}
```

——— Program's Output ———
The default fill character is ' '.
ABCD
ABCD$$$$$$
######ABCD
0X**ABCD**
+1.2E+34**

14.6 Adding User–defined Flag Bits

The following member functions are used for declaring additional flag bits and user words:

```
static long    bitalloc()
static int     xalloc()
long&          iword(int)
void*&         pword(int)
```

ios::bitalloc() is a static function and it is used to acquire a new flag bit. This function returns a long with a single bit set, which represents the newly allocated bit.

ios::xalloc() is a static function and it returns the index of a previously unused word in an array that is used to hold your own state variables.

iword(int) is a member function and it takes an argument that is one of the indexes returned by xalloc(). It returns a reference to the word indexed by the argument.

pword(int) is a member function and it takes an argument that is one of the indexes returned by xalloc().

14.7   Other Member Functions

rebuf() is a member function that returns a pointer to the streambuf associated with a stream object. This function is used to find an object's streambuf when the object's constructor is implicitly assigned a buffer.

ios::sync_with_stdio() is a static function that returns a void and it is used when mixing iostream I/O with standard C (stdio) I/O to preserve the order of I/O. If this is not done, problems will occur. When this function is first called, it switches cin, cout, cerr, and clog to use stdiobufs. Then, when they perform I/O, they are correctly synchronized with the corresponding FILEs stdin, stdout, stderr, and stderr. This function also forces cout and cerr to use unit buffering (see ios::unitbuffer).

tie() is a member function that returns the tie variable, is an ostream pointer.

tie(ostream*) is a member function that sets the tie variable to its argument and returns the previous value. The purpose of a tie variable is to support automatic buffer flushing. If the tie variable is not null and the stream needs more characters or has characters to be consumed, the stream pointed to by the tie variable is flushed before the operation. A sequence of streams can be tied together and they will get flushed down the chain. A typical example of tied streams is tying cin to cout so that a message that prompts for input is seen (flushed to the screen) before the system inputs the data that are being requested.

operator void*() is a conversion function that converts an ios object or an object derived from ios, like the ostream object cout, to a void pointer. The void* value returned is the object's address if the object's I/O state variable has 0 values for the flags failbit, badbit, and hardfail, meaning all is fine; otherwise, a 0 is returned. It is important to notice that the condition of the eofbit does not affect this conversion function. This conversion is very important and it is used to implicitly check the state of an I/O operation. The following example uses this implicit type conversion:

```
#include <iostream.h>

main()
{
    char word[500];
    while(cin.good() && cin >> word)
        cout << word << endl;
    return 0;
}
```

In this code, the while statement will loop, reading a word (stripping leading whitespace), and writing it on a separate line. When you enter a Control–D character (the Control–Z or F6 on a PC DOS system), the program terminates. An inspection of the code will explain why this happens. When using a stream it is important to make sure a stream is good before using it. If cin is good and the input succeeds, the body of the while loop is executed; otherwise, the while loop terminates.

The expression cin >> word reads a character string into word and the operator>> returns the stream object cin. At this point, the while statement sees the equivalent of

> **while(cin)**

Because while expects an integral type and is given an stream object, the compiler implicitly converts the object to an integral type by using the iostream conversion function that converts stream objects to a void* pointer and then a standard conversion converts the void* to an integral number. If cin's I/O completes, cin's address is returned as an integral number which tests as true in the while statement and the while loop continues. If an EOF was signaled by you entering a Control–D, the cin is converted to a NULL pointer and the NULL pointer is then converted to 0 by a standard conversion; the 0 is false and the while loop terminates. Thus, the iostream–defined conversion from stream objects to a void* makes it very easy and natural to check I/O operations with no extra effort. In fact, I/O operations are likely to be checked more often in C++ than they were in C because of this feature of the iostream library.

operator!() is a member function that returns the int value returned by the member function fail(). Thus operator! checks the value of the I/O state variable and returns true (non–zero) if a fail bit, a bad bit, or both bits are set; otherwise, it returns false (0). This operator is used to determine if a file was successfully opened. The following program illustrates the use of operator void* and operator! to copy words from standard input to the file my_file:

```
#include <iostream.h>

main()
{
    ostream os("my_file");              // Open the output file
    if(!os) {                           // Use operator!
        cerr << "Error: Could note open file my_file. \n";
        exit(1);
    }
    char word[500];
```

```
    while(cin.good() && cin >> word)    // use operator void*
        cout<< word << endl;
    return 0;
}
```

If you look in the iostream header files, you will find additional functions that we did not discuss. Many of these are self–explanatory.

14.8   Using the iostream Width Manipulator to do Formatted I/O

The following program uses the iostream width manipulator to do formatted I/O:

```
#include <iostream.h>
#include <iomanip.h>        // For manipulators like setw(int)
#include <stdio.h>          // For exit

(int)const width_max = 20;

main()
{
    double d = 1.23456789;
    // Preserve I/O order when mixing streams and stdio
    // which means using "cout << " and "printf" in same program
    cout.sync_with_stdio();
    cout << endl;
    for (int i = 0; i < width_max; i++) {
        cout << setw(i) << d
            <<    "Printed using cout << setw(" << i << ")" << endl;
        printf( "%*fPrinted using printf(\"%%*f with * value of\
                %d\n",i,d,i);
    }
    return 0;
}

——— Program's Output ———
1.234568Printed using cout << setw(0)
1.234568Printed using printf("%*f with * value of 0
 1.234568Printed using cout << setw(1)
```

1.234568 Printed using printf(″%*f with * value of 1
1.234568 Printed using cout << setw(2)
1.234568 Printed using printf(″%*f with * value of 2
1.234568 Printed using cout << setw(3)
1.234568 Printed using printf(″%*f with * value of 3
1.234568 Printed using cout << setw(4)
1.234568 Printed using printf(″%*f with * value of 4
1.234568 Printed using cout << setw(5)
1.234568 Printed using printf(″%*f with * value of 5
1.234568 Printed using cout << setw(6)
1.234568 Printed using printf(″%*f with * value of 6
1.234568 Printed using cout << setw(7)
1.234568 Printed using printf(″%*f with * value of 7
1.234568 Printed using cout << setw(8)
1.234568 Printed using printf(″%*f with * value of 8
1.234568 Printed using cout << setw(9)
1.234568 Printed using printf(″%*f with * value of 9
1.234568 Printed using cout << setw(10)
1.234568 Printed using printf(″%*f with * value of 10
1.234568 Printed using cout << setw(11)
1.234568 Printed using printf(″%*f with * value of 11
1.234568 Printed using cout << setw(12)
1.234568 Printed using printf(″%*f with * value of 12
1.234568 Printed using cout << setw(13)
1.234568 Printed using printf(″%*f with * value of 13
1.234568 Printed using cout << setw(14)
1.234568 Printed using printf(″%*f with * value of 14
1.234568 Printed using cout << setw(15)
1.234568 Printed using printf(″%*f with * value of 15
1.234568 Printed using cout << setw(16)
1.234568 Printed using printf(″%*f with * value of 16
1.234568 Printed using cout << setw(17)
1.234568 Printed using printf(″%*f with * value of 17
1.234568 Printed using cout << setw(18)
1.234568 Printed using printf(″%*f with * value of 18
1.234568 Printed using cout << setw(19)
1.234568 Printed using printf(″%*f with * value of 19

14.9   Left and Right Justification Formatting

This program illustrates left and right justification formatting:

```
#include <iostream.h>
#include <iomanip.h>

main()
{
    char stars[] = ”****”;
    cout << stars << setw(5)                                  << ”ABC”;
    cout << stars << setw(5)    << setiosflags(ios::left  )   << ”DEF”;
    cout                        << resetiosflags(ios::left  );
    cout << stars << setw(5)    << setiosflags(ios::right )   << ”GHI”;
    cout                        << resetiosflags(ios::right );
    cout << stars << setw(5)    << setiosflags(ios::left  )   << ”JKL”;
    cout                        << resetiosflags(ios::left  );
    cout << stars << setw(5)    << setiosflags(ios::right )   << ”MNO”;
    cout                        << resetiosflags(ios::right );
    cout << stars << endl;
    return 0;
}
```

——————— Program's Output ———————
**** ABC****DEF **** GHI****JKL **** MNO****

14.10 A Comprehensive File I/O Example

The following example, uses File I/O and iostream manipulators to produce a report from an exercise log for exercising. The program treats lines that begin with # as comments and ignores them. This technique allows you to put your documentation inside your data files. The information will come from a file called exercise.dat and the following is a sample file:

```
/* Sample input data follows:
# exercise.dat – Art's exercise record for 1990
#
```

```
#    April 1990
#  S M Tu W Th F S
#  1 2 3 4 5 6 7
#  8 9 10 11 12 13 14
# 15 16 17 18 19 20 21
# 22 23 24 25 26 27 28
# 29 30

#km    mm:ss pulse  date  ski   arm    Weight

1.7   12:00   0    4/9    15    3.5
5.0   41:56   0    4/10   15    3.5
2.0   14:25   0    4/16   15    3.0     158
2.0   14:14   0    4/19   15    3.5

*/

#include <iostream.h>
#include <fstream.h>
#include <iomanip.h>
#include <stdlib.h>

main()
{
    char* file_name = "exercise.dat";

    ifstream ifs(file_name);
    if(!ifs) {
        cerr << "Error: Could not open file " << file_name << endl;
        exit(1);
    }

    double distance;
    int    mm, colon, ss;             // Time field
    const  rem_size = 200;
    char   rem[rem_size];             // Remainder of the line

    char   c;
    int    i;
```

```
double time, pace;                    // Calculated values
int   mmkm, sskm;

while (ifs.good()) {

    // Skip line if it begins with #
    if ((i = ifs.peek()) == '#') {
        ifs.getline(rem, rem_size);
        continue;
    }
    if (i == EOF)
        break;

    // Skip an all blank line
    ifs >> c; // note, \n is whitespace too
    if (c == '#') {
        ifs.getline(rem, rem_size);
        continue;
    }
    if (!ifs.good())
        break;
    ifs.putback(c);

    ifs >> distance >> mm;
    ifs.get((signed char)colon);
    ifs >> ss;
    ifs.getline(rem, rem_size);

    // Calculate mm:ss per km

    time = mm + ss / 60.0;

    pace = time / distance;
    mmkm = pace;
    sskm = (pace – mmkm) * 60;

    // Output a line of the report

    cout << '\t'
        << setw(4)
```

```
                    << setprecision(1)
                    << setiosflags(ios::showpoint)
                    << distance
                    << resetiosflags(ios::showpoint)

                    << '\t'
                    << mm
                    << ':'
                    << setw(2) << setfill('0')
                    << ss

                    << '\t'
                    << mmkm
                    << ':'
                    << setw(2)
                    << sskm
                    << setfill(' ')

                    << '\t'
                    << rem

                    << endl;

        }
        cout << endl;

        return 0;
    }
```

—— Program's Output ——

1.7	12:00	7:03	0	4/9	15	3.5	
5.0	41:56	8:23	0	4/10	15	3.5	
2.0	14:25	7:12	0	4/16	15	3.0	158
2.0	14:14	7:06	0	4/19	15	3.5	

14.11 Example of Incore Data Formatting

The following example shows how to do incore I/O using the strstream.h defined class ostrstream, which is analogous to using the C library function sprintf(). The following program formats a number to have a comma every three digits:

```
#include <iostream.h>
#include <strstream.h>

main()
{
    long n = 12345678;

    // Format the long with commas for readability
    const size_a = 30;
    char  a[size_a];
    char  b[size_a];

    // Using ostrstream
    ostrstream s(a, size_a);
    s << n;
    int ndigits = s.pcount();  ostrstream t(b, size_a);
    for (int i = 0; i < (ndigits – 1); i++) {
        t << a[i];
        if ((ndigits – i – 1) % 3 == 0)
            t << ',';
    }
    t << a[i] << ends;

    // Output the results
    cout << "The number " << n << " with commas is " << b << endl;

    return 0;
}
```

——————— Program's Output ———————
The number 12345678 with commas is 12,345,678

14.12 Example of Using Manipulators to Format a Table

The following example uses manipulators to format a conversion table that converts miles to kilometers:

```
#include <iostream.h>
#include <iomanip.h>

main()
{
    double km_per_mi = 2.54 * 12 * 5280 * 0.00001;
    double mi_per_km = 1/km_per_mi;
    cout    << "           " << km_per_mi
            << " is kilometers per mile  \n ";
    cout    << "          " << mi_per_km
            << " is miles per kilometers \n\n";
    double km, mi;
    int   i = 0;                          // To control number of columns
    cout.setf(ios::showpoint);
    for (km = 0; km <= 10; km += .1) {
        mi = km * mi_per_km;
        i++;
        if ( i == 1) {
            cout << "           " << setprecision(1) << setw(4) << km;
        }
        cout   << " " << setprecision(2) << setw(4) << mi;
        if (i == 5) {
            i = 0;
            cout << endl;
        }
    }
    cout << endl;
    return 0;
}
```

——— Program's Output ———

1.612087 is kilometers per mile
0.620314 is miles per kilometers

0.0   0.00   0.06   0.12   0.19   0.25
0.5   0.31   0.37   0.43   0.50   0.56
1.0   0.62   0.68   0.74   0.81   0.87

1.5	**0.93**	**0.99**	**1.05**	**1.12**	**1.18**
2.0	**1.24**	**1.30**	**1.36**	**1.43**	**1.49**
2.5	**1.55**	**1.61**	**1.67**	**1.74**	**1.80**
3.0	**1.86**	**1.92**	**1.99**	**2.05**	**2.11**
3.5	**2.17**	**2.23**	**2.30**	**2.36**	**2.42**
4.0	**2.48**	**2.54**	**2.61**	**2.67**	**2.73**
4.5	**2.79**	**2.85**	**2.92**	**2.98**	**3.04**
5.0	**3.10**	**3.16**	**3.23**	**3.29**	**3.35**
5.5	**3.41**	**3.47**	**3.54**	**3.60**	**3.66**
6.0	**3.72**	**3.78**	**3.85**	**3.91**	**3.97**
6.5	**4.03**	**4.09**	**4.16**	**4.22**	**4.28**
7.0	**4.34**	**4.40**	**4.47**	**4.53**	**4.59**
7.5	**4.65**	**4.71**	**4.78**	**4.84**	**4.90**
8.0	**4.96**	**5.02**	**5.09**	**5.15**	**5.21**
8.5	**5.27**	**5.33**	**5.40**	**5.46**	**5.52**
9.0	**5.58**	**5.64**	**5.71**	**5.77**	**5.83**
9.5	**5.89**	**5.96**	**6.02**	**6.08**	**6.14**
10.0	**6.20**				

15

Porting C Applications to C++

15.1 Reasons for Porting Applications

Why would you want port an application to C++? The presence of the new features of C++ programming are useful, but do they justify the effort of porting your C applications to C++? A major reason would be to gain the benefits of object–oriented programming, which is supposed to increase productivity through the extensions to the language by the creation of abstract data types and through inheritance, which promotes reusability. Proponents of object–oriented programming maintain that this technique will make program maintenance easier and thereby reduce the cost of code maintenance (a large portion of today's software cost). If everything said of object–oriented programming is true, from a management perspective, it makes sense to use this technique. But what language to use?

Many software packages today are written in C and use software interfaces that are also written in C. For example, windowing systems that run on a workstation are typically written in C and use the interface that is provided by X Windows, Xt, Motif, or Open Look, which are also written in C. The decision to port these applications to Smalltalk would involve the learning of a new language and a major rework of code. Porting to Objective–C would also necessitate the learning of a new language and major changes to the software. Although the porting of applications to C++ would not be a trivial effort, C programmers would easily learn the new features of C++ and the porting would be a straightforward effort. Clearly, in the future, many C applications will be ported to C++. When to do the porting is another question. As a general rule of thumb, *if it isn't broke, don't fix it*. Wait until there are many changes that you must make to the software package and then plan to port at that time. However, any new features that are to be added to a software could be added using C++.

15.2 Considerations when Porting Applications

There are two considerations a developer must keep in mind when porting applications. They are

    1) Is your original application written in C or ANSI C?

    2) Are you going to port to the 1.2, 2.0, or 2.1 version of C++?

Programs developed on many workstations use the pre–ANSI version of C. Porting these applications will require more effort than porting applications from ANSI versions of C. For example, ANSI C supports function prototyping and the use of constants; both of these features are found in C++. Therefore, porting from ANSI C presents fewer problems (however, constants are handled differently in ANSI C and C++). However, neither of these features are found in pre–ANSI C and therefore, the programmer doing the port must create function prototypes. Another difference results from the inclusion of the header file <stdlib.h>, which is present in ANSI C and is not present in pre–ANSI C. Because of function prototyping this header file must be included in C++. There has been a substantial change in the implementation of C++ between versions 1.2 and 2.0/2.1. Porting a C application to version 1.2 would require the user to pay particular attention to function name overloading. Because of type–safe checking and mangling (changing the identifiers) of all function identifiers, which is present in version 2.0, the porters would not have to concern themselves with order when mixing C and C++ function identifiers. In practice, you should port to the latest available version of the C++ compiler.

15.3 Differences Between C and C++

Keywords

Perhaps, the first item to which a porter must attend is making sure that no identifier used in the code to be ported is a keyword in the C++ language. The following are keywords in C++, and are not keywords in pre–ANSI C:

asm	**class**	**const**	**delete**
friend	**handle**	**inline**	**new**
operator	**overload**	**private**	**protected**
public	**signed**	**template**	**this**
virtual	**volatile**		

The following is the list of keywords found in C++ that are not found in ANSI C:

class	delete	friend	handle
inline	new	operator	overload
private	protected	public	template
this	virtual		

If these keywords were used as identifiers in an original C program, they would have to be changed. Once these identifiers are changed, other important porting issues can be addressed.

Namespaces

A second important issue has to do with namespaces in the two languages: in C, the tag name of a struct is in a different namespace than a variable identifier. In C++, both the tag name and the identifier are in the same namespace. The following code fragment is legal in C and imposes an extra coding effort in C++:

```
struct namespace {
    int argument;
 };


char namespace[25];
```

In C++, the name of a struct becomes a user–defined data type that extends the language and you should not use the name of a data type as an identifier. The following combinations of declarations would not be legal in C++:

```
int            float;
namespace      example;
char           namespace[25];
```

It is obvious that you cannot use the keyword *float* as a variable identifier. It is also true in C++ that you should not use the name of a user–defined data type as a variable identifier. C++ also does not allow a name to be declared as both a structure tag name and a different typedef name if they are in the same scope. For example, the following code fragment is legal in C, but generates a compiler error in C++:

```
struct namespace {
    int newName;
};


typedef float namespace;
```

If a program contains many typedef declarations, you must carefully check to determine whether any typedef name conflicts with any user–defined data type. Therefore, whenever a program is going to be ported to C++, you must very carefully check the code being ported to make sure that there will be no namespace conflicts in the new program.

Type Checking

C++ provides stronger type checking than either pre–ANSI C or ANSI C. In C++, you must declare a function before it can be used. In C++, a function declaration must specify the type of arguments passed to a function when a declaration is made (function prototype). The following declaration is valid in C, but would generate an error in C++:

    int printf();

The valid declaration for C++ would be:

    int printf(char* ...)

which indicates that printf takes one required argument, a control string, and an unspecified number of additional arguments. The following program fragment is valid in C, but will not compile in C++:

```
extern int countCharacters();
main()
{
    int x, y;
    x = countcharacters("William Heinze");
    y = countWords("I am legion.");
}
```

The fragment would have to be changed to the following in C++:

```
extern int countCharacters(char*);
extern int countWords(char*);

main()
{
    int x, y;
    x = countcharacters("William Heinze");
    y = countWords("I am legion.");
}
```

A major amount of effort, if not the most effort in porting will be spent on determining the proper function prototypes that are needed to port the programs. This may require modification of all header files used by the program. For example, when a software provider ships a C++ compiler, new header files for window applications are included. These header files contain the new function prototypes that allow C++ applications to use the window functions.

Calling C Functions from a C++ Program

You can escape type checking by adding ellipses to function declarations (this is not a good idea but may be done to quickly port an existing application as long as you later provide the proper function prototypes). For example,

char *malloc(...);

turns off type checking for the malloc() function. The program containing this declaration will compile, but not link because the name has been mangled and the linker cannot find the function identifier in the C Standard Library under the new name. To get the program to compile and link, you must tell the compiler not to mangle the function name. This is done as follows:

extern "C" char *malloc(unsigned);

malloc() will now link with libc.a. You can use this approach to turn off name mangling for a series of functions.

```
extern "C" {
    printf(...);

    puts(...);
}
```

You can even include an entire header file.

```
extern "C" {
    #include <stdio.h>
}
```

If you want to use C and C++ functions in the same program, you can use the predefined macro __cplusplus (this is underbar underbar cplusplus in version 2.0 and later versions. The macro _cplusplus with one underbar can also be used.)

```
#ifdef __cplusplus
    extern "C" char *malloc(long);
#endif
#inndef __cplusplus
    char *malloc();
#endif
```

With __cplusplus, you can intermix C and C++ code.

Constants

In ANSI C, the default linkage of a constant is extern (external linkage), whereas in C++ the default linkage is static (internal linkage). This difference can cause problems where a constant is declared in one file and is used in another file. The C code may have to be changed. For example, the following code fragment works well in C, but will not link in C++:

```
// file1.c

const int bill = 57;
```

```
// file2.c

extern int const bill;
```

To fix this code for C++, it must be modified as follows:

```
// file1.cc

extern const int bill = 57;
```

```
// file2.cc

extern const int bill;
```

The keyword *extern* had to be used where the constant was first declared to change the default linkage from internal to external. Now, the constant behaves like a global variable and memory is allocated for it – it can be seen in both files.

Goto Statements

Although programmers are not supposed to use gotos in their programs, many still do. There is an important difference in the treatment of goto in C and C++. In C++, a goto statement cannot jump over a declaration of a struct or class with an explicit initializer, unless the declaration is contained in a block and the entire block is jumped. Because this constraint is not present in C, the use of goto statements in a C program must be analyzed to make sure that they are working properly in C++.

15.4 Differences Between Version 1.2 and Versions 2.0/2.1 of C++

Although there are many differences between the two release versions of C++, the one that impacts portability most is the linkage to other languages and the impact of function name overloading. In release 1.2, when a function name was overloaded, the first time the function was encountered, the function identifier was not mangled. All subsequent overloadings led to changes in the identifiers (name mangling). If the function name that was being overloaded was one in a C standard library, the C function name might not have gotten encoded and a link error could have occurred. If printf() were to be overloaded in release 1.2, one version for C and the other version for C++, the following sequence of steps must occur in the given order:

First, declare printf() as an overloaded function

overload printf;

Next, make sure that the C version is the first one encountered

#include <stdio.h>

Finally, make the declarations that will be included for C++

#include "printFunctions.h" // This includes new printf

Another consideration to make when combining libraries with overloaded function identifiers in release 1.2, is that you must make sure that the overload keyword is used before the first instance of the function name. For example, if myClass.h overloads abs(), and graphics.h overloads asin(), we could have the following:

```
// myClass.h

overload abs;

#include <math.h>
adt abs(adt);

// graphics.h

overload asin;
#include <math.h>
```

If the developer writes:

```
// myHeader.h

#include "myClass.h"
#include "graphics.h"
```

the above code would get an error because asin() was first seen in the math.h which is part of myClass.h and is read before overload asin, which is in graphics.h. To be sure, you must look in all header files that are to included in the port and make sure that a proper header file is created:

```
// myHeader.h

overload abs;
overload asin;
#include "myClass.h"
#include "graphics.h"
```

Whenever any header file is to be included, you must check to make sure that it declares a function as overloaded before it overloads it. In 2.0, these problems were removed. All function names are mangled and the keyword overload is not required. You no longer need to spend time checking dependencies in header files.

15.5 Porting Strategies in C++

You have seen that there are many small issues that must be considered when attempting to port an application from C to C++. Most of these issues do not affect most porting efforts, but they must be kept in mind. Therefore, as previously suggested, before, wait until there is a need to port an application before attempting to do so. If you decide to port an application, do it in stages and do not try to do everything at once. we suggest the following three–stage approach:

1)   Use the C extension features of the C++ language first. If you can get a program to compile and execute with minor changes, you have solved many of the previously described problems.

2)   Use the data abstraction features of the language next.

3)   Finally, use the object–oriented features of the language.

C Language Extensions

Look through header files and see if symbolic constants are created through macro expansions of preprocessor #define directives. These directives can be converted to const types and placed in the program where they will obey the scoping rules of the language, can be type checked, are known to the compiler, can be included in debug symbol tables, and can have pointers to them.

Next, check to see if you are creating macros with #define preprocessor directives to mimic functions. These macros are chosen because they avoid the overhead of a function call. Rewrite these macros as standard functions and then inline the functions. These functions can have their arguments type checked, are known to the compiler, can be included in debug symbol tables, can have pointers to them, and can be passed as arguments to functions, yet in most cases, they avoid the cost of a function call.

Check to see if you can overload function names in your application. If you can, and there are differences in their arguments lists, overload the function names. A warning: It is easy to get carried away with function name overloading. Only functions that carry out related tasks should have their names overloaded.

Check to see if some function arguments can be assigned default values in your function declarations. If they can, assign default values in the function parameter list.

This first phase will produce a workable port of your existing C code and also allow you to use the advanced features of C++.

Data Abstraction

As you look at the new functionality that your application requires, try to achieve a design that allows you to encapsulate your data and the functions that operate on those data. Use the

C++ feature, the class, to create abstract data types. Check to see if parts of your program can be rewritten to take advantage of the class concept. Time spent in this step will produce more efficient and more easily maintainable code than was present in the C version. Beware. It is just as easy to develop bad classes in C++ as it is to develop bad algorithms in C. Time spent in this step is not wasted. Also, be prepared to start over again if you discover that your present classes are not sufficient. The most important thing to be gained in this stage is the development of truly usable classes.

Inheritance and Virtual Functions

When you have finally developed the classes that you require, try to extend them with derived classes and add new functionality to them. When later changes to your program must be made, use inheritance from existing classes to add the changes.

Appendix A: Program Sizeof

The following program can be used to display the size of fundamental types and the results are machine–dependent:

```
#define NL        << "\n"
#define TAB       << "\t"

#include <stream.h>
#include <stdlib.h>                // For exit(0)
main()
{
    cout << sizeof(char          )    << "\tis sizeof( char        )"    NL;
    cout << sizeof(short         )    << "\tis sizeof( short       )"    NL;
    cout << sizeof(int           )    << "\tis sizeof( int         )"    NL;
    cout << sizeof(long          )    << "\tis sizeof( long        )"    NL;
    cout << sizeof(float         )    << "\tis sizeof( float       )"    NL;
    cout << sizeof(double        )    << "\tis sizeof( double      )" NL;
    cout << sizeof(long double   )    << "\tis sizeof( long double)" NL;
    cout << sizeof(void *        )    << "\tis sizeof( void*       )" NL;
    exit(0);
}
```

——— Program's Output ———
```
1     is sizeof( char        )
2     is sizeof( short       )
2     is sizeof( int         )
4     is sizeof( long        )
4     is sizeof( float       )
8     is sizeof( double      )
10    is sizeof( long double)
4     is sizeof( void*       )
```

Appendix B: Program to Determine Implicit Conversions

This program determines the system–dependent implicit arithmetic type conversions that occur for binary and unary arithmetic operators.

Some binary Arithmetic Operators are

*	/	%	*=	/=	%=
+	–	+=	–=		
<	>	==	!=	<=	>=

Note: when this program is compiled, warning messages will to occur because the functions intentionally do not use their arguments:

```
#define NL  << "\n"
#define TAB << "\t"

#include <iostream.h>
#include <string.h>                    // For strcpy

char*    type (char x);
char*    type (short x);
char*    type (int x);
char*    type (long x);
char*    type (unsigned char x);
char*    type (unsigned short x);
char*    type (unsigned int x);
char*    type (unsigned long x);
char*    type (float x);
char*    type (double x);
char*    type (long double x);
char*    type (char* x);
```

```
main()
{
        char            c;
        short           s;
        int             i;
        long            l;
        unsigned char   uc;
        unsigned short  us;
        unsigned int    ui;
        unsigned long   ul;
        float           f;
        double          d;
        long double     ld;
        char*           cs;

        cout << "type( c +  c)" TAB << type( c +  c)    NL;
        cout << "type( c +  s)" TAB << type( c +  s)    NL;
        cout << "type( c +  i)" TAB << type( c +  i)    NL;
        cout << "type( c +  l)" TAB << type( c +  l)    NL;
        cout << "type( c + uc)" TAB << type( c + uc)    NL;
        cout << "type( c + us)" TAB << type( c + us)    NL;
        cout << "type( c + ui)" TAB << type( c + ui)    NL;
        cout << "type( c + ul)" TAB << type( c + ul)    NL;
        cout << "type( c +  f)" TAB << type( c +  f)    NL;
        cout << "type( c +  d)" TAB << type( c +  d)    NL;
        cout << "type( c + ld)" TAB << type( c + ld)    NL;

        cout << "type( s +  c)" TAB << type( s +  c)    NL;
        cout << "type( s +  s)" TAB << type( s +  s)    NL;
        cout << "type( s +  i)" TAB << type( s +  i)    NL;
        cout << "type( s +  l)" TAB << type( s +  l)    NL;
        cout << "type( s + uc)" TAB << type( s + uc)    NL;
        cout << "type( s + us)" TAB << type( s + us)    NL;
        cout << "type( s + ui)" TAB << type( s + ui)    NL;
        cout << "type( s + ul)" TAB << type( s + ul)    NL;
        cout << "type( s +  f)" TAB << type( s +  f)    NL;
```

```
cout << "type( s +  d)" TAB << type( s +  d)   NL;
cout << "type( s + ld)" TAB << type( s + ld)    NL;

cout << "type( i +  c)" TAB << type( i +  c)   NL;
cout << "type( i +  s)" TAB << type( i +  s)   NL;
cout << "type( i +  i)" TAB << type( i +  i)    NL;
cout << "type( i +  l)" TAB << type( i +  l)    NL;
cout << "type( i + uc)" TAB << type( i + uc)  NL;
cout << "type( i + us)" TAB << type( i + us)  NL;
cout << "type( i + ui)" TAB << type( i + ui)   NL;
cout << "type( i + ul)" TAB << type( i + ul)   NL;
cout << "type( i +  f)" TAB << type( i +  f)   NL;
cout << "type( i +  d)" TAB << type( i +  d)  NL;
cout << "type( i + ld)" TAB << type( i + ld)   NL;

cout << "type( l +  c)" TAB << type( l +  c)   NL;
cout << "type( l +  s)" TAB << type( l +  s)   NL;
cout << "type( l +  i)" TAB << type( l +  i)    NL;
cout << "type( l +  l)" TAB << type( l +  l)    NL;
cout << "type( l + uc)" TAB << type( l + uc)  NL;
cout << "type( l + us)" TAB << type( l + us)  NL;
cout << "type( l + ui)" TAB << type( l + ui)   NL;
cout << "type( l + ul)" TAB << type( l + ul)   NL;
cout << "type( l +  f)" TAB << type( l +  f)   NL;
cout << "type( l +  d)" TAB << type( l +  d)  NL;
cout << "type( l + ld)" TAB << type( l + ld)   NL;

cout << "type(uc +  c)" TAB << type(uc +  c) NL;
cout << "type(uc +  s)" TAB << type(uc +  s) NL;
cout << "type(uc +  i)" TAB << type(uc +  i) NL;
cout << "type(uc +  l)" TAB << type(uc +  l) NL;
cout << "type(uc + uc)" TAB << type(uc + uc) NL;
cout << "type(uc + us)" TAB << type(uc + us) NL;
cout << "type(uc + ui)" TAB << type(uc + ui) NL;
cout << "type(uc + ul)" TAB << type(uc + ul) NL;
cout << "type(uc +  f)" TAB << type(uc +  f) NL;
cout << "type(uc +  d)" TAB << type(uc +  d) NL;
```

```
cout << "type(uc + ld)" TAB << type(uc + ld) NL;

cout << "type(us +  c)" TAB << type(us +  c) NL;
cout << "type(us +  s)" TAB << type(us +  s) NL;
cout << "type(us +  i)" TAB << type(us +  i) NL;
cout << "type(us +  l)" TAB << type(us +  l) NL;
cout << "type(us + uc)" TAB << type(us + uc) NL;
cout << "type(us + us)" TAB << type(us + us) NL;
cout << "type(us + ui)" TAB << type(us + ui) NL;
cout << "type(us + ul)" TAB << type(us + ul) NL;
cout << "type(us +  f)" TAB << type(us +  f) NL;
cout << "type(us +  d)" TAB << type(us +  d) NL;
cout << "type(us + ld)" TAB << type(us + ld) NL;

cout << "type(ui +  c)" TAB << type(ui +  c) NL;
cout << "type(ui +  s)" TAB << type(ui +  s) NL;
cout << "type(ui +  i)" TAB << type(ui +  i) NL;
cout << "type(ui +  l)" TAB << type(ui +  l) NL;
cout << "type(ui + uc)" TAB << type(ui + uc) NL;
cout << "type(ui + us)" TAB << type(ui + us) NL;
cout << "type(ui + ui)" TAB << type(ui + ui) NL;
cout << "type(ui + ul)" TAB << type(ui + ul) NL;
cout << "type(ui +  f)" TAB << type(ui +  f) NL;
cout << "type(ui +  d)" TAB << type(ui +  d) NL;
cout << "type(ui + ld)" TAB << type(ui + ld) NL;

cout << "type(ul +  c)" TAB << type(ul +  c) NL;
cout << "type(ul +  s)" TAB << type(ul +  s) NL;
cout << "type(ul +  i)" TAB << type(ul +  i) NL;
cout << "type(ul +  l)" TAB << type(ul +  l) NL;
cout << "type(ul + uc)" TAB << type(ul + uc) NL;
cout << "type(ul + us)" TAB << type(ul + us) NL;
cout << "type(ul + ui)" TAB << type(ul + ui) NL;
cout << "type(ul + ul)" TAB << type(ul + ul) NL;
cout << "type(ul +  f)" TAB << type(ul +  f) NL;
cout << "type(ul +  d)" TAB << type(ul +  d) NL;
cout << "type(ul + ld)" TAB << type(ul + ld) NL;
```

```
cout << "type( f +  c)" TAB << type( f +  c) NL;
cout << "type( f +  s)" TAB << type( f +  s) NL;
cout << "type( f +  i)" TAB << type( f +  i) NL;
cout << "type( f +  l)" TAB << type( f +  l) NL;
cout << "type( f + uc)" TAB << type( f + uc) NL;
cout << "type( f + us)" TAB << type( f + us) NL;
cout << "type( f + ui)" TAB << type( f + ui) NL;
cout << "type( f + ul)" TAB << type( f + ul) NL;
cout << "type( f +  f)" TAB << type( f +  f) NL;
cout << "type( f +  d)" TAB << type( f +  d) NL;
cout << "type( f + ld)" TAB << type( f + ld) NL;

cout << "type( d +  c)" TAB << type( d +  c) NL;
cout << "type( d +  s)" TAB << type( d +  s) NL;
cout << "type( d +  i)" TAB << type( d +  i) NL;
cout << "type( d +  l)" TAB << type( d +  l) NL;
cout << "type( d + uc)" TAB << type( d + uc) NL;
cout << "type( d + us)" TAB << type( d + us) NL;
cout << "type( d + ui)" TAB << type( d + ui) NL;
cout << "type( d + ul)" TAB << type( d + ul) NL;
cout << "type( d +  f)" TAB << type( d +  f) NL;
cout << "type( d +  d)" TAB << type( d +  d) NL;
cout << "type( d + ld)" TAB << type( d + ld) NL;

cout << "type(ld +  c)" TAB << type(ld +  c) NL;
cout << "type(ld +  s)" TAB << type(ld +  s) NL;
cout << "type(ld +  i)" TAB << type(ld +  i) NL;
cout << "type(ld +  l)" TAB << type(ld +  l) NL;
cout << "type(ld + uc)" TAB << type(ld + uc) NL;
cout << "type(ld + us)" TAB << type(ld + us) NL;
cout << "type(ld + ui)" TAB << type(ld + ui) NL;
cout << "type(ld + ul)" TAB << type(ld + ul) NL;
cout << "type(ld +  f)" TAB << type(ld +  f) NL;
cout << "type(ld +  d)" TAB << type(ld +  d) NL;
cout << "type(ld + ld)" TAB << type(ld + ld) NL;
```

```
// Implicit conversion for arithmetic unary operators

cout << "type( c++)" TAB << type( c++) NL;
cout << "type( s++)" TAB << type( s++) NL;
cout << "type( i++)" TAB << type( i++) NL;
cout << "type( l++)" TAB << type( l++) NL;
cout << "type(uc++)" TAB << type(uc++) NL;
cout << "type(us++)" TAB << type(us++) NL;
cout << "type(ui++)" TAB << type(ui++) NL;
cout << "type(ul++)" TAB << type(ul++) NL;
cout << "type( f++)" TAB << type( f++) NL;
cout << "type( d++)" TAB << type( d++) NL;
cout << "type(ld++)" TAB << type(ld++) NL;

return 0;
}

char* type (char x)
{
    char* t = new char [5];
    strcpy(t,"char");
    return t;
}

char* type (short x)
{
    char* t = new char [6];
    strcpy(t,"short");
    return t;
}

char* type (int x)
{
    char* t = new char [4];
    strcpy(t,"int");
    return t;
```

```
    }

char* type (long x)
{
    char* t = new char [5];
    strcpy(t,"long");
    return t;
}

char* type (unsigned char x)
{
    char* t = new char [14];
    strcpy(t,"unsigned char");
    return t;
}

char* type (unsigned short x)
{
    char* t = new char [15];
    strcpy(t,"unsigned short");
    return t;
}

char* type (unsigned int x)
{
    char* t = new char [13];
    strcpy(t,"unsigned int");
    return t;
}

char* type (unsigned long x)
{
    char* t = new char [14];
    strcpy(t,"unsigned long");
    return t;
}
char* type (float x)
```

```
{
     char* t = new char [6];
     strcpy(t,"float");
     return t;
}

char* type (double x)
{
     char* t = new char [7];
     strcpy(t,"double");
     return t;
}

char* type (long double x)
{
     char* t = new char [12];
     strcpy(t,"long double");
     return t;
}

char* type (char* x)
{
     char* t = new char [6];
     strcpy(t,"char*");
     return t;
}
```

——— **Program's Output** ———
type(c + c) char
type(c + s) short
type(c + i) int
type(c + l) long
type(c + uc)unsigned char
type(c + us)unsigned short
type(c + ui) unsigned int
type(c + ul) unsigned long
type(c + f) float

```
type( c +  d) double
type( c + ld) long double
type( s +  c) short
type( s +  s) short
type( s +  i)  int
type( s +  l)  long
type( s + uc)short
type( s + us) unsigned short
type( s + ui) unsigned int
type( s + ul) unsigned long
type( s +  f)  float
type( s +  d) double
type( s + ld) long double
type( i +  c)  int
type( i +  s)  short
type( i +  i)  int
type( i +  l)  long
type( i + uc) int
type( i + us) unsigned short
type( i + ui) unsigned int
type( i + ul) unsigned long
type( i +  f)  float
type( i +  d) double
type( i + ld) long double
type( l +  c)  long
type( l +  s)  long
type( l +  i)  long
type( l +  l)  long
type( l + uc) long
type( l + us) long
type( l + ui) long
type( l + ul) unsigned long
type( l +  f)  float
type( l +  d) double
type( l + ld) long double
type(uc +  c)unsigned char
type(uc +  s)short
```

```
type(uc +  i) int
type(uc +  l) long
type(uc + uc)unsigned char
type(uc + us)unsigned short
type(uc + ui)unsigned int
type(uc + ul)unsigned long
type(uc +  f) float
type(uc +  d)double
type(uc + ld)long double
type(us +  c)unsigned short
type(us +  s) unsigned short
type(us +  i) unsigned short
type(us +  l) long
type(us + uc)unsigned short
type(us + us)unsigned short
type(us + ui)unsigned int
type(us + ul)unsigned long
type(us +  f) float
type(us +  d)double
type(us + ld)long double
type(ui +  c) unsigned int
type(ui +  s) unsigned int
type(ui +  i) unsigned int
type(ui +  l) long
type(ui + uc)unsigned int
type(ui + us)unsigned short
type(ui + ui)unsigned int
type(ui + ul)unsigned long
type(ui +  f) float
type(ui +  d)double
type(ui + ld)long double
type(ul +  c) unsigned long
type(ul +  s) unsigned long
type(ul +  i) unsigned long
type(ul +  l) unsigned long
type(ul + uc)unsigned long
type(ul + us)unsigned long
```

type(ul + ui)unsigned long
type(ul + ul)unsigned long
type(ul + f) float
type(ul + d)double
type(ul + ld)long double
type(f + c) float
type(f + s) float
type(f + i) float
type(f + l) float
type(f + uc)float
type(f + us) float
type(f + ui) float
type(f + ul) float
type(f + f) float
type(f + d) double
type(f + ld) long double
type(d + c) double
type(d + s) double
type(d + i) double
type(d + l) double
type(d + uc)double
type(d + us)double
type(d + ui)double
type(d + ul)double
type(d + f) double
type(d + d)double
type(d + ld)long double
type(ld + c) long double
type(ld + s) long double
type(ld + i) long double
type(ld + l) long double
type(ld + uc)long double
type(ld + us)long double
type(ld + ui)long double
type(ld + ul)long double
type(ld + f) long double
type(ld + d)long double

```
type(ld + ld)long double
type( c++)char
type( s++)short
type( i++)int
type( l++)long
type(uc++)unsigned char
type(us++)unsigned short
type(ui++)unsigned int
type(ul++)unsigned long
type( f++)float
type( d++)double
type(ld++)long double
```

Appendix C: iostream Library Synopsis

filebuf

Attach	Attach this filebuf to opened file descriptor.
	filebuf* attach(int);
close	Flush and close file.
	filebuf* close();
fd	Return the file descriptor.
	int fd();
filebuf	Constructor.
	filebuf(int);
	filebuf(int _f, char*, int);
filebuf	Make a closed filebuf.
	filebuf();
is_open	Is the file open.
	int is_open();
open	Open named file with mode and protection, attach to filebuf.
	filebuf* open(const char*, int, int = filebuf::openprot);
overflow	Perform the streambuf function on a filebuf.
	virtual int overflow(int = EOF);
seekoff	Perform the streambuf function on a filebuf.
	virtual streampos seekoff(streamoff, ios::seek_dir, int);
setbuf	Perform the streambuf function on a filebuf.
	virtual streambuf* setbuf(char*, int);
sync	Perform the streambuf function on a filebuf.
	virtual int sync();
underflow	Perform the streambuf function on a filebuf.
	virtual int underflow();
~filebuf	Destructor.
	~filebuf();

fstream

fstream	Constructor.	
		fstream();
		fstream(const char*, int, int = filebuf::openprot);
fstream	Constructor , continued from above.	
		fstream(int _f, char*, int);
		fstream(int);
open	Open.	
		void open(const char *, int, int = filebuf::openprot);
rdbuf	Rdbuf read the buffer contents.	
		filebuf* rdbuf();
~fstream	Destructor.	
		~fstream();

fstreambase

attach	Attach.	
		void attach(int);
close	Close.	
		void close();
fstreambase	Constructor.	
		fstreambase();
		fstreambase(const char*, int,
		int = filebuf::openprot);
		fstreambase(int, char*, int);
		fstreambase(int);
open	Open.	
		void open(const char*, int, int = filebuf::openprot);
rdbuf	Rdbuf read the buffer contents.	
		filebuf* rdbuf();
setbuf	Setbuf set the buffer contents.	
		void setbuf(char*, int);
~fstreambase	Destructor.	
		~fstreambase();

global functions

dec	Set conversion base to decimal.
	ios& dec(ios&);
endl	Insert newline and flush.
	ostream& endl(ostream&);
ends	Insert null to terminate string.
	ostream& ends(ostream&);
flush	Flush the ostream.
	ostream& flush(ostream&);
hex	Set conversion base to hexadecimal.
	ios& hex(ios&);
oct	Set conversion base to octal.
	ios& oct(ios&);
ws	Extract whitespace characters.
	istream& ws(istream&);

ifstream

ifstream	Constructor.
	ifstream();
	ifstream(const char*, int = ios::in,
	int = filebuf::openprot);
	ifstream(int _f, char*, int);
	ifstream(int);
open	Open.
	void open(const char*, int = ios::in,
	int = filebuf::openprot);
rdbuf	Rdbuf.
	filebuf* rdbuf();
~ifstream	Destructor.
	~ifstream();

ios

bad	Stream's state: non–zero if error occurred.
	int bad();
bitalloc	Stream's user defined flags: acquire a
	new flag bit, value returned.
	static long bitalloc();
clear	Stream's state: set the stream state.
	void clear(int = 0);
eof	Stream's state: non–zero on end of file.
	int eof();
fail	Stream's state: non–zero if an operation failed.
	int fail();
fill	Padding character reading.
	char fill();
fill	Padding character reading & setting.
	char fill(char);
flags	Format flags reading.
	long flags();
flags	Format flags reading & setting.
	long flags(long);
good	Stream's state: non–zero if no state bits set.
	int good();
ios	Constructor.
	ios(streambuf*);
iword	Stream's user defined flags: return the nth
	user word as an int.
	long& iword(int);
operator void*	Stream's state: zero if state failed.
	operator void* ();
operator!	Stream's state: non–zero if state failed.
	int operator! ();
precision	Digits of floating precision reading.
	int precision();
precision	Digits of floating precision reading and setting.
	int precision(int);
pword	Stream's user defined flags: Return the nth

user word as a pointer.
>   void*& pword(int);

rdbuf   Stream's assigned streambuf: get it.
>   streambuf* rdbuf();

rdstate   Stream's state read.
>   int rdstate();

setf   Flags reading & setting.
>   long setf(long);
>   long Setf(long,long);

skip   Obsolete, for streams 1.2 compatibility.
>   int skip(int);

sync_with_stdio Synchronizes iostream I/O with FILE I/O.
>   static void sync_with_stdio();

tie   Ostream tied to this stream.
>   ostream* tie();

tie   Ostream tied to this stream.
>   ostream* tie(ostream*);

unsetf   Flags reading & modifying.
>   long unsetf(long);

width   Field width reading.
>   int width();

width   Field width reading & setting.
>   int width(int);

xalloc   Stream's user defined flags: acquire a
>   new user word, index returned.
>   static int xalloc();

~ios   Destructor.
>   virtual ~ios();

iostream

iostream   Constructor.
>   iostream(streambuf*);

~iostream   Destructor.
>   virtual ~iostream();

iostream_withassign

iostream_withassign Constructor.
                                 iostream_withassign();

operator=   Associates streambuf with stream
                      and does entire initialization.
                      iostream_withassign& operator= (streambuf*);

operator=   Gets buffer from stream and does entire initialization.
                      iostream_withassign& operator= (ios&);

~iostream_withassign Destructor.
                      virtual ~iostream_withassign();

istream

gcount   Number of unformatted chars last extracted.
                      int gcount();

get   Extract a single character.
                      int get();
                      istream& get(signed char&);
                      istream& get(unsigned char&);

get   Extract characters into a streambuf up
                to termination char.
                      istream& get(streambuf&, char = '\n');

get   Unformatted extraction.
                      istream& get(signed char*, int, char = '\n');
                      istream& get(unsigned char*, int, char = '\n');

getline   Extraction of chars into an array up to termination char.
                      istream& getline(unsigned char*, int,
                                    char = '\n');
                      istream& getline(signed char*, int, char = '\n');

ignore   Extract and discard chars but stop at delimeter
                      istream& ignore(int = 1, int delimeter = EOF);

ipfx   Input prefix function.
                      int ipfx(int = 0);

ipfx0	Same as ipfx(0).	
	int ipfx0();	
ipfx1	Same as ipfx(1).	
	int ipfx1();	
isfx	Unused input suffix function.	
	void isfx();	
istream	Constructor.	
	istream(streambuf*);	
istream	Obsolete constructor re 1.2.	
	istream(streambuf*, int _sk, ostream* _t=0);	
	istream& operator>> (streambuf*);	
	istream(int _fd, int _sk=1, ostream* _t=0);	
operator>>	Extract from this istream, insert into streambuf.	
	istream(int _sz, char*, int _sk=1);	
operator>>	Formatted extraction operation for the parameter.	
	istream& operator>> (signed char&);	
	istream& operator>> (signed char*);	
	istream& operator>> (unsigned char&);	
	istream& operator>> (unsigned char*);	
	istream& operator>> (short&);	
	istream& operator>> (int&);	
	istream& operator>> (long&);	
	istream& operator>> (float&);	
	istream& operator>> (double&);	
	istream& operator>> (long double&);	
	istream& operator>> (ios& (*_f)(ios&));	
	istream& operator>> (istream& (*_f)(istream&));	
	istream& operator>> (unsigned int&);	
	istream& operator>> (unsigned long&);	
	istream& operator>> (unsigned short&);	
peek	Return next char without extraction.	
	int peek();	
putback	Push back char into input.	
	istream& putback(char);	
read	Unformatted extraction.	
	istream& read(unsigned char*, int);	
	istream& read(signed char*, int);	

seekg	Set the stream's position.
	istream& seekg(streamoff, seek_dir);
	istream& seekg(streampos);
sync	Synchronize the internal data structures with
	The external source of characters.
	int sync();
tellg	Get the streams position.
	streampos tellg();
~istream	Destructor.
	virtual ~istream();

istream_withassign

istream_withassign	Constructor.
	istream_withassign();
operator=	Associates streambuf with stream and does entire
	initialization.
	istream_withassign& operator= (streambuf*);
operator=	Gets buffer from istream and does entire initialization.
	istream_withassign& operator= (istream&);
~istream_withassign	Destructor.
	virtual ~istream_withassign();

istrstream

istrstream	Constructor.
	istrstream();
	istrstream(char *, int);
~istrstream	Destructor.
	~istrstream();

ofstream

ofstream	Constructor.
	ofstream(const char*, int = ios::out,
	int = filebuf::openprot);

	ofstream();
	ofstream(int _f, char*, int);
	ofstream(int);
open	Open.
	void open(const char*, int = ios::out,
	int = filebuf::openprot);
rdbuf	Rdbuf.
	filebuf* rdbuf();
~ofstream	Destructor.
	~ofstream();

ostream

flush	Flush the ouptut stream's buffer.
	ostream& Flush();
operator<<	Dispatcher for simple manipulators.
	ostream& operator<< (ios& (*_f)(ios&));
	ostream& operator<<
	(ostream& (*_f)(ostream&));
operator<<	Extract from streambuf, Insert into this ostream.
	ostream& operator<< (streambuf*);
operator<<	Formatted output for the parameter.
	ostream& operator<< (signed char);
	ostream& operator<< (unsigned char);
	ostream& operator<< (double);
	ostream& operator<< (float);
	ostream& operator<< (int);
	ostream& operator<< (long double);
	ostream& operator<< (long);
	ostream& operator<< (short);
	ostream& operator<< (unsigned int);
	ostream& operator<< (unsigned long);
	ostream& operator<< (unsigned short);
operator<<	Insert character representation of the
	value of the pointer.
	ostream& operator<< (void*);

operator<<	Insert the null–terminated string.
	ostream& operator<< (const signed char*);
	ostream& operator<< (const unsigned char*);
opfx	Output prefix function.
	int opfx();
osfx	Output suffix function.
	void osfx();
ostream	Constructor.
	ostream(streambuf*);
ostream	Obsolete constructors for streams 1.2.
	ostream(int _sz, char*);// use strstream
ostream	Obsolete constructors, for streams 1.2 compatibility.
	ostream(int _fd); // use fstream
put	Insert the character.
	ostream& put(char);
seekp	Set/read the put pointer's position.
	ostream& seekp(streamoff, seek_dir);
seekp	Set/read the put pointer's position.
	ostream& seekp(streampos);
tellp	Read the Stream's position.
	streampos tellp();
write	Insert the string.
	ostream& write(const signed char*, int);
	ostream& write(const unsigned char*, int);
~ostream	Destructor.
	virtual ~ostream();

ostream_withassign

iostream_withassign	Constructor.
	ostream_withassign();
operator=	Associates streambuf with stream and does entire initialization.
	ostream_withassign& operator= (streambuf*);
operator=	Gets buffer from istream and does entire initialization.
	ostream_withassign& operator= (ostream&);

ostream_withassign   Constructor.
                         ostream_withassign();
~ostream_withassign Destructor.
                         virtual ~ostream_withassign();

ostrstream

ostrstream   Constructor.
                         ostrstream();
                         ostrstream(char*, int, int = ios::out);
~ostrstream   Destructor.
                         ~ostrstream()

streambuf

do_sgetn   Implementation of sgetn.
                         virtual int do_sgetn(char *, int);
do_sputn   Implementation of sputn.
                         virtual int do_sputn(const char, int);
dbp   For debugging streambuf implementations.
                         void dbp();
in_avai   Number of avail chars in buffer.
                         int in_avail();
out_waiting   Number of unFlushed chars.
                         int out_waiting();
overflow   Flush buffer and make more room.
                         virtual int overflow(int = EOF);
pbackfail   Implementation of sputbackc.
                         virtual int pbackfail(int);
sbumpc   Return current char and Advance.
                         int sbumpc();
seekoff   Move to the specified position in the stream.
                         virtual streampos seekoff(streamoff, ios::seek_dir,
                                       int = (ios::in I ios::out));

seekpos	Move to the specified position in the stream.
	virtual streampos seekpos(streampos,
	int = (ios::in | ios::out));
setbuf	Use the provided char array for the buffer if possible.
	virtual streambuf * Setbuf(signed char *, int);
	streambuf* Setbuf(unsigned char *, int);
setbuf	Obsolete, for streams 1.2 compatibility.
	streambuf* Setbuf(char *, int, int);
sgetc	Peek at next char.
	int sgetc();
sgetn	Get next n chars.
	int sgetn(char *, int);
snextc	Advance to and return next char.
	int snextc();
sputbackc	Return char to input.
	int sputbackc(char);
sputc	Put one char.
	int sputc(int);
sputn	Put n chars from string.
	int sputn(const char *, int);
stossc	Advance to next character.
	void stossc();
streambuf	Constructor.
	streambuf();
	streambuf(char *, int);
sync	Synchronize internal structures with external sources of data.
	virtual int sync();
underflow	Fill empty buffer.
	virtual int underflow();
~streambuf	Destructor.
	virtual ~streambuf();

strstream

str	Str.	
	char* str();	
strstream	Constructor.	
	strstream()	
	strstream(char *, int, int);	
~Strstream	Destructor.	
	~strstream();	

strstreambase

rdbuf	Return the address of the buffer.
	strstreambuf* rdbuf();

strstreambuf

doallocate   Doallocate.

           virtual int doallocate();

overflow   Flush buffer and make more room.

           virtual int overflow(int=EOF);

seekoff   Seekoff.

           virtual streampos seekoff(streamoff, seek_dir,

                           int = (ios::in | ios::out));

setbuf   Use the provided character array for buffer .

           virtual streambuf* Setbuf(char*, int);

streambuf   Constructor.

           strstreambuf();

           strstreambuf(int);

           strstreambuf(void*(*a)(long), void (*f)(void *));

           strstreambuf(signed char*, int,

                signed char* = 0);

           strstreambuf(unsigned char*, int,

                unsigned char* = 0);

underflow   Character input: fill empty buffer.
                                    virtual int underflow();

~streambuf   Destructor.
                                    virtual ~streambuf();

Index

Symbols

::, 30, 73
   Multiple inheritance, 330
::*, 279
(), 279
[], 272, 279
&, 279
*, 279
=, Multiple inheritance, 311
<<, 382
>>, 382
_new_handler, 65

A

Abstract base class, 361

Abstract data type, 139
   Built–in double, 206
   Concepts, 205
   Data representation, 205
   Functions and operators, 206

Access, Class members, 173

Access regions, 80
   Private, 77, 80
   Protected, 77, 80
   Public, 77, 80

Adding user–defined flag bits –
   member functions
   bitalloc(), 430
   iword(), 430

pword(), 430
xalloc(), 430

Aggregate names in C, 31
   enum, 31
   struct, 31
   union, 31

Aggregate names in C++, 34
   class, 36
   enum, 34
   struct, 34
   union, 34

Aggregates, class, struct, union, 141

Aliases, 282

Assignment operator, Operator overloading, 267

Associativity, 106, 258

Associativity rule, 113

B

Base class, 80, 301

Binary operator, 107

Binary operator, Operator overloading, 265, 266

Built–in data types, 121

Built–in manipulators
   dec, 409
   endl, 410
   ends, 410
   flush, 410